THE JOY OF GERANIUMS

Other Books by Helen Van Pelt Wilson

House Plants for Every Window (in collaboration with Dorothy
H. Jenkins)

The Complete Book of African Violets (1951)

The Joy of Flower Arranging

Perennials Preferred (1952)

Climbing Roses

Roses for Pleasure (in collaboration with Richard Thomson)

The New Perennials Preferred (1961)

The Flower Arrangement Calendar (1947–1966)

The New Complete Book of African Violets (1963)

The Joy of Geraniums

(Original title: Geraniums—Pelargoniums for Windows and Gardens)

THE STANDARD GUIDE TO THE SELECTION, CULTURE, AND USE OF THE PELARGONIUM

Helen Van Pelt Wilson

William Morrow & Company, Inc., New York, 1972

3 4 5   77 76 75 74

For my dear family
Cynthia and Ben
Susanna and Eric
Who give moral support to all my ventures,
sensible—and otherwise

Contents

	My Thanks—Again	xi
one.	*Geraniums—Plants for All Seasons, All People*	1
two.	*The Amazing Species*	18
three.	*Handsome Zonals and Their Groups*	34
four.	*The Lovely Single and Double Zonals*	51
five.	*Treasures for the Collector*	69
six.	*Winter-flowering Pot Plants and Their Culture*	81
seven.	*Fancy-leaved Zonals for Contrast*	98
eight.	*The Irresistible Dwarfs*	108
nine.	*The Intimate Appeal of the Scenteds*	125
ten.	*Culture and Use of the Scenteds*	148
eleven.	*The Elegant Ivy-leaveds*	161
twelve.	*Distinguished Regals for East and West*	182
thirteen.	*Care in California*	192

x · Contents

fourteen. *New Plants from Cuttings*   202

fifteen. *New Plants from Seed, Cross, and Mutation*   210

sixteen. *Tree Forms, Baskets, Bonsai, and Espaliers*   218

seventeen. *For Urns, Tubs, Planters, and Window Boxes*   233

eighteen. *How to Succeed in Business with a Little Trying*   247

nineteen. *How to Photograph Your Geraniums*   262

twenty. *Pest and Disease to Avoid or Control*   268

twenty-one. *Societies, Magazines, and Shows*   281

Finder's List of Species and Selected Varieties   292

Plants that are Illustrated   293

Unscented Species and Latin-named Hybrids   296

Zonal Geraniums   300

Fancy-leaved Zonal Geraniums   311

Dwarf Zonal Geraniums   316

Scented-leaved Species, Latin-named Hybrids, and Varieties   320

Ivy-leaved Geraniums   329

Regal Geraniums   333

Glossary   339

Sources of Plants   344

Index   349

My Thanks—Again

As I complete my work on this practically new book on Geraniums—I have rewritten more than two-thirds of the former book, added new chapters and new illustrations, updated all lists, and reported the latest research—I am overwhelmed with thankfulness. First, I rejoice that the manuscript is finished.

Then I am thankful to all who have so generously contributed information for this book. Geraniums are a complex subject and it seems to me that the six classifications have required me to write six books in one. On this account, I did, indeed, need help, and it was always forthcoming, from Maine to California, from England and Australia.

I have not forgotten those who helped me with the 1946 book and the 1950 and 1957 revisions, and again I thank them, particularly Dorcas Brigham. In her home and greenhouses at Village Hill in Williamsburg, Massachusetts, I wrote the greater part of my first geranium book in 1945. In the winter of 1963 in her Florida home, I commenced my work on this one.

For assistance on this 1965 book, I am most grateful to:

Fred A. Bode, Jr. In an extensive correspondence he has answered a multitude of questions, advised me soundly, and volunteered interesting information about plants and the people associated with them. Anyone who has corresponded with Fred knows the delightful quality of his letters and remembers their humor. When one of Fred's piercing comments comes suddenly to mind, I laugh aloud no matter where I am. And Alice Bode's marginal notes have been by no means the least of the pleasure of these letters.

Holmes C. Miller. He has devoted many hours to my text, furnished many dates of introduction of plants, and greatly increased my knowledge of the zonal geraniums—standard type, fancy-leaved, and particularly the dwarfs. I appreciate the fresh point of view he presented to me on the smaller geraniums, and I am indebted to him also for the Geranium Family Tree he prepared to show the years of hybridizing required to produce fine varieties like his.

William E. Schmidt. He generously shared his knowledge of the ivy-leaved and the regal classes that include many of his own handsome hybrids. He read the chapters on these groups and also advised me on the Finder's List.

Mary Ellen and Irvin Ross of Merry Gardens. I enjoyed an informative visit with them. Their collection of geraniums of all types is not equaled in the East, and these plants gave me an opportunity to compare and evaluate a great many varieties in a short time. Mary Ellen also conferred with me on the Finder's List, and her gift of small regal plants opened my eyes to their value as spring-blooming house plants in the East.

Mrs. Bruce Crane. I had a fine day studying her extensive collection of dwarf varieties and enjoying the beauty of the great baskets of ivy-leaved geraniums for which she is so justly famous. She kindly read the chapters dealing with both classes.

Elenore Rober Hamlin. She wrote a wonderful letter sharing

with me memories of her father, Ernest Rober, whom I had the privilege of meeting in California in 1945 when he named a geranium for me.

W. Howard Wilson of Wilson Brothers. He gave me excellent information on culture of geraniums in the Midwest and suggested suitable garden varieties for that area.

Robert Warner, Manhattan Garden Supply and President of the International Geranium Society. I appreciated his enthusiastic support and very much enjoyed the plants he sent me, including 'Lady Lavender'.

F. J. Eisenbart of Guse's Flowers. He supplied the dates I had been seeking of introduction of the Fiat varieties with serrated petals.

Mrs. Early F. Mitchell of Memphis, Tennessee; Mrs. J. B. Hall of Tampa, Florida; and Mrs. John D. West of Manitowoc, Wisconsin. I am most grateful for the regional information each of them supplied.

Ada L. Both of Sydney, Australia. I was pleased to have her account of the hybridizing work of her late husband, Ted Both, and the lists she provided of his varieties.

The Australian Geranium Society, and especially Mr. W. H. Heytman, the foreign correspondent. I enjoyed the complete file of their publications and his informative letters about geraniums in Australia.

Charles F. Lawrance of New Zealand. I found most interesting his account of the zonal geranium he named 'Mrs. Lawrance' for his mother.

Prof. Frank P. McWhorter, Oregon State University. He supplied a great deal of helpful information on the diseases of geraniums, especially verticillium wilt, and his letters were lively even though they were concerned with what is certainly a rather grim subject.

Dr. Seymour Shapiro. I was interested in his account of the

irradiation work he did on geraniums while he was at Brookhaven National Laboratory.

Albert O. Paulus, Donald E. Munnecke, the late Philip A. Chandler, for "Diseases of Geraniums in California," a publication of the University of California. This brief account provided insight into some of the California problems.

Contributors to "Geraniums," a publication of the Penn State Geranium Clinic, 1961. This collection of papers was an invaluable source of information.

David M. Hutt, University of California. His list of species was useful to me.

Hubert R. Smith, University of Melbourne. The report of his work on bacterial blight was most interesting.

Derek Clifford. I appreciated permission to use from his book "Pelargoniums" (Blandford Press, London, 1958) dates of introduction of certain species that arrived in England after Aiton's list appeared in "Hortus Kewensis" in 1789; also dates of introduction of some of the fancy-leaved zonal geraniums.

William J. Dress, Editor of "Baileya," and Prof. Harold E. Moore, Jr., Director of the Liberty Hyde Bailey Hortorium at Cornell University and author of "Pelargoniums in Cultivation." I owe special thanks for permission to reproduce from "Baileya" Vol. III, 1955, illustrations drawn by Mitsu Nakayama. These include original drawings reproduced in Figures 12 (right) and 44, and the following adaptations from earlier botanical illustrations: Figures 12 (left), 32, and 35 redrawn from Cavinelles' "Dissertationes"; Figures 5 (upper), 6, and 43 adapted from L'Heritier's "Geraniologia"; Figures 10 and 42B adapted from Curtis's "Botanical Magazine"; Figure 5 (lower) adapted from Knuth in "Das Pflanzenreich"; Figure 38 adapted from "Refulgium Botanicum"; Figure 42A, C, D adapted from Robert Sweet's "Geraniaceae".

The artists: I appreciate the many lovely new line drawings Elaine Ruth Harman has made for this edition; and I thank Natalie

Harlan Davis again for her drawings which were used in the earlier editions.

Paul Arnold. He strayed from his favorite Gesneriads to give me technical assistance and to interpret botanical data, and I thank him, indeed, for the information he collected and also for his careful editing of many of these pages.

Elaine Cherry. I am grateful for her meticulous editorial attention to detail to insure the accuracy and reliability of this complicated manuscript and to bring all the names of garden varieties in conformity with the International Code of Nomenclature for Cultivated Plants.

Helen B. Krieg, my secretary and friend. Her humor and continuing optimism have been wonderfully helpful through the long effort of this book.

Of course, the biggest "thank you" goes to the geraniums themselves. These have been a joy to me for many years and the varied forms never cease to give me pleasure. I appreciate particularly their gay greeting every morning—rain, mist, or shine—as I come downstairs into the Plant Room with trays, shelves, and brackets full of the colorful flowers and bright foliages of geraniums.

Helen Van Pelt Wilson

Westport, Connecticut
January, 1965

THE JOY OF GERANIUMS

Chapter ONE

Geraniums—
Plants for All Seasons, All People

If there is one plant that makes me wish I had more than one life to live, surely it is the geranium in its many lovely manifestations. All my life I have grown geraniums of one kind or another but especially since the early 1940s. And I find the longer our acquaintance, the greater the fascination—like association with a good friend. Some years I favor one classification, some years another. Yet even when the Plant Room overflows and all the broad window sills in my home are filled, if I visit the greenhouses of a specialist in winter, spring, summer, or fall, I cannot resist adding a few more geraniums! In every season, these are irresistible plants.

The appeal is due partly to the beauty of the flowers, partly to the diversity of the plants. There is such contrast, for instance, between the tiny greenish-yellow night-fragrant blooms of the species, *Pelargonium gibbosum* (Figures 1, 7), and the big cream-white to coral-pink blooms of the zonal, 'Always' (Figure 1); between the tricolor foliage of the fancy-leaved 'Skies of Italy' and

1

Figure 1. In her Plant Room in late spring, Helen Van Pelt Wilson holds a pot of the geranium 'Magnificent'. On the pebble trays are 'Always', 'Party Dress', 'Clorinda', *P. gibbosum,* some small regal plants, and various scented-leaved geraniums. From baskets trail the ivy-leaved 'Santa Paula' and 'Mexican Beauty'; the center shelf holds small pots of fancy-leaved geraniums. Photo by Bradbury.

the trailing mint-scented velvety *P. tomentosum* (Figures 25, 33). As for stature, 'Black Vesuvius' (Figure 27) might stay 3 inches tall for a couple of years while 'Rollisson's Unique' (Figures 37, 62) would grow to 5 feet in that time. Indeed every lover of plants finds favorites among the geraniums with their rich colors and interesting foliages.

By Any Name

This plant we see everywhere and call a geranium because our grandmothers did is not traveling under its right name. True, it is of the *Geraniaceae* family, but its particular genus is rightly *Pelargonium*. It was commonly called Storksbill by early enthusiasts for some real or fancied resemblance of its seed case to the long and slender form of a stork's bill. Within the family another genus, the *Erodium*, was designated Heronsbill; a third retained the name *Geranium* and was called Cranesbill.

Between *Geranium* and *Pelargonium* there is this botanical difference: the *Geranium* is "regular," the *Pelargonium* is "irregular." The five *Geranium* petals are evenly formed and regularly spaced; the *Pelargonium*, particularly in its early forms before man tampered with nature, had two- and three-petal groupings, the upper two petals often larger and more richly colored than the lower. In the species this differentiation remains. It often disappears from the varieties. The *Pelargonium* is also blessed with a nectar tube adnate—meaning "congenitally grown together"—to the flower stalk for almost the whole length. This is the most marked of the differences of form. As for locality, the *Geranium* is an herbaceous perennial of the northern hemisphere (also found in Africa and South America), a recurring lavender-pink pleasure in spring along the paths of my fern garden. The *Pelargonium* is generally a subshrub that hails from the southern hemisphere and, though some are hardy in California and Oregon, the genus is not hardy in gardens of our northern states.

With apologies, then, to botanists, in this book I will use pelargonium and geranium interchangeably—except sometimes in the case of the regals that *everyone* calls pelargoniums. Somehow I cannot discard a name so dear and meaningful as geranium.

Life Story

Geraniums were famous long before our grandparents' day. About the time the Maryland colony was being founded the forerunner of the clan, *Pelargonium triste,* the "sad or dull one" (sweetly aromatic at night) was taken to England from South Africa by the botanist and plant hunter, John Tradescant. I have seen his statue on the stairs at Hatfield House in England where he was gardener to Charles I. Soon many other species arrived via Dutch and English navigators who were engaged in the 1700s defending Britain's supremacy of the seas.

People took to geraniums at once and geraniums took to people. In England, and later in America, the plants grew and thrived, intercrossing with and without the hand of man, until Harvey and Sonder's "Flora Capensis" of 1859 listed 163. The latest monograph, Knuth's in 1912, mentions 232, while one checklist in 1945 compiled over 4,000 species and varieties. A revision today might well be twice that long.

Tracing the genealogy of the geranium is a fascinating, though admittedly frustrating, experience. While happily engrossed in studying the family tree I came upon this wistful statement in Andrews' 1805 monograph, "Geraniums":

> The principal difficulty annexed to this undertaking arises from the introduction of the African species within the last twenty years from the Cape of Good Hope, whose prolific character seems to know no bounds, in the production of endless seminal varieties, which, Proteus-like appear in ever-varying forms, and for which numerous variations we are indebted to the industrious bee; which, in its unceasing researches after nectariferous

Figure 2. Geraniums in a basket—cut flowers or potted plants—are always attractive. Here, set in coarse sphagnum moss, pots of pale pink geraniums bring a warm note of welcome to a small entrance porch of brick and concrete. Photo by Roche.

juice, constantly conveys the pollen, or farina, from one plant to another; which certainly disorganizes the symmetry of the sexual system, but at the same time more amply proves its real intrinsic merit by displaying the great power which is annexed to the seminal character of plants and that Nature, in spite of all the irregularities caused by this casual intermixing, evidently on the *externa facie* of the whole tribe still stamps Geranium! under which title we shall ever place it, regarding every unnecessary increase of genera as the direct road to confusion.

How sympathetically any modern student of geraniums must view this remarkably long sentence of the Andrews' preface. In subsequent months I read it again, comforting myself that mine was not a new dilemma. Geraniums evidently have no intention of lending themselves to the cool disciplines of science.

Yet, geraniums have not lacked historians to depict their progress in beauty through three centuries. In the library of the Massachusetts Horticultural Society, I studied many of the old records. As early as 1732, in King George II's time, J. J. Dilennius, botanist and professor at Oxford University, gave an account of the famous garden of James Sherard at Eltham—an account which, with proper dignity, he calls "Hortus Elthamensis"—and included among his handsome engravings half a dozen species of geraniums. His descriptions, which challenged my almost forgotten "classical education," are given in lengthy Latin. *Pelargonium* × *glaucifolium* (Figure 42) and *P. cucullatum* (Figures 43, 44) were already among those present.

Some twenty years later, in 1753, Linnaeus in his "Species Plantarum" brought the geranium list up to twenty-five. Many species that exist today had arrived in England by that time. Such plants as *P. inquinans* and *P. zonale*, progenitors of our familiar garden varieties, had taken up residence. The yellow-flowered night-fragrant *P. gibbosum* had appeared, as had that famous parent of the ivy-leaved varieties, *P. peltatum*; and such leaf-scented kinds as the lemon-scented *P. crispum,* the apricot-scented *P. scabrum,* and the apple-scented *P. odoratissimum* were already delighting English gardeners.

Near the end of the eighteenth century, the geranium record made significant progress. In 1792, the French botanist L'Héritier in his popular "Geraniologia" used the name *Pelargonium,* distinguishing this plant group from the *Erodium* and *Geranium.* His writings and twenty-nine engravings of pelargoniums, as Prof. Moore points out, could not form the basis of the genus *Pelargonium* under the International Code because of an earlier publication of the name with valid and legitimate descriptions by William Aiton in "Hortus Kewensis" Vol. 2, 1789. I found among L'Héritier's plates two of the oak-leaf *P. quercifolium* varieties, the rose-sweet *P. Radula* and *P. grœveolens,* and several other scented-leaveds; also the sticky *P. glutinosum* or Pheasant's Foot Geranium (Figures 28, 43), the square-stemmed *P. tetragonum* (Figure 8), and another parent of the ivy-leaveds, *P. lateripes* or Side Foot.

Biographers Andrews and Sweet

Then in 1805 came Henry Andrews' gloriously illustrated volume, "Geraniums," and between 1820 and 1830 the noble work of Robert Sweet: five truly-beautiful volumes of hand-colored plates with Latin names given to species and to the distinct garden hybrids. Both Andrews and Sweet produced such completely fascinating works that they have been my undoing. With outlined research to do and full of righteous intent, I have gone to the Pennsylvania Horticultural Society Library. There I have chanced to pick up a volume of Sweet "just for a moment." Twice it happened that hours passed while I dwelt enchanted on page after page of those exquisite paintings. In the interest of progress I finally requested the sympathetic librarian to hold the volumes from me unless I gave proof of specific need for their reference.

If you do not know the work of the painstaking Robert Sweet

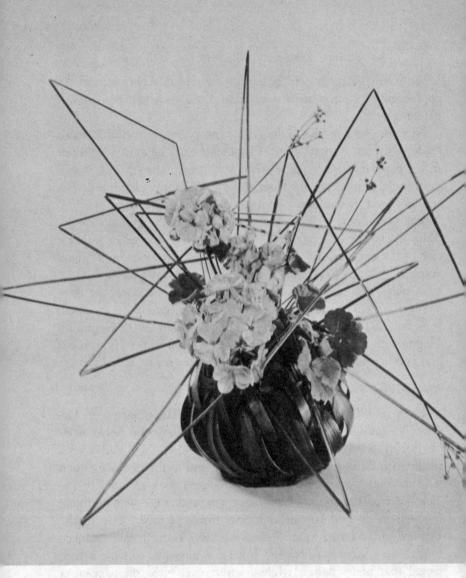

Figure 3.   Clusters of bright red 'Flame' geraniums, with their own leaves, and many-angled groups of marsh reeds are used by Lee Early Quinn in a sophisticated Japanese free-style arrangement. This abstracted design is a far cry from the more usual approach to geraniums as nostalgic Victorian bouquet flowers. Photo by Boice Studio.

who in 500 renderings covers the geranium story of the early nine-teenth century, by all means seek it out. Rare copies still exist in the larger libraries and in some private collections. Sweet found his subjects mainly at the nursery of Colville and Sons in Chelsea where for the first time, according to Loudon, hybridization was no longer left to chance but was managed "by manipulation."

You will be amazed at the differences between the plants de-picted by Andrews and Sweet and those commonly grown today. Perhaps you have thought of the geranium only as a scarlet crepe-paper ball of a flower for park beds and window boxes. In these 150-year-old books, it appears in multiform glory. Hundreds of varieties are shown and described—dwarfs and giants, smooth- and cut-leaved, and flowers of white, pink, lavender, near-yellow, and red colors.

It was from Andrews that I learned of *P. crassicaule* (Figure 5), discovered by Antoni Pantaleo Hove who was sent out by His Majesty in 1785 on a botanical expedition to Africa. There on the southwest coast in the bay of Angra Peguena, in a chasm of white marble rock where apparently there was no earth, he found a thick-stemmed, unknown geranium with roots several yards long. They were "naked and hard as wire and the heat was so intense on the rocks as to blister the soles of the feet." Yet this lovely white-flow-ered, round-leaved *P. crassicaule* was blooming there in mid-April as freely as if it were growing in a well-tended English garden. The plants "appeared to have received their nourishment solely from the moistness lodged there during the rainy season, assisted by a little sand drifted by the wind into the cavities," wrote Andrews. It is from such robust, tolerant ancestors that today's geraniums draw their strength.

In Sweet's "Geraniaceae" I read the story of the Duchess of Gloucester's *P. solubile*. This was so called because she discovered that water accidentally spilled on the petals dissolved their color. Sweet has little to say of the common or zonal geraniums. Yet in his time, Lady Grenville started the fashion of using geraniums as summer bedding plants. This innovation soon became popular. Her plants were fancy-leaved varieties, not the large-flowering types we modern gardeners use as bedding plants.

From 1750 On

Turning the pages of the old books, I can well appreciate the geranium furor of the early 1800s. The agitation subsided, but appreciation of geraniums lasted all through Queen Victoria's reign so that today many of us think of geraniums as primarily Victorian plants. However, they arrived in England long before her era.

Most geraniums are of South African origin with a few representatives from the north of Africa, Australia, and Asia Minor. *P. cotyledonis* (Figure 6) comes from St. Helena where the introduction of goats nearly caused its demise. Though distantly born, geraniums proved adaptable to the climate and the excellent gardeners of Britain.

In Colonial times, by 1750 in fact, the geranium flourished in America, too. And by 1806 it was mentioned in an encyclopedia of gardening published that year in Philadelphia. By 1877, Hansford in Columbus, Ohio, listed 159 species and varieties in his catalog; by 1893, Saul in Washington, D. C. had collected 392 of them. Certainly the rose- and other scented-leaved geraniums have long been dear to us, and fine collections of these and the fancy-leaved types continue to be made today, especially in the East.

From 1850 on, in California where warm days and cool nights approximate the climate of the Cape of Good Hope, splendid varieties of zonal, ivy-leaved, and regal geraniums have been developed. The last owe much of their present state of grace to such Germans as Carl Faiss, Max Burgers, and Richter of "Edel Pelargonium" fame. They developed magnificent varieties that were grown widely in America by 1925.

Much of the progress with garden and ivy-leaved varieties has been based on plants of French origin, for it happened that in 1863 in France an accidental seedling, produced in the garden of Henri Lecoq at Clermont-Ferrand, had flowers of double form. Thus, fortunately, the forebears of the spectacular garden geranium we enjoy today appeared in the time of the great hybridizer, Victor Lemoine. 'Floire de Nancy', 'Madame Lemoine', and 'Victor Lemoine' were among the varieties he developed from the pollen sent to him from that first double-flowered plant. The variety, 'Victor Lemoine', became the common seed parent used by English growers. Meanwhile, in another French garden, Mr. Jean Sisley crossed a single white and a double red to produce in 1872 the first double white.

Ten dollars apiece this new variety, 'Aline Sisley', cost our early California growers. Soon, however, James Hutchinson of Bay Nurseries in Oakland offered the plant in this country for $1.50. In their catalogs, Henry A. Dreer, Peter Henderson, William C. Walker, and R. D. Fox devoted pages to many beautiful varieties such as 'L'Aube', 'Madame Jaulin', 'Beaute de Poitevine', 'Charles Turner', 'Madame Thibault', 'Hall Caine', 'S. A. Nutt', 'New Life', 'General Grant', and 'Happy Thought'. Some of these are still cherished. Many have been superseded since progress never ceases when there is so diverse a heritage as that of the geranium.

Geraniums Today

Indeed, improvements continue to be phenomenal. To realize the possibilities you need only to read "Geraniums Around the World," the magazine of the International Geranium Society, or visit the nurseries of specialists. I shall always remember my talks with the late Ernest Rober of Los Angeles whose work with the zonals, particularly dwarf types, was so remarkable. I shall always be grateful, too, that he named a lovely lavender-pink single geranium for me. At my window in winter, on the terrace in summer, it reminds me of a happy encounter.

Figure 4. Lovely for simple long-lasting arrangements like this one by Catherine Cutler, white geraniums in bud and bloom are used with their own leaves in a white milk-glass vase of the same Victorian feeling as the flowers. However, the design is contemporary with its open outline and loose elongated focal area. Photo by Roche.

The late Richard Diener of Oxnard, California, produced an excellent strain of regals, and this type was also the particular concern of R. M. Henley of Indiana, and of Paul Howard of California.

The names of Dr. Charles Piper Smith, who published "Geranium Records"; Professor H. M. Butterfield of the University of California; Mrs. William H. Bohannon, Professor Stafford Jory, Mr. and Mrs. A. H. Cassidy, and the late Clara Sue Jarrett are all significant in pelargonium progress.

In the last twenty-five years William E. Schmidt of Palo Alto, California, a talented hybridizer, has offered us a fine selection of regals, ivy-leaveds, and zonals of which a few are dwarfs. In Los Altos, Holmes C. Miller has produced, particularly for the hobbyist, zonals in the most melting shades, both standard and dwarf types; and a number of excellent fancy-leaved varieties as well. His contribution to our pelargonium world is tremendous. Mr. and Mrs. Harry May of Long Beach are responsible for some fine ivy-leaveds and regals; and Fred Bode, Jr., the largest wholesale grower of geraniums in the world, has produced at Southern California Geranium Gardens some zonals, ivy-leaveds, and regals of fame and merit.

In the Midwest, at Roachdale, Indiana, a business started by Cully Wilson in a makeshift hothouse at the back of a general store continues almost fifty years later as Wilson Brothers. The firm sells more than a million plants yearly, and the Wilsons have produced some lovely varieties of their own.

In the East, pelargoniums flourished for years in the hands of Dorcas Brigham at Village Hill Nursery in Williamsburg, Massachusetts. Her collection of scented- and colored-leaved varieties was outstanding. In the same state Richard P. Stiles has brought together a representative group of geraniums. Joy S. Logee developed hybrids at Danielson, Connecticut. In New Jersey, Mrs. R. N. Vandivert, as a hobbyist, assembled an imposing collection.

Figure 5.   Thick-stemmed *Pelargonium crassicaule,* above, has white flowers, with or without spots, and spines at the stem tips. Found only in specialists' collections, *P. xerophyton,* below, is a sprawling, woody plant with tiny leaves and long-spurred flowers at the tips of short branches.

Among commercial enterprises, Merry Gardens at Camden, Maine, is outstanding. The collection there includes a great number in each classification: zonals of both standard and dwarf varieties, ivy-leaveds, regals, scented- and fancy-leaveds.

Mrs. Bruce Crane at Sugar Hill Nursery in Dalton, Massachusetts, seems to have all the dwarf varieties known to man both in England and America, and a superb collection of ivy-leaveds.

Overseas

The late Ted Both in Sydney, Australia, did significant work in the fields of dwarf zonals and *Pelargonium frutetorum* hybrids, and in developing varieties of complex parentage that he named Zonquils. He also produced pelargoniums he considered crosses of zonals and *P. staphysagroides,* though his was not the same as Sweet's *P. staphysagroides.* He experimented with 'Fingered Flowers', the small bushy plant that is a true zonal but does not look it. Mr. Both's death in 1963 was a blow to geranium enthusiasts everywhere, for he brought tremendous energy and imagination to his hybridizing work.

The contributions of English hybridizers are too numerous to mention, going back as they do through centuries of interest and enthusiasm. Today there is a continuous interchange of information—and visits too—among American, Australian, and English growers.

At Colleges and Universities

In areas all over the country, research is going on to improve the pelargonium; to cope, as at Pennsylvania and Oregon State Universities, with the problems of pest and disease; to develop varieties suited to the exigencies of our summer weather, as very dry heat and very high humidity, or long cold spells followed by long torrid periods. Several geraniums of notable quality for the Midwest have been produced at Iowa State University. Efforts have been made

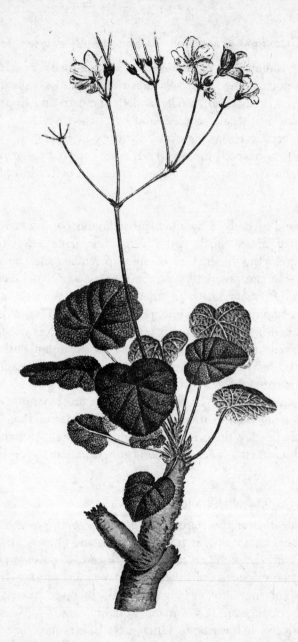

Figure 6. A rare Pelargonium from the Island of St. Helena is *P. cotyledonis* which differs from other thick-stemmed species in having almost undivided leaves covered by white hairs underneath. The flowers are white.

to untangle the twisted skeins of nomenclature. In the Bailey Hortorium at Cornell University, Prof. Harold E. Moore, Jr., has clarified the nomenclature of the species and Latin-named hybrid pelargoniums available from dealers in the United States.

Duplicate Naming of Geraniums

Duplication of names can be a frustration and even lessen our delight in the plants. At times I have felt more despair than pleasure when faced with a variety that roamed the country under five different names, or with two completely different geraniums with the same name. Like a rose, under any name a geranium is a sweet delight. 'Mary Ann' may be called 'Wilhelm Langguth' or 'Bijou', and still be an attractive plant; but, for the benefit of us all, I hope the promiscuous naming of plants will cease. In the interests of exactness, I have tackled French, German, and Latin monographs. I do not doubt Dutch treatises also contain invaluable information, but my mild linguistic abilities have already been seriously strained.

Six Useful Classifications

In this book I will discuss geraniums under six broad classifications: *Species,* especially the cactus and climbing types; *Single and Double Zonals,* also known as Fish, Horseshoe, Garden, and Common geraniums, botanically the *P. × hortorum* group, and including certain unusual forms and both standard and dwarf varieties; *Fancy-leaved zonals; Scented-leaved zonals; Ivy-leaved* or trailing, *P. peltatum; Regals,* known also as Lady Washington, Fancy, or Show geraniums, scientifically as the *P. × domesticum* group.

I apologize, for the last time, for so often calling these proper pelargoniums "geraniums." As in other aspects of life, I *know* better than I *do*. The point is, a plant I grew up with as a geranium is still that to me and, as Leigh Hunt remarked,

Everything is handsome about the geranium, not excepting its name.

Chapter TWO

The Amazing Species

Like the proverbial taste for olives, pleasure in the species and interspecific hybrids apparently must be acquired. For myself, I can say only that there are no plants in my window gardens, even ugly ones like the tortured *Pelargonium carnosum,* that interest me more. I value few of the species for their bloom, although the flowers of some like *P. gibbosum* and *P. × rutaceum* are pretty, and the possibilities of those two as parents of yellow, night-scented offspring always come to mind when they produce their long-petioled clusters of yellow-green or yellow-rimmed maroon bloom. What fascinates me is the amazing contrast of the species' foliages and growth habits to those of the more usual geraniums.

Confront almost anyone with the thick-stemmed, succulent ferny *P. dasycaule,* the stark square-stemmed *P. tetragonum,* or the thorny stalks of *P. fulgidum* and the reaction is the same: "That can't be a geranium!" Yet these strange plants belong to the family *Gera-*

18

niaceae and the genus *Pelargonium* as surely as the familiar zoned-leaf garden plant or the ivy-leaved geranium trailing over the window box. The scented-leaved species, also, often are odd if you come right down to it, but they are accepted more readily as geraniums, perhaps because the rose-fragrant *P. graveolens,* peppermint-scented *P. tomentosum,* and many others have been with us for such a long time.

The pelargonium species (some of them climbers, some quite cactuslike with their sharp spines) are only, I suppose, for way-out enthusiasts like me. If you are a collector of geraniums, you surely will want a few species and if you are botanically minded you may prefer them to all others. Your window garden or greenhouse will not be so pretty, but it certainly will be interesting. However, there are a number of species that are quite attractive except when they are dormant. Then they are a sight, and I retire them behind a tree. For some reason, curious guests always seem to discover them there and think I am concealing my dying failures. In their prime, the tall species like *P. gibbosum* look fine against a greenhouse wall or trained as an espalier. The flowers of others are charming in bouquets, and I use them to add fineness to a composition, as baby's-breath often is combined with garden flowers. In my bean-pot bouquet you can see the sprays of *P.* × *Stapletonii* and *P.* × *rutaceum* (Figure 20). It is amazing how exactly these species fit the old descriptions. So similar, too, are the plants in the old paintings that today's plants might well have sat for portraits made almost a century and a half ago.

Climbing Types

Pelargonium × *rutaceum* is the Rue-scented Storksbill of Sweet III, 279 (Figures 20, 42). There is a fragrance, perhaps of rue, to the gray-green ferny leaf and a sweet scent to the evening flowers. This plant has a tuberous root and, as Sweet indicates, "a fruticose stem unequally knotty in irregular swellings." I have seen one 30

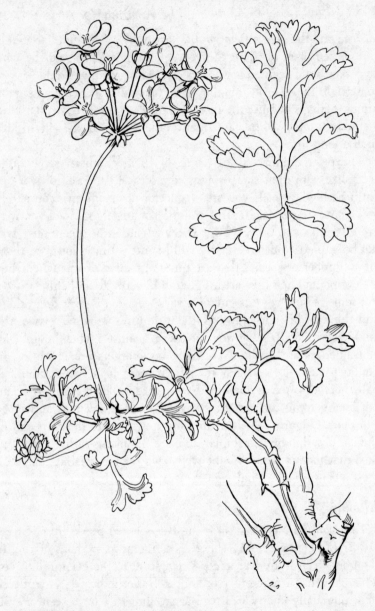

Figure 7.   The knotted or Gouty Storksbill, *P. gibbosum,* is a night-scented climber with greenish yellow flowers, gray-green brittle foliage, and tan, corky, jointed stems that show noticeable swellings.

inches high with 10- to 12-inch flower stems, growing in a 6-inch pot. The 3-inch umbel was made up of tiny maroon-petaled flowers with a yellow rim and yellow base of good clear color. According to Sweet, *P.* × *rutaceum* is a hybrid raised from seed of *P. multi-radiatum*, fertilized by pollen of *P. gibbosum* from which it inherited, among other characteristics, its strong evening scent. *P.* × *rutaceum* blooms in summer and is extremely succulent, requiring little water except when in blossom or full growth. My plant blooms in spring, seems loath ever to go dormant, and hangs on to some foliage all the time. I have trained it over a narrow 3-foot wire arch thrust into the pot. In its flowering season, this is a fine figure of a plant and an interesting contrast among the other geraniums.

When *P. gibbosum* (Figures 1, 7) lacks leaf and bloom, it presents a stark framework and has a wooden *feel*. Where the tan, corky stems are jointed, the swellings measure ¾ of an inch across. Sweet states that *P. gibbosum* has been in cultivation since 1712, and Andrews mentions that it is one of the African species enumerated by Willdenow.

Pelargonium × *glaucifolium* is also a tuberous-rooted climber that I have liked (Figures 28, 43). Not mentioned by Andrews, it is described by Sweet I, 354. Its flowers—maroon, yellow, and green—resemble *P.* × *rutaceum* but are darker. The leaves are large and ruffled, pinnately divided, and the night scent is powerful and sweet. Low-growing, it works during fall and winter and ends its year in spring with clusters of small flowers.

The plant we hear of as *P. orithnifolium* or *criterifolium* is probably *P. crithmifolia* of Sweet II, 179. *Crithmifolia* means samphire-leaved and the foliage does resemble samphire. Philip M. Post had this rare plant in his collection and described it as "an odd looking thing with a succulent green stem an inch or more in diameter, and just about as thick at the tip as at the base. When dormant, it might easily pass for some xerophytic euphorbia. The deciduous foliage is almost as finely compound as carrot tops, and it produces

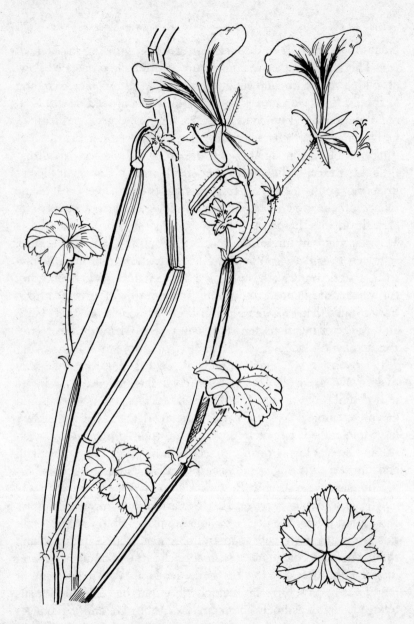

Figure 8.   Square-stalked cranesbill, *P. tetragonum*, is unusual in every way. This climber has a quadrangular stem, the two upper petals conspicuous; other petals of the rose-and-white flowers are scarcely noticeable.

huge clusters of pink-striped, white flowers." I have seen the plant when not in bloom. It was ugly but interesting, with a leaf the image of the Sweet painting.

Pelargonium tetragonum is a plant only a collector could love, at least when out of bloom. But I must say I find it fascinating, like a homely woman with a lot of personality. Absolutely nothing is usual about it. It has even lost a petal and offers but four, violating the rule of five petals for pelargoniums. Called Square-stalked Jenkinsonia by Sweet I, 99 and the Square-stalked Cranesbill by Andrews, it went from the Cape to Kew Gardens in London about the time of our Declaration of Independence. Curtis's "Botanical Magazine" in 1789 had this to say of *P. tetragonum*: "A vein of singularity runs through the whole of this plant, its stalks are unequally and obtusely quadrangular, sometimes stems more evidently triangular, its leaves few and remarkably small; its flowers on the contrary are uncommonly large and what is more extraordinary have only four petals; previous to their expansion they exhibit also an appearance somewhat *outre,* the body of the filaments being bent so as to form a kind of bow.

"When it flowers in perfection, which it is not apt to do in all places, the larger of its blossoms renders it one of the most ornamental of the genus. There is a variety of it with beautiful colored leaves." This one is no longer with us but *P. tetragonum* with round, crenate, stiff green leaves that have a rubbery feeling is not too scarce. Figure 8 was drawn in May, although June to September is the usual flowering time.

Pelargonium scandens has a round, crenate, slightly-zoned shiny dark leaf. The medium-sized magenta flower clusters are loose and spidery looking and the single flowers are made up of rather linear petals. It is known popularly as the Climbing Geranium, and is perhaps the easiest to grow and the most easily obtained of the species pelargoniums. It branches freely and makes an attractive well-formed pot plant, although the color of the petals does not arouse

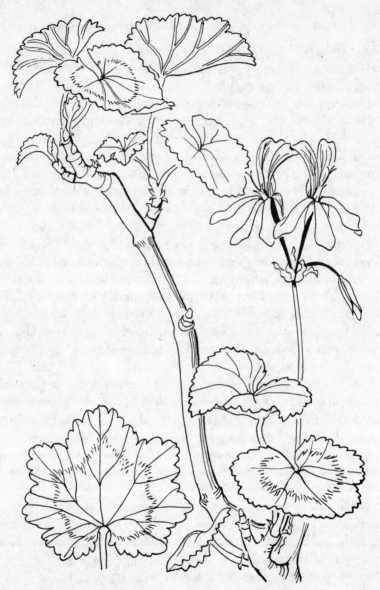

Figure 9.   Climbing Geranium, *P. scandens*, bears spidery, magenta flower clusters that rise above the shiny, slightly-zoned dark leaves.

much enthusiasm in those who see it in bloom; it is shown in Figure 9.

This Climbing classification is arbitrary. Almost all the stronger varieties of pelargoniums will climb if supported. The pepper-scented 'Rollisson's Unique', given half a chance, makes immediately for the top of a greenhouse or the frame of a window. 'Lavender Ricard' and other strong zonals, and the scented-leaved 'Clorinda', if offered cord, stake, or strong wire arch or iron grill for support, soon progress upward. Some plants of *P. peltatum*, the ivy-leaved geranium, would just as soon climb as trail, and they make excellent espaliers.

If you keep in mind this climbing quality of both the oddities and the standards, the geranium becomes a plant of even greater possibilities. Against lath-house or greenhouse wall it can be exciting in bloom or simply among those present while dormant. Large plants may be trained to frame a sunny window garden. In California exuberant varieties reveal their decorative ability to cover a trellis, mask an unattractive wall, or grace a patio stair.

Cactus Types

These are so called because of their sharp pointed stipules that resemble those of certain cacti. This group is to be distinguished from the cactus-*flowered* geraniums which are zonals. Among the cactus types, the Prickly-stalked Geranium, *P. echinatum* (Figure 10) is to a T the plant pictured by Sweet I, 54 and by Andrews. Out of flower and leaf it is scarcely worth a glance. "Betwixt the blowing of the first and last umbels—there are usually four, although some plants flower almost constantly except for brief summer dormancy—it is, indeed, a lovely thing," states Andrews. Petals are a clean white, the upper two brilliantly marked crimson, and the clusters are showy and graceful. The grayish stems of *P. echinatum* are fleshy with many recurved brownish spines; roots are tuberous and "the leaves silky, between heart-shaped and roundish;

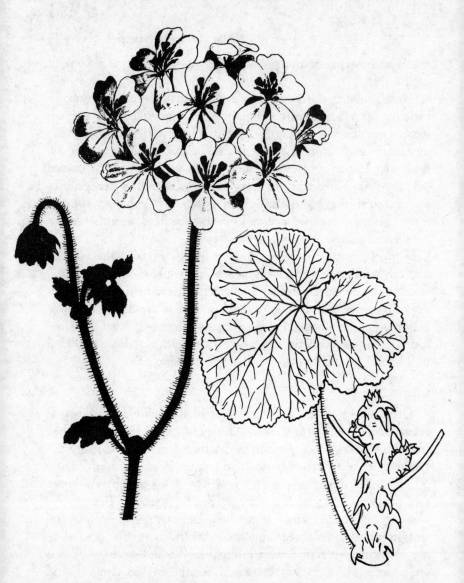

Figure 10. The Sweetheart Geranium, *P. echinatum,* has sturdy upright growth and large pale-lavender flowers. It blooms from early winter into spring.

from three to five lobes, toothed." Purple flowers may also appear with whites on the same plant.

Sweet considers the beautiful *P. echinatum* "one of the most desirable plants of the genus for any collection, as it begins to flower in autumn, after most other kinds have done, and if kept in a warm situation; it will continue to bloom till late in spring." In New England, *P. echinatum* blooms toward spring, rather than in winter; but in some greenhouses it has given a longer account of itself, and has been colorful from December to May. Certainly, it makes an excellent and interesting pot plant with flowers lovely as an orchid. Flowers measure more than an inch across and petals are notched. The upper petals are maroon-marked to form a heart and so give the plant the common name, Sweetheart Geranium. In whatever season flowering commences, spring or autumn, it continues for a long time and the dormancy of a mature plant is usually only a matter of weeks while young plants in their first year rest not at all.

Slow-growing, *P. echinatum* produces two kinds of stems. The permanent main ones are gray, short, and stubby with brief laterals and hard spiny stipules to justify the name *echinatum,* which means spiny. Long-stalked, silvery leaves grow in tufts at the ends of the branches. Flowering stems are slender and branching with but a few small leaves at the lower points. A stem will produce from 3 to 12 umbels of bloom. Then the stem dies back.

Even the tubers of *P. echinatum* are fascinating. Of spherical form they are placed like "beads on a string." On one 6-inch plant recorded in "The Pelargonium Bulletin," 77 such tubers were counted, yet the specimen was only in its second year.

The tuberous-rooted *P. fulgidum,* the Celandine-leaved Storksbill of Sweet I, 69 and the Refulgent-flowered Cranesbill of Andrews, is included in the cactus types (Figure 42). The *P. fulgidum* plant I have seen is much like the old ones pictured, except that the modern flower is smaller and less prominently marked. (Sometimes one reads of *P. fulgidium,* which is probably only a misspelling.) 'Old Scarlet Unique' is a scented-leaved variety of P. *fulgidum* showing a definite relationship in habit of growth (Figure 45). It has more striking, larger flowers, red with black markings.

The P. *fulgidum* I know has an oblong, wooly, grayish-green, 3-lobed toothed leaf with an elongated and divided terminal lobe. Each smaller lobe is twice indented. The plant is tall and thick-stemmed with prominent, pointed stipules. Flowers are fairly small but a rich and lovely crimson. In summer P. *fulgidum* is dormant but toward September it comes alive again and makes a plant as tall as the climbers.

P. × *saepeflorens,* the Frequent-flowered Storksbill of Sweet I, 58, is by Andrews called Frequent-flowering Prickly-stalked Cranes-bill, a title to suggest one of those endless German words like *Schnellnachrichtenverkehr,* meaning Special Delivery! Anyway, the modern plant, very rare, is the same as Sweet's and Andrews' with rosy, red-spotted flowers much like the white, red-spotted blossoms of P. *echinatum.* This cultivated material may be a cross of P. *echinatum* with "its relative species the *reniforme,*" as Andrews suggests. Its wonderful habit of flowering the greater part of the year, with only a brief midsummer slump, makes it as valuable today as yesterday. The shrubby, brown stem is fleshy and spiny, the flat, cordate leaves are bluntly notched, tomentose below and pubescent above. P. × *saepeflorens* is a handsome plant worth having for other reasons than oddity.

Pelargonium × *Stapletonii* is the child of P. *echinatum* and P. × *saepeflorens* (Figure 20). Not mentioned by Andrews, it was named by Sweet III, 212, Miss C. Stapleton's Storksbill, "in compliment to Miss C. Stapleton of Grey's Court, Henley on Thames, a lady much attached to the *Geraniacae* and to whom we feel much obliged." The flowers are similar to those of P. *echinatum* except the petals are not white but suffused carmine with large purple spots on the upper ones. However, these are white near the base. The barked stem is shrubby and glossy with spiny stipules. The

Figure 11. A form of *P. frutetorum* with somewhat the same leaf blotch as 'Dark Beauty' but with a different leaf shape and a much fuller umbel of salmon-pink flowers.

5-lobed leaves, their points bent downwards, are cordate and wavy. They are more lobed and crenate than those of P. *echinatum*.

Frutetorum Group

Pelargonium frutetorum is a fairly recent discovery. It was found in Cape Province, South Africa, in 1931 and named and described by R. A. Dyer in 1932. In the wild apparently it sprawls and clambers among shrubby plants. In baskets, stems spread and droop, turning up at the ends and not hanging loosely. Typical plants are rather long-jointed and only moderately branching, inclined to rank and weedy growth. Its particular value is in the bold clean zoning of the prominently lobed leaf. Zoning is actually more pronounced than in P. *zonale,* and this unfortunately has led to *frutetorum* derivatives sometimes being called horseshoe geraniums. It seems to me this should be avoided since for more than a century the name "horseshoe geranium" has been applied commonly to P. *zonale* and *its* varieties.

The rambling species *frutetorum* is hardly a showy plant. Only three or four of the single salmon-pink flowers are normally open at one time and these have quite narrow petals though not so linear as those of P. *acetosum.* 'Dark Beauty' is a mutant form with shorter joints and denser growth, a strong grower but more amenable as pot or basket plant or for spreading out in a garden bed. Holmes Miller has used it since 1946 in his hybridizing. His 'Medallion' is a fine, fancy-leaved basket plant. 'Filigree' is good for a small basket. 'Greetings' is a stiffer grower of excellent coloring. 'Sorcery' is low and spreading, smaller than the others.

Miss Frances Hartsook, a hybridizer of Baja California, is working with P. *frutetorum* to increase foliage color in her varieties and to get wider range of hue in the flowers. 'Royal', introduced in 1960, is a small plant for baskets but still with single salmon flowers. Many more varieties are promised from her hybridizing. Figure 11 is a form of P. *frutetorum* drawn from a plant grown by Dorcas

Figure 12. The Heart-leaved Storksbill, *P. cordifolium,* left, has sturdy, up-right growth and large pale lavender flowers. Low-growing *P. Endlicheri-anum,* right, from a basal rosette sends up stalks bearing flowers with upper petals so much larger than the lower ones the flowers seem to have only two.

Brigham some years ago at Village Hill.

The late Ted Both of Australia used *P. frutetorum* extensively in his hybridizing program. Two of his varieties, 'Magic Lantern' and 'Mosaic', came to us in 1962 from Fred Bode. They make excellent basket plants with single salmon flowers, those of 'Mosaic' larger and more freely produced.

In time we may be getting from Australia the Both Hybrid Staphs, a series based on the apparently native Chinese cactus-type geranium known as 'Fiery Chief'. To Mr. Both the closest ancestor to this seemed to be the species *P. staphysagroides,* which Sweet illustrated in his Volume V. Although Mr. Both was in error about *P. staphysagroides,* these so-called Staphs are lovely with large star-like flowers. In Australia they are available in a wide selection of named varieties, as 'Fairy Queen', 'Dawn Star', and 'Bright Pixie'.

It has been found that *P. frutetorum* crosses readily with culti-vars normally accepted as zonal geraniums, so the hybrids may well be considered within *P. × hortorum,* as defined by Bailey. This botanical group now includes the whole hybrid class of zonals, whether or not foliage is actually zoned.

Other Species

Lost species and Latin-named hybrids are coming to light all the time, and I get them as I can locate them. I have enjoyed *P. × ardens* with its bright scarlet glow. *P. cordifolium,* the Heart-leaved Storksbill of Sweet, with lavender flowers is a pretty foliage plant out of bloom (Figure 12). *P. reniforme* makes a delightful cascade for a geranium tub in summer, its thin wiry stems covered with small gray-green leaves and a nice scattering of bright purple flow-ers (Figure 46).

A favorite is *P. tricuspidatum,* which may be a form of *P. scabrum* or a *P. scabrum* cross but does not look so. I like it for the terrace plantstand in summer when it produces small white flowers, the two upper petals carmine-brushed. Nothing, of course, could look less like a geranium.

Pelargonium × *coriandrifolium* makes a choice bracket plant for me, trailing down the west casement in the Plant Room; it would be pretty in a basket with its ferny foliage like refined parsley and its small single lavender-to-white flowers. This is a pleasing change from ivy and philodendron vines, and we do need trailers for grace in our window gardens.

Pelargonium australe is common in Australia but with no source I know of in this country, although a rather dull-scented cross was sold here as 'Australis'. There is a story that P. *australe* came to Australia from Capetown through seed in mud clinging to the hooves of cattle. It felt so much at home that it became naturalized up and down the coast in the vicinity of Sydney. I am told it is a pretty thing with heart-shaped leaves and flowers with narrow blush red-spotted and feathered upper petals (Figure 43).

These species and others are described more fully in the Finder's List. Many of the scented-leaveds are also species but they are not so odd as some we have just been discussing. The scented-leaved species and varieties are described in the Finder's List on page 320; the other species are described separately in the Finder's List on page 296. As is obvious, I grow the species as pot plants simply for my pleasure. If you want a more serious view, consult Derek Clifford's excellent reference book, "Pelargoniums." It is published in England but is available here through growers. Mail-order houses do not always list all their species because of short supply and limited demand, but an inquiry often reveals a source for a wanted plant. Merry Gardens has a good number of species.

Chapter THREE

Handsome Zonals and Their Groups

Chances are, if you know geraniums at all, you recognize those called "common," although they are most uncommonly handsome. True, they are the ones most commonly seen—the double zonals of proud heritage and form with colors so brilliant they have few rivals in the whole plant world. Indeed these geraniums have so long adorned the American scene from public park to private fire escape that it is possible for a city child never to have seen a tree and yet to know intimately the leaves and flowers of these old-fashioned plants.

The zonals are so named for the usually dark circular marking on the green scalloped leaf. But there are fancy-leaved zonals, too, with richly colored and patterned foliage; and there are zonals with single as well as double blooms; and many fascinating flower forms as in the Bird's Egg, Rosebud, and Cactus-flowered groups. With these the collector can be enslaved, and assuredly we all begin with the

Figure 13. The old-fashioned geranium can be used to plant a garden island as here in a graveled area outside the dining room of a contemporary
home. Friede R. Stege, L. A. Photo by Molly Adams.

zonals. Properly they are called *Pelargonium* × *hortorum*, a group name given to them by Liberty Hyde Bailey.

Early in the eighteenth century the progenitors of this famous race went to England. They were elegantly sponsored, one by the Duchess of Beaufort in 1710 and the other by Bishop Compton in 1714. *Pelargonium inquinans*, the "staining" geranium, still exists in America. I have seen plants of it, the leaves not so sticky as Linnaeus indicated in "Species Plantarum" of 1753. They are handsome, stalwart growers with the same single, graceful flowers of a clear, beautiful vermilion shown in the old engraving. As an ancestor, *P. inquinans* was worth a portrait and may still be claimed with pride by its many descendants. The other parent, *P. zonale*, provided the leaf markings. Zonal geraniums today are derived mainly from the mingling of the various forms of *P. inquinans* and *P. zonale*, and their mutations, although other species have contributed to lesser degree.

Standard, French, and Other Types

Among zonals, there are two major types, Standard and French, based on chromosome count. In his catalog, Holmes Miller still lists them separately, and for the hybridist the distinctions are significant. Looking at a group of typical zonals in bloom, we do not find it too hard to differentiate them.

Standard zonals are usually thinner-stemmed diploids with a chromosome count of 18. (Dwarf and fancy-leaved zonals also have 18 chromosomes.) If flowers are double, they are usually fully double. In the Standard types, sometimes called English, we find the greater range of hues and flower forms. Singles that are closest to English and Australian taste—and preferred by many collectors here as well—are round-flowered like 'Honeymoon', not the "primitive" type of 'Mrs. E. G. Hill', which has the 2- and 3-petal groupings.

The French type, presumably tetraploidal forms (having a

chromosome count of 36), occurred spontaneously from the Standard type in Poitiers, France, about 1880. The French type has been called variously the Bruant Race, the Gigantea Section, the Gros Bois Geraniums or Heavy-Wooded Type. In "Les Geraniums," Paris, 1897, Dauthenay described them thus: "Umbels ordinarily 4 to 5 inches in diameter: flowers very large; petals roundish, or sometimes triangular, the limb always very large and giving the corolla a remarkably round contour: leaves very large, thick and coriaceous, . . . their diameter averaging about 5 inches, pedicels large and short: peduncles large, rigid, and projecting beyond the foliage: wood soft, fleshy, very large, often 1½ inches around."

As Holmes Miller describes them, "They are more vigorous, with larger, rougher, and more sharply toothed leaves, larger stems, and, on the average, larger and more irregular flowers on much heavier stalks. The petals generally are heavy and firmly attached, making the flowers very durable. *All* the differences are not always present."

Paul Bruant did not originate the race but he did produce a number of varieties of it, as 'Alphonse Ricard', 'Beaute Portevine', 'Fiat', and the single-flowered 'Mrs. E. G. Hill'. The name Bruant is probably founded on his 1882 variety called 'Bruant', a semidouble red. Many of Bruants' varieties, as 'Berthe de Presilly' and 'Marguerite de Layre' were not of the French type.

The heavy-wooded French type proved hardy and resistant to heat and disease, and the mostly semidouble flowers in many pink and salmon shades with a few reds and at least one orange, are very popular. The brilliant red 'Alphonse Ricard', a Bruant introduction of 1894, was a favorite into the 1940s. 'Improved Ricard', a French type but not one of Bruant's, was introduced about 1949 and is still popular. A soft medium shade of red with large semidouble flowers on a strong fairly tall plant, it is a sport of 'Madame Landry'. 'Orange Ricard', whose origin is obscure, has large double orange-to-scarlet flowers on a big free-flowering plant and is a handsome example of the French type.

Of less importance to us now—but of considerable future promise —are various other types that we might term German, Oriental, and Czechoslovakian. Geraniums also occur in Lapland and Siberia. Fred Bode hopes some day to visit these countries and "possibly bring back northern varieties that will bloom well for us indoors through the winter."

Of the German type Fred Bode says, "This group, also with 36 chromosomes, is unusually beautiful and dependable. Here belong the double soft rose-colored slightly-marked 'Marktbeherrscher' or 'Market Leader' and 'Schöne Schwarzwälderin', which we offer as 'Forest Maid'." I have this lovely one with big round fully-double rose-pink flowers and soft green foliage, a pretty pot plant in my window in winter and on the south terrace steps in summer. 'Forest Maid' shows no upper-petal markings and appears more ivylike than the Standard or French types. In maturity it makes a nice cascading basket plant.

Fred Bode also describes an Oriental type that he has seen but that is not available here yet, with "gigantic flowerheads having rarely more than four flowers, but these measuring 2¼ inches across."

Family Matters

The zonals also can be divided into a number of groups, some like the Irenes with an ever-increasing progeny; others like the Double Drydens or the Bird's Eggs or the Peltato-Zonals ('Alliance' is one of these) with only a few survivors of a once-extensive group. These groups have developed in two ways. They come from lines of mutation appearing on one variety or on mutations of that variety, and members closely resemble each other, as in the Better Times group where plant and flower form are almost identical. Groups also are developed by hybridizers who use one plant consistently for the seed or pollen parent; members of such a group differ from each other a little more than members of a mutation group, but still the group resemblance is strong, again as among the Irenes.

The Irene Group

Among commercial growers and florists who supply the early spring market with flowering gift plants and the summer market with geraniums for window boxes, garden beds, and terrace pots and tubs, the Irenes, a group of the French type, are favorites at present. Only in the South where early bloom is less of a problem than in the North are other varieties more popular. Indeed there are now so many Irenes and they have proved so satisfactory that Fred Bode's wholesale Southern California Geranium Gardens puts out a supplementary catalog of Irenes alone. In it the selection of reds is wide, from the orange-scarlet 'Lollipop' to the dark crimson 'Apache'.

My own brief acquaintance with newer Irenes, like the lovely rose-pink 'Party Dress' and the enormous scarlet 'Toyon', whose size so amazed the visitors to a flower show here, has been satisfactory winter and summer. However, while acknowledging their worth, and by all means *wanting some of them,* I think hobbyists may be drawn more to unusual flower forms; nor does great size have much appeal to the real-gone collector. However, for the large or small commercial grower the increasing tribe of Irenes is of great importance.

Charles Behringer of Warren, Ohio, originated the Irenes in the early 1940s. His were weedy open plants, a far cry from the newer compact selections like 'Radiant'. As a rule, the Irenes produce masses of semidouble flowers that are loose-petaled; some are inclined to shatter. Modern crosses are destined to correct this and certainly my newer varieties do not scatter, and they are of more compact and formal appearance than the older Irenes. Constant bloom indoors and out, ruggedness, heat endurance, and reasonable pest resistance are Irene characteristics.

About 1953, following Mr. Behringer's death, David Agate of Elm Road Greenhouses, also in Warren, acquired and advertised the Irenes, and they became the most popular of all commercial varieties. Some of them were seedlings, many were sports or sports from sports. In the early 1960s, Wilson Brothers introduced 'Blaze'.

Meanwhile, Fred Bode developed a most tremendous enthusiasm for the Irenes. The first mutation he introduced was 'La Jolla' in 1959; 'Party Dress', 'Toyon', 'Jeweltone', and 'Seventeen' are among his handsome newer ones. The older 'Salmon Irene' (known in England as 'Cal') has long been popular; also 'Springtime', a lighter salmon-pink shade. In all there are now more than twenty varieties of Irenes including:

'Apache'	'Lollipop'
'Blaze'	'Party Dress'
'Buccaneer'	'Penny'
'Corsair'	'Radiant'
'Dark Red Irene'	'Red Meteor'
'Firebrand'	'Rose Irene'
'Genie'	'Salmon Irene'
'Irene'	'Seventeen'
'Jolly Roger'	'Springtime'
'Jeweltone'	'Toyon'
'La Jolla'	'Warrior'

Better Times Group

Before the 1960s, this was the important commercial group, and today's 'Better Times' itself, apparently a 1935 sport of 'Edmond Blanc' found in a New York greenhouse, still commands major sales. The group is popular in the Pacific Northwest, and to a lesser degree throughout Ohio and elsewhere.

This group is also notable for mass bloom, dependable for colorful winter flowers, and useful for its compact (not cabbagelike) neat, low-growing plant form. It is hardy where temperatures do not fall for a long period below 50 degrees F. Commercial growers sometimes complain of the constant winter cleanup of old flowers and the disbudding required, but hobbyists value such a dependable winter succession of bloom. Flowers are fully double and of medium size. Spider mites can be a problem but plants are reasonably resistant to stem-rot and not prone to botrytis.

Members of the Better Times group are almost identical except for flower colors. These run from magenta through red to rose and cerise. 'Better Times' itself is a rich crimson. There are no whites, no clear pink, salmon, or orange shades among them. Here is the group:

'Better Times'   'Glamour'
'Conquistador'   'Magenta Ruby'
'Edna'   'Royal Times'
'Galli Curci'

Radio Group

This Standard group is famous for red varieties that still appear on big commercial lists but no longer in specialists' catalogs. On the whole, 'Dark Red Irene' and other reds are preferred. Once 'Radio Red', introduced about 1920, was a favorite for its habit of late blooming with double flowers of brilliant vermilion on a tall small-wooded plant. 'Scarlet Princess', a patented and probably a tetraploid variety with heavy wood, followed. This one was also called 'Hasse's Scarlet Princess', 'Hasse's Scarlet', and probably also 'TV Red'. Two sports, 'ABC Red' and 'Avalon Red', are still around but recommended only where seasons are short and weedy growth not objectionable.

Figure 14. For her own small, delightful formal garden, the landscape architect, Friede R. Stege, selected the dark pink zonal geranium 'Fiat Supreme' (synonym 'Dawn') and light pink 'Fiat Enchantress' as summer bedding plants to follow the early display of tulips. The perennial edging of *Veronica incana* is a pleasant foil to the dark green of the geranium foliage. Photo by Molly Adams.

Fiat Group

The progenitor of this French group, 'Fiat', was introduced by Bruant in 1908. Very likely that was the same lovely salmon-pink semidouble we enjoy today. *Apparently* Bruant's 'Fiat' was a sport of a plant now known as 'Gorgeous', a geranium that has had a checkered career, appearing also as 'Jennifer Jones' and 'Avalon Beauty', and no longer important to trade or hobbyist. Fred Bode says that about one in every 200 plants of 'Fiat' is a reversion to 'Gorgeous'. Sometimes 'Fiat' itself is called 'Pink Fiat' to distinguish it from 'Red Fiat', which, to make matters interesting but I hope not confusing, is *not* a Fiat but a relative of another notable French group, the Alphonse Ricards. Furthermore, there may well have been a 'Pink Fiat' that was not the same as the present-day 'Fiat'. In 1950, K. G. Schulze claimed that in 1919 he had originated 'Pink Fiat' from a cross between 'Ronsard' and 'Madame Laporte Bicuit'. In the history of the Fiats, fact and speculation are indeed mixed, but this does not affect our enjoyment of the many varieties now known as Fiats.

From 'Fiat' has come a fine series of sports and sports of sports. These, despite the acknowledged delicacy of some varieties like 'Fiat Enchantress', are great favorites, especially those with serrated petals. Some scientists consider these to be virus mutations, thus the results of disease; if true, it does not seem to affect their performance.

Characteristics of the Fiats are soft gray-green foliage and compact short-jointed growth. Under cool conditions, outdoors or in a greenhouse, they are superb. For winter bloom, bloom in the shade, in sheltered pots or window boxes, they are exquisite—and dependable. In the open garden, they are too often failures, resenting heat, intolerant of very dry or very wet conditions, and subject to botrytis. However, in my garden where plants are in pots packed in peatmoss, the variety 'Fiat' has thrived and bloomed luxuriously through

some of the worst New England summers in the memory of man.
But I have placed the plants in protected locations out of full sun
(in full sun they are inclined to bloom themselves to death), and
they have never lacked water. If you select some of the beautiful
Fiats, keep in mind that their need for water and fertilizer is
greater than that of most other geraniums. These are all said to
belong to the Fiat group:

'Camellia Fiat'	'Fiat Queen'
'Cameo Fiat'	'Fiat Supreme'
'Dawn'	'Gorgeous'
'Fiat' ('Pink Fiat')	'Princess Fiat'
'Fiat Enchantress'	'Royal Fiat'
'Fiat King'	

Alphonse Ricard Group

The Ricards are also of French origin. Introduced by Bruant in
1894, the free-blooming, semidouble red 'Alphonse Ricard' has long
been popular, especially since the introduction of a fine strain of it
in the mid 1950s. However, this one is not 'Improved Ricard',
which is no relative of the group. The Ricards are a robust group
but do not flower well in winter. One of the finest of the orange
varieties, lately so very popular, is the bright semidouble 'Orange
Ricard', which makes a somewhat smaller plant than 'Alphonse
Ricard', and this is an advantage. These are notable, supposedly
Ricard varieties:

'Aphonse Ricard'	'Orange Ricard'
'Helen Michel'	'Red Fiat'
'Improved Red Fiat'	'Seabright'
'Lavender Ricard'	'Wyona'

Figure 15. Pink geraniums in clay pots, fastened by ring-holders against a board fence, serve to break the stark expanse of wood and associate it pleasantly with the delphiniums and other perennials in the garden of Mrs. Gordon W. Roaf, Marblehead, Massachusetts. Photo by Taloumis.

Painted Lady Group

The original Cyclops pelargoniums, aptly named long ago by Paul Bruant for the race of giants with one prominent eye, apparently do not exist today. The distinguishing feature was a large *sharply-defined* white center in both single and double varieties. Today we have plants that around 1950 were classified as the Painted Lady group. They are mostly singles with the white area displacing more color on the upper petals than on the lower. The white is not constant, being more noticeable in warm than in cold weather and the white area is not clearly defined as in the original Cyclops group. However, there is certainly a resemblance and very likely a continuity.

These are among the loveliest of pelargoniums and particularly dear to collectors. One variety in this group is called 'Apple Blossom'. I remember the plants of it at Village Hill. They seemed to me to have no superiors, so large and beautifully formed were the trusses, so exquisitely shaded the flowers. These blended from pure white centers to deep pink edges, like the apple blossoms of the Pennsylvania orchards. 'Apple Blossom' is a choice winter pot plant, and looks well with salmon-pink and scariet varieties but is not pleasing alongside crimsons or bluish pinks.

In 1907 Mr. Bruant remarked of his Cyclops geraniums: "This set represents a continuance toward perfection in this race of geraniums with a giant white eye. Cyclops was first raised in our establishment. Our efforts have been to improve the growth, the habit, the greatness and beauty of the flowers having a large and pure white center in distinct circle." In 1908 semidoubles and doubles with white centers were introduced. By 1913 at least twenty of these were cataloged.

In 1909 this statement appeared in the R. Vincent Jr. and Sons' catalog: "When we introduced to the trade, under the name 'Cyclops', the original of this series, we pointed out the interest attached to this new stock from which we would produce a whole generation of new varieties with white centers. Our predictions have been realized, and we have the satisfaction of offering this year seven new fine varieties with single and semidouble flowers, of varied coloring, ornamented with a very decided white center. The semidouble varieties are distingushed from the other geraniums by the particular shape of the flower. The petals are elegant and showy, and leave the white center visible in a very marked manner."

By 1913 the *singles* that we now call Painted Ladies had become immensely popular. The better nursery catalogs listed some twenty-two varieties. Fred Bode states that his records include more than a hundred. In the Miller catalog the term is not used, but the single varieties under "Scarlet and Red with White Centers" might well be considered Painted Ladies. Admittedly this is an arbitrary classification but the name continues to be appealing. It is best applied only to single varieties of Standard type.

Today more than a dozen Painted Ladies are available, including 'Ann Sothern', 'Lady of Spain', and 'Linda Arce'. One of the loveliest and most dependable for winter bloom is 'Souvenir de Mirande'. This was originated by a Monsieur Herlaut, a grower in Mirande, France; it is not a French type but a short-jointed plant of small to medium size.

These are some of the so-called Painted Ladies, and I am afraid the one gentleman commemorated here would resent this title.

'Alice of Vincennes'	'Holiday'
'Ann Sothern'	'Lady Dryden'
'Apple Blossom'	'Lady of Spain'
'Berkeley Belle'	'Linda Arce'
'Bougainvillea'	'Nouvelle Aurore'
'Cheerio'	'Painted Lady'
'Fantasy'	'Salmon Queen'
'General Leonard Wood'	'Souvenir de Mirande'

Figure 16. Zonal geraniums in handsome terra-cotta containers accent the three important entrances of this garden and contribute to the balanced formality of the design with their repeated asymmetric placements. Photo by Molly Adams.

Zonal Geraniums from Holmes Miller

Among the finest newer zonal geraniums of our time are those that have come from Holmes Miller. Whether these constitute a group is indeed a question, but in this general consideration of zonals, I would like to say a word about these varieties that I admire so much. Of both Standard and French types, they are distinct from most other zonals and appeal tremendously to collectors. A few of them like 'Always', 'Glory', and 'White Magic' are also important commercially.

Many of the Miller varieties are pastels—those I think of as the "tender shades"—often with a slight metallic luster. In Figure 59, the family tree of a number of Mr. Miller's varieties is shown. In the orange range the Miller varieties are outstanding. Such large-flowered, large-clustered zonals as 'Always', 'Joy', 'Fanfare', 'Maytime', 'Glory', 'Treasure', 'Fortune', 'White Magic', 'Nimbus', 'Shimmer', 'Coralglow', 'Blossomtime', 'Halloween', 'Indian Summer' are the hobbyist's joy, excellent winter bloomers, superb pot plants, as a group perhaps the best for shows and exhibits. I am told that they are so distinct in type that a foreign variety grown among them in a field can be spotted immediately and that in such field culture, they can be recognized at some distance.

From different strains is another Miller group that includes 'Debonair', 'Gallant', 'Inspiration', and 'Summer Cloud'. Successful in the outdoor garden, these bloom well in winter, too. Most of them are fully described in the Finder's List on page 300; they are too wonderfully numerous even to list here.

Zonal-Ivy Group

Among the most beautiful of geraniums are those that were introduced by Vincent in 1906 as the Peltato-Zonals type. Listed were 'Alliance', 'Achievement', and 'Alpha', but this may not be the 'Alpha' we know, since there is some doubt that the present-day

'Alpha' is a zonal-ivy. I understand that in England 'Alliance' is known as 'Milford Gem' and 'Pink Alliance' as 'Lady Gertrude'.

'E. H. Trego', also called 'Louise', is certainly lovely, double with rosebudlike buds opening to enormous flowers of brilliant orange-red with a metallic cast. The fine plant has a large glossy leaf, hairy on the reverse. Vincent stated that this group had the best qualities of both parents, *Pelargonium peltatum* and *P. zonale*. Where mites are not a problem, these zonal-ivies are a fine choice. And they are free of rust, which makes them favorites in Australia and England where rust can be a problem. Many zonals besides these are related to *P. peltatum* and the group as a whole is also the result of a mixed ancestry.

Chapter FOUR

The Lovely Single and Double Zonals

The Victorians planted the zonal geraniums so lavishly in their formal gardens of balanced beds with iron deer, single-spout fountains, and cannas, that many people still associate them with such unimaginative use. Today window boxes of red or pink geraniums with periwinkle vines are ubiquitous. Then there are the park beds, set out with dull red doubles that seem to get duller as the heat goes up and the rain goes down. These zonal geraniums have such decorative possibilities it seems a great pity not to make them count for more in our gardens and on our terraces than as impromptu fill-ins.

Gardens Featuring Zonals

In my memory are stored many lovely garden pictures of zonals. Driving through Boston one July, I was struck with the mass beauty of double salmon-pink zonals, growing by the hundreds in a small city park outside the Christian Science Church on Huntington

51

Figure 17. In boxes on the sea-wall garden of Mr. and Mrs. Howard A. Colby, Marblehead Neck, Massachusetts, where summer days are hot and breezy but mornings and evenings are cool, bright red geraniums thrive and bloom all through the holiday season with white petunias and variegated vinca. Photo by Taloumis.

Avenue. In a setting of rich green grass long rectangles of solid brilliance were regularly and dramatically interrupted by taller specimen geraniums grown as low standards (tree geraniums). To every city-weary soul they brought refreshment through the hot summer days.

I recall a multicolored sunporch bower of 6- and 7-foot plants enjoyed by an elderly lady in Massachusetts. She trimmed her plants back a little each year, fed them generously spring and summer, and from about November to March stored them in an unheated cellar where there was an earth floor and some little sunlight from the windows. With temperatures sometimes down to 35 degrees F., little water was required by the almost-dormant plants.

Dorcas Brigham told me of her visit to the English garden of Sir Herbert Jekyll, brother of the late Gertrude Jekyll, one of the finest gardeners of our time. At Godalming, Sir Herbert used tall geraniums to full advantage against a clipped yew hedge some 10 feet high. Where niches were cut into the hedge for the usual placement of statuary, Sir Herbert with real imagination had inserted 5-foot plants of glowing red geraniums. Silhouetted against the darkness of the yew, they offered dramatic and colorful contrast.

With dwarf English boxwood, zonals can be used charmingly as I saw them in one small formal Eastern garden crossed by white pebble paths. The triangular, box-edged beds held tulips in the early spring. These were followed by plantings of double white geraniums that held blooms well above the evergreen boundaries. Tulip bulbs had been set 8 to 10 inches deep and spaced widely enough for the young geraniums to be inserted among them without disturbing the proper maturing of the tulip foliage. As tulip flowers faded, the developing geraniums soon covered their passing. Standard plants of 'Masure's Beauty' geraniums were set in the corners of the garden and around the center birdbath was a collection of rose- and mint-scented geraniums.

For effective use of color, I recall a striking effect on a willow-shaded terrace in New Jersey. The furnishings were in quiet colors. Shaded beds of ferns had been inserted into the brick floor on the wall side. The awning and chair coverings were green, the dining-table a dark polished brown. These muted tones offered a cooling summer retreat. Only one thing was needed, a little warm color to enliven. It was supplied by the flowing single orange-scarlet 'La Fiesta' geranium, planted in four Italian terra-cotta urns. Placed at the edge of the terrace where the sunshine reached them, the plants bloomed richly all summer, providing just that splash of brilliance with which every knowing decorator touches off a cool effect.

In California Gardens

In California it is easy to plant pelargoniums in interesting rela-tionships. So many sections are frost-free or nearly so that with a modicum of care geraniums go on living a brilliant life year after year. I think, for instance, of a great steep bank in Golden Gate Park alive with the massed brilliance of the single orange 'Maxime Kovalevski', and of this same variety used as a foundation against a cream-colored house in San Francisco. Yellow calceolarias were set to the fore of the brilliant geraniums and impressive gray-blue agaves spaced among them for accent.

I recall another garden adorned by double pink pelargoniums in-terplanted with the lovely lavender *Aster Frikarti;* and another with pink pelargoniums and the small *Begonia semperflorens* 'Pink Pearl', edged by the purple bellflower, *Campanula carpatica* and white sweet alyssum. Never to be forgotten was a planting sur-rounding a drive at the top of a mountain estate near Belvedere. The white and lavender bells of the trumpet vine *Distictis cineraria* trailed down from the retaining wall among plants of dark 'Empress of Russia' regals, while stalwart specimens of lavender *Statice lati-folia* blended the whole into a gracious composition.

I think, too, of the Mission garden at Carmel where so many pelargoniums were richly set. One deep planting held yellow

Two apparently effortless arrangements by Lee Early Quinn show strong Japanese influence and feature red geraniums with green pine in bamboo containers. Figure 18, above, is a double design with short-needled pine and 'Dark Red Irene' geraniums.. Figure 19, below, includes the airy long-leaf pine, stems of dark red-berried wild rose, and a cluster of bright red 'Flame' geraniums. Photos by Boice Studio.

acacias, salmon geraniums, and plants of old-fashioned lavender. Another pleasant harmony included enormous plants of pink geraniums combined with banana and palm trees, the purple shrub *Salvia leucantha* brought in by priests from Mexico, tall white marguerite daisies, and the large, lavender *Impatiens oliveri*. I noticed within this Mission close, rosebud-type geraniums used as foundation shrubs. They were larger and lovelier than any of this kind I had ever seen before.

These are other possibilities you will find delightful for borders: the salmon-apricot geranium 'Emile Zola', interrupted by groups of the red hot poker plant (*Kniphofia*); salmon 'Springtime' planted with blue lily-of-the-Nile (*Agapanthus umbellatus*) or with Siberian iris 'Perry's Blue'. Among regals the deep salmon 'Grossmama Fischer' looks well in a border of *Nemesia* 'Blue Gem', with the dark lavender campanula, 'Telham Beauty', nearby. The purple-striped white 'Mrs. Mary Bard' geranium grows in loveliness bordered by the dwarf pomegranate, and this same variety with the rosy-pink 'Heartbeat' geranium is enchanting edged by violets. For the foreground of such shrubs as *Osmanthus ilicifolium* and silver-bud Rhamnus a planting of 'Orange Ricard' geranium is really exciting.

As for geranium hedges, Californians seem to consider these too common to be worth mentioning. To my Eastern eyes they will never be a negligible aspect of Western gardening. Perhaps it was another Easterner, gardening in San Francisco, who also valued them and planted her boundary line with them to such brilliant advantage. She set there a hedge of double scarlet and white pelargoniums, 'Olympic Red' and 'Madame Buchner', and then spread before them a great carpet of waxen white camellia-flowering tuberous begonias. I shall never forget the clear brilliance of the effect.

When it comes to pot plants, the Western gardener does respect the pelargonium and uses it delightfully. Three pictures remain from a Sunday afternoon in Carmel, where every tiny house rests in a mass of beautifully tended flowers. The first was the dooryard of a house called "The Dockery," built of rose-and-gray brick with an occasional blue one tucked in. The entrance terrace was fashioned of the same softly blended material. Around the edge were tellingly set, at regular intervals, dark blue pots of perfectly grown double white zonal geraniums. A ribbon bedding of small pink begonias running before them intensified their more spectacular form. White pots of coral fuchsias stood beside the door of this inviting place with a magnificent corner tub of flame and yellow tuberous begonias introducing a bit of warm color. This small paradise was entered through a blue gate set in a white fence and the whole was predicated on a minute section of perfectly nurtured green lawn.

Then there was the small open garden so close to the road I could almost reach into it from the car. Whoever possessed it was an original designer, for its small confines were set off by a rosy brick wall 3 feet high and skillfully serpentined. Within each curve had been sunk a section of concrete pipe some 30 inches in diameter holding, as of course you have guessed, great green plants of pelargoniums flaunting masses of pink bloom in perfect accord with the mellow tones of the brick.

Finally in Carmel, I saw a pink-and-yellow consonance that demanded an artist's paint box. The small house was white with yellow blinds and an entrance arch and gate wreathed by that exuberant creamy climbing rose, 'Mermaid'. Beside the steps were great yellow urns of handsome bright pink pelargoniums and the entrance walk was edged with the same colorful variety. Elsewhere in the garden grew pink tuberous begonias to complete a picture that was memorable even in lovely Carmel.

For seashore gardens, East or West, the zonals and other pelargoniums are treasures. If you temporarily occupy a cottage you can quickly produce a garden with pots of geraniums set in log or more conventional planters, as in Figures 17 and 65. Geraniums thrive by the sea, their color more sparkling and vivid in the salt air.

Figure 20.　This bean-pot bouquet is a simple long-lasting arrangement of scented-leaved geraniums: *P. crispum* 'Prince Rupert', *P. radens* 'Skeleton Rose'; zonals: 'Apple Blossom Rosebud', 'Madame Jaulin', 'Snowflake'; the cactus-type geranium *P.* × *Stapletonii* (lower right) and the climber *P.* × *rutaceum* at top and lower left. Photo by Cushing-Gellatly.

We might take note, too, that geraniums of all kinds are wonderful keepers when cut and provide delightful and varied material for those who make simple arrangements for their homes or stylized compositions for exhibition. For this use I think the geranium has been too long overlooked. I see a few set pieces at flower shows but I believe the skilled and imaginative designers have hardly discovered them. Geraniums offer a wealth of lovely, even unusual, flowers and also fine foliages for designing in various styles or for bouquets. The fancy-leaveds and the scented-leaveds, also the species, have interesting possibilities, and I know one enthusiast who devotes a greenhouse bench to a collection of pelargoniums just to have them for cutting.

For Tucson, Memphis, and Tampa

Reports of good varieties for special areas always interest me. In "Geraniums Around the World," VII, 4, Charles P. Tullis of Tucson, Arizona, reports on his successful culture of certain zonals in 4-inch pots. From May 15 to September 20, when temperatures may go to 110 degrees F., he grows plants on a bench under extra heavy lathhouse shade with filtered sunlight reaching them early in the morning and late in the afternoon. Plants are misted in the morning and watered, and watered again as periodic checking through the day indicates the need. No fertilizer is given.

After September 20, the extra lath shade is removed to admit filtered sun all day long. Leggy plants are then cut back and repotted as required, and a feeding schedule is started for all the plants. About November 1, when frost is a possibility, plants are transferred to a lightly shaded glasshouse with a 55 degree F. minimum temperature. Good bloom occurs from early September on, with a fine display from Christmas to April 15 on these varieties: 'Berkeley Raspberry', 'Better Times', 'Dreams', 'Fanfare', 'Flame', 'Honeymoon', 'Lady of Spain', 'Marguerite de Layre', 'Mrs. E. G. Hill', 'Reverie', 'Romany', 'Salmon Supreme'.

Figure 21. Sprays of deep pink ivy-leaved geraniums describe a lovely curve in this simple, natural arrangement by Marguerite Bozarth. The blue bronze vase is elevated on two brown bases that set off the charming composition. This vining pelargonium, hardly discovered yet by arrangers, offers beautiful material for designs in many styles. Photo by C. Fanders.

Writing to me from Memphis, Tennessee, where summer temperatures may go to 100 degrees F., Mrs. Early Mitchell believes that plants should go outdoors as soon after frost as possible so they can get well established before hot weather. She plants in well-drained beds with plenty of lime and chicken manure mixed in the soil, and some 0-20-20 fertilizer. Outdoors in summer she has found that plastic foam pots and drinking cups with holes punched for good drainage provide excellent insulation against the baking sun so that plants are still blooming when September comes. These have been satisfactory zonals for her: 'Better Times', 'Blaze', 'Canadian Pink and White', 'Dark Red Irene', 'Fiat', 'Gallant', 'La Fiesta', 'Madame Landry', 'Souvenir de Mirande'.

Indoors, she adds 'Fiat Enchantress', 'Peaches and Cream', and 'Welcome'; and she has enjoyed a number of the fancy-leaveds as 'Carleton's Velma', 'Miss Burdett Coutts', 'French Lace', 'Happy Thought', and 'Mrs. Parker'. These fancy-leaveds and the spring cuttings are in a room air-conditioned through July and August, the pots set on trays of crushed oyster shells kept damp to increase humidity. Mrs. Mitchell feels that her earlier failures indoors can be traced to low humidity. She likes to use her plants decoratively and has made a unique grouping in her fireplace. With fluorescent lights above and behind the plants, and in front where they are concealed by the brass fender, she has made a pretty picture with 'Berkeley Belle' ("that is in constant bloom"), 'Miss Burdett Coutts', 'French Lace', and the ivy-leaved 'L'Elegante'. Mrs. Mitchell has shared her great pleasure in geraniums through a therapy project she has developed in a local mental hospital.

From Tampa, Florida, Helen Hall, who has a plant business there, writes that the best zonals for outdoor growing are: 'Gregerson's White', 'Improved Ricard', 'Jean Viaud', 'Lavender Ricard', 'Madame Landry', 'New Ruby', and 'Radio Red'. These can be successfully planted in beds during October for quality bloom in cool weather. Protect if frost threatens. Other varieties do better in

Figure 22. This home greenhouse in Ireland with one long bench devoted to a collection of geraniums offers an invitation not to be refused on a winter day. Photo by Roche.

containers that can be moved to cooler locations as the heat increases and the rains come. No geraniums make good house plants in Florida, but a great many do well on patios and the old-fashioned porch or carport. A loose porous soil is essential in her area and Mrs. Hall packages a good mixture for her customers. I have liked it too. She finds ivy-leaved varieties do well the year around with full sun in winter, some shade in summer, and well-controlled watering. She recommends: 'Cliff House', 'Comtesse de Grey', 'Corden's Glory', 'Galilee', 'Mexican Beauty', 'Mrs. Banks', and 'Santa Paula'.

Garden Zonals for the Midwest

I asked Mr. W. Howard Wilson of Wilson Brothers in Roachdale, Indiana, to recommend zonal varieties for outdoor planting in the Midwest. He tells me that the smaller varieties, the dwarfs, are just not big enough for bedding out. The fancy-leaveds are very popular, especially 'Alpha', 'Distinction', 'Happy Thought', Madame Langguth', and 'Mrs. Parker'. The bronze fancy-leaveds as 'Double Mrs. Pollock' and 'Skies of Italy' grow well but do not keep their color through the summer. These are the standard zonals that Mr. Wilson recommends: 'A. M. Mayne' ('Springfield Violet'), 'Apple Blossom' ('Madame Jaulin'), 'Blaze', 'Dark Red Irene', 'Flame', 'Improved Ricard', 'Irene', 'Olympic Red', 'Penny Irene', 'Pink Cloud', 'Salmon Irene', 'Snowball', 'Springtime Irene'.

Incidentally, Mr. Wilson does not recommend regals for this area because they will not bloom throughout the summer. The scented-leaved varieties are favorites there and the ivy-leaved geraniums increasingly so.

Selecting the Zonals

Now, which of the many lovely zonals will you choose? They are such a handsome and varied group, it is not easy to reduce enthusiasm to the practicalities of space, and today we must also consider strength since so little garden help is available to us. I reduce my agonies of decision by planting different varieties in the garden every spring with no attempt to hold them over winter. Limiting the number of year-round pot plants is something else, since there is just so much space in the Plant Room, and the zonals must share the broad window sills elsewhere in the house with the scented- and fancy-leaveds, and with the species.

Since most of us select by color, I offer at the end of this chapter lists of varieties in color groupings. I make note here that light, temperature, and soils do alter colors somewhat. I have included as many singles as doubles.

If you are just entering this thralldom of the geranium, you may not realize that the doubles are far from the whole story. There are numerous singles that are utterly beautiful. These are just as easy to grow as the doubles and, particularly among the paler ones, the color range is entrancing. In form the singles are the ultimate in geranium grace. Furthermore, while scarcely any of the doubles produce well-formed flowers under unduly cool conditions, many of of the singles do; and tightly potted, they make fine winter-flowering house plants. Reports from the Midwest indicate that the singles often make better summer garden plants there than the doubles. Mrs. John D. West of Manitowoc, Wisconsin, writes that the singles endure quite a lot of rain and fog with little damage and that they stand up well through the hot humid weather in late July and August. She particularly likes 'Gertrude Pearson', 'Lady Ruth', and 'Mrs. E. G. Hill'. Alas, my namesake, "of divine color, grows too tall and is too brittle for the windy exposure."

In the short lists that follow I do not distinguish between semi-double and double, and apparently there is no accepted standard. The extra petals in all of the doubles vary considerably in number and size with growing conditions, but what conditions cause the decrease in number of petals is not known. Holmes Miller says that for him flowers are least double in late summer and early fall.

Figure 23. Double-white, light and dark pink to single red geranium flowers with their own foliage are informally arranged by Myra E. Brooks and placed in perfect association with the homely things of life—the basket for bread, the carafe of wine. Photo by Roche.

Every variety on these lists has been selected for quality and relative ease of culture as well as for beauty. Here are the typical mainly self-colored forms—all more fully described in the Finder's List on page 300. Your local florist will probably carry only a few of them, and perhaps none of the singles, but mail-order specialists can supply them.

Double and Single Zonals by Color

WHITE

DOUBLE	SINGLE
'Merry Gardens White'	'Marguerite de Layre' or
'Summer Cloud'	'Starlight'
'Verite'	
'White Magic'	

PALE TINTS

'Always'	'Carmel'
'Joy'	'Ecstasy'
'Madame Jaulin'	'New Phlox'
'Nimbus'	

CORAL- AND SALMON-PINK

'Dreams'	'Cheerio'
'Festival'	'Elenore S. Rober'
'Fiat'	'Emile Zola'
'Fiat Supreme'	'Flare'
'Inspiration'	'Fred Bean'
'Lullaby'	'Honeymoon'
'Magnificent'	'Lady of Spain'
'Shimmer'	'Mrs. E. G. Hill'
'Springtime'	
'Tresor'	
'Welcome'	

ROSE-PINK AND CARMINE

'Frances Perkins'   'Afterglow'
'Genie'   'Gertrude Pearson'
'Party Dress'   'Luster'
'Pink Giant'
'Shocking'

LAVENDER-PINK TO PURPLE-ROSE

'Debonair'   'Fantasy'
'Lavender Ricard'   'Helen Van Pelt Wilson'
'Patience'   'Persian Rose'

ORANGE

'Halloween'   'Harvest Moon'
'Orange Ricard'   'Nouvelle Aurore'
                           'Token'

RED WITH WHITE CENTERS

'Challenge'   'Alice of Vincennes'
'Double Dryden'   'Holiday'
'Radiance'   'Souvenir de Mirande'

SCARLET AND VERMILION

'Aztec'   'Flame'
'Fireglow'   'La Fiesta'
'Gallant'   'Paul Crampel'
'Garnet'
'Pride of Camden'
'Toyon'

CRIMSON

'Apache'   'Thomas E. Stimson'
'Gypsy'   'Velma'
'Masure's Beauty'
'My Beauty'

CRIMSON-PURPLE

'A. M. Mayne'   'Bougainvillea'
'Magenta Ruby'   'Lady Ruth'
'Marquis de Montmort' 'Will Rogers'

Chapter FIVE

$\mathcal{T}$ reasures for the $\mathcal{C}$ ollector

When I hear of all the big things people are deprived of to-day, certain smaller deprivations also come to mind. I thought of this one August day when some 700 garden enthusiasts visited me and I discovered that not one I talked with had ever seen before what I consider the treasures of the geranium world. Imagine plant-lovers not knowing the Bird's Egg or Rosebud or Painted Lady pelargoniums. Imagine never having had at your window the picot-edged 'Jeanne 'or the astoundingly beautiful 'Nouvelle Aurore', or any of the others the catalogs list as "Unusual and Fine-flowering." Don't you agree that this is deprivation of a horti-cultural kind?

These are exquisite zonals, deviating from the more familiar singles and doubles in form, marking, or blending of colors. These are the geraniums every collector or window gardener can enjoy winter and summer, in pots or on the terrace, in tubs and on plant

69

stands. They are hardly suited to bedding but give most pleasure when their individual beauty can be observed close at hand. I never enter my front door in summer without an appreciative glance at these unique geraniums flowering in pots on the graystone entrance terrace that was constructed, in fact, with this setting in mind. And all winter I have the early morning pleasure of seeing these plants the very first thing when I come down the stairs to the light and color of the Plant Room.

The Bird's Egg Group

From 1892 on, the Bird's Egg pelargoniums have appeared in and out of records. It is characteristic of this group that the petals, particularly the lower ones, are stippled a darker color than the rest of the flower and usually rose-red. In winter the speckles are not so pronounced. These are varieties that have beauty as well as novelty but not many are available today. However, I do not doubt that some are grown as unnamed plants in hobby collections particularly through New England.

'Double Pink Bird's Egg' is really lavender-pink, white toward the center with petals spotted rosy red, though not very prominently. The large flowers come in large clusters and the plants are free-blooming. Then there are three single pinks, the flowers similar but each kind worth acquiring by the collector. Fred Bode has developed superior strains of these and two are usually offered as 'Bode's Light-Pink Bird's Egg', the lavender-rose speckling prominent on the pale petals, and 'Bode's Coral-Pink Bird's Egg', which has large flowers in large clusters, some white towards the centers and conspicuous rose-red dots. 'Single Rose-Pink' or 'Single Pink' (it is listed both ways and seems to be the same plant) is a strong grower. 'Mrs. J. J. Knight' is probably the freest-flowering of the Bird's Eggs, white to very pale pink, all petals well spotted, and lovely but very slow growing.

Before World War I, Bird's Egg geraniums were not nearly so scarce. Evidently of French origin and very likely from Victor Lemoine, they were freely offered in American catalogs. Peter Henderson, of New York, in 1901 listed three: light pink 'Bobolink', carmine-pink 'Nightingale', and snow-white, rose-dotted 'Skylark'.

The catalog stated: "New Bird's Egg Geraniums. The most unique advance in any class of plants for years has been obtained in this new race. We have given a distinct, and we believe, an appropriate title to them. They are dwarf in habit, very free blooming, especially suited for growing in pots . . . we have taken the liberty to give the names of birds to the separate varieties instead of the practically meaningless French names given by the raiser." A quaint picture of four stippled bird's eggs in a nest accompanies the illustration of the flowers.

The next year, 1902, the Henderson catalog listed seven, with only one "bird" among them:

'Bandalaire'. Single, clear rose, white center, crimson dots.

'Daumier'. Single, soft rose-lilac, rose-aniline dots.

'David d'Angers'. Bright pink, dotted with carmine.

'Skylark'. Single, snow-white, dotted with rosy carmine.

'Theophile Gautier'. Single, carmine and white, rosy dots.

'Abel Le Franc'. Double, delicate shades of lilac-white, petals dotted with carmine-violet.

'Rosamond'. Double, deep rose, dotted carmine.

Then in 1910 R. Vincent, Jr. & Sons' Co., of White Marsh, Maryland, had this listing:

'Abel Le Franc' (Lemoine 1905). Splendid large flowers of perfect form and size; lilac-white, lower petals liberally covered with rose-lilac dots. One of the most attractive of the dotted sorts.

'Bariolage' (Bruant 1906). Dwarf, vigorous and free flowering, clear rose, lower petals blotched crimson, upper petals blotched white.

Figure 24. These are geraniums of unusual form. Above, 'Double Poinsettia' has red linear petals of different lengths; below, 'Jeanne' is salmon-pink with notched petal edges.

'Marthe Dupuy' (Bruant 1907). Single flowers of a pretty bright rose mauve, spotted and dotted with carmine-violet, the upper petals maculated with white at the base.

'Curiosa' (Bruant 1908). Plant short, trusses of medium size, beautiful double rose-mauve, spotted carmine dots, center white.

Considering both the beauty and the reliability of these lovely varieties, we rejoice that some of the larger commercial growers are today taking them in hand and making them readily available to us. I have enjoyed them in a window garden where they offer interesting contrast to other geraniums there. But, of course, all these unusual flowering types do that.

Carnation-flowered Group

Not so rare as the Bird's Egg is a serrated-petal group with flowers like those of the carnation. In England, 'Jeanne' is called 'Skelly's Pride'. No pelargonium is more free-flowering than 'Jeanne'. I have counted five fully-opened, five-petaled blossoms and two maturing buds on plants in 4½-inch pots. Flowers are rather small, not over an inch and a quarter, and the truss itself and the plant are of medium size.

Dr. Charles Piper Smith in "Geranium Records" had this to say of 'Jeanne': "We have yet to learn of its origin, but occasional plants develop 'sport-branches' called reversions, which very probably represent the ancestral form from which 'Jeanne' itself developed as a sport. We have yet to see a blossom of 'Jeanne' set seed; but the larger and deeper salmon flowers of the 'reversion branches' produce abundant, self-pollinated seeds."

Numerous other pelargoniums of the 'Jeanne' type have appeared. 'Seabright' is red-petaled, dentate, and probably of French origin. It was found in the nursery of E. H. Eisley at Seabright, near Santa Cruz in California, but only a small percentage of the flowers sport to carnation-type petals.

'Fiat King', 'Fiat Queen', 'Princess Fiat', and 'Royal Fiat', all four semidouble to double with serrated petals and in soft salmon-pink shades, are handsome sports of the very fine "sporting" Fiat group.

'Madame Thibaut', a very old single variety, is white in the bud, pink in the flower, and with sharply cut edges. 'Cerise Carnation', "the most carnation-like of the group" with deeply notched petals is a delicate though rapid grower but hardly profuse of bloom.

Exactly what causes these serrated petals in mutations is not known. Because so many of these varieties are dwarfed and show a viruslike pattern in the foliage during part of the year, some pathologists have concluded that serration of petals is the result of virus, but this has not been proven and the plants certainly are good growers and in most cases free-flowering as well.

The Rosebud Group

These are among the most appealing of all the unusual geraniums. Each flower is very double, like a tiny rambler rosebud before it has opened flat. Perhaps 'Apple Blossom Rosebud' is the prettiest, its white flowers carmine-rimmed. I once saw a whole sunny window garden filled with this one variety and will never forget how delightful it appeared. For me 'Apple Blossom Rosebud' blooms well and each cluster lasts for weeks. Everyone admires this one.

There are at least three other Rosebuds in light-to-dark shades, and variously designated. 'Pink Rosebud' is a light, rosy red and the most free-flowering. 'Red' or 'Scarlet Rosebud' is of somewhat deeper tone, and 'Crimson' or 'Magenta Rosebud', which I can't say I admire, is quite dark, and never flowers well. However, all the Rosebuds are good growers and, of course, you will want at least one of them. Mrs. West reports that in Wisconsin 'Apple Blossom Rosebud' and 'Red Rosebud' put on a wonderful show early in the season but fail in wet weather, as blossoms can't keep up with leaves."

Very likely these Rosebuds are old varieties that once had other names. Derek Clifford thinks that 'Magenta Rosebud' may be the old 'Le Negre' of the 1870s. 'Pink Rosebud' is known to many whose grandmothers cherished it as 'The Rosebud Geranium'. 'Red Rosebud', which originated in England about 1870, might be the old variety 'Jewel'. It was listed and illustrated in the 1878 catalog of Charles T. Starr of Avondale, Pennsylvania. But this is not the 'Jewel' grown in England today.

Cactus-flowered Group

These are mainly doubles with narrow often uneven twisted petals. Aside from the dwarf types, to be described later, there are six doubles you might collect, along with the one single, the white 'Silver Star'. 'Double Poinsettia' is bright red with pointed linear petals of different lengths; 'Pink Poinsettia' has shorter broader petals of bluish pink, a ragged looking thing, I think, and of poor color. 'Morning Star' is prettier, a soft salmon; 'Noel' is white; 'Starlet', coral-pink, and 'Star of Persia', purple-crimson. 'Tangerine' is one of the prettiest. Although these seem very popular, I myself am not mad about them, as I certainly am about the Bird's Eggs and the Rosebuds.

Phlox Group

These are singles with dark eyes, so called, I suppose, for their resemblance to the flowers of garden phlox. There are at least three Phlox varieties and all are excellent. 'Ecstasy' is a beautiful large-flowering variety, one of the loveliest of all single geraniums, cream-white with a pale coral center. 'New Phlox' is white with a bright vermilion eye and sometimes a suffusion of pink. This one is unusually free-blooming, indoors and out, with large flower clusters. 'Phlox New Life', also included in the New Life group, is white sometimes pink-flushed with a coral center. Flowers are not so large but in constant procession and the plant is compact, a sport of 'New Life' and very pretty indeed.

It is difficult to give accurate descriptions of the Phlox group since the ground color of newly-opened flowers is nearly pure white for all of them but intensifies as the flower ages, particularly outdoors. 'Ecstasy' colors the least and 'New Phlox' the most.

New Life Group

Here are interesting variations for the collector. Flowers always catch the attention in a window garden, their narrow flecked and striped petals in pleasing contrast to the rounded selfs. The single 'New Life' or 'Peppermint Stick' is particularly variable, sometimes producing on the same plant an all-scarlet bloom or an all-white one with a pink eye and these along with the more usual pattern of stripes. 'Double New Life' is picturesquely called 'Stars and Stripes' and 'Flag of Denmark'.

Holmes Miller has this to say of the New Life group: "This group originated with the introduction of the variety 'Vesuvius' in England in 1868. 'Vesuvius' soon produced a double-flowered sport, called 'Wonderful'. Sometime prior to 1884 'Vesuvius' produced another sport with flaked or variegated flowers. This was called 'New Life' and is the most interesting of the group. 'New Life' soon sported again, and still does fairly frequently, to the form that I call 'Phlox New Life'. This may have had an earlier name, but so far I have not been able to discover it. About 1892, 'Wonderful', the double-flowered sport of 'Vesuvius', produced a sport with variegated flowers, called 'Double New Life'. Although the flowers are quite different in each, the plants are all the same, healthy and vigorous, but bushy and compact, and very free flowering."

Painted Lady Group

In contrast to the dark-eyed Phlox varieties, the Painted Lady group, which includes some of the loveliest of all the singles, is characterized by large white centers or eyes. These were classified by Bruant as the Cyclops pelargoniums, a term not used today. Actually about half the singles are white-centered and thirty varieties could easily be included in this group, which is hardly well-defined. Nor is 'Painted Lady' itself typical, since the white area is veined. Little is known of the origin of this one which is probably a very old variety arbitrarily renamed 'Painted Lady' about 1940.

'Souvenir de Mirande', originated by Herlaut in 1886, was the first geranium of this type but there is no certainty that we have the original 'Souvenir de Mirande'. The early descriptions are confusing. Dauthenay characterizes the group as "Les Varieties a Grand Centre Blanc," and we could more appropriately list "Singles with Large White Centers." However, the Painted Lady name for the group is now so widely used and such a pretty designation that we keep it despite inaccuracy.

To complicate matters more, in the East this group is often called the Apple Blossom group. The 'Apple Blossom' variety itself is one of the loveliest of pelargoniums and seems to me to have among the singles no superiors, so large and beautifully formed are the trusses, so exquisitely shaded the flowers. These blend from pure white centers to deep pink edges, like the apple blossoms of our Pennsylvania orchards. This is an excellent variety for window boxes and choice as a winter pot plant too. It goes well with salmon-pink and scarlet varieties but is not pleasing near crimsons or bluish pinks.

Including the varieties 'Painted Lady' and 'Apple Blossom', there are at least a dozen very fine Painted Ladies, and I love them all. 'Alice of Vincennes' (who hails from Indiana and not France), is red shading to a white center. 'Ann Sothern' blends from scarlet to veined white. 'Berkeley Belle' is light red to white; 'Bougainvillea', purple-crimson to white; 'Cheerio', salmon-coral to white; 'Fantasy', purple-rose to white; 'Holiday', soft red to white; 'Lady of Spain', coral-pink to white, and such a beauty; 'Nouvelle Aurore', orange to white, difficult but worth all effort; and 'Souvenir de Mirande' is red to white.

Other Unusual Geraniums

With these less usual types we might include two more that at this point defy precise classification. From Japan has come 'Fingered Flowers' or 'Formosa' with clusters of semidouble linear flowers of a soft salmon shade. Leaves are deeply lobed on a plant about a foot high. This is hardly for the window garden since it drops its leaves in winter but it is interesting.

Then there is 'Mr. Wren', very free of bloom with flowers different and most attractive, single scarlet with a variegated white edge brushed onto the deeper color, and sometimes reverting to all red.

These geraniums of less usual appearance make a collection all the more interesting. If you wish, you might concentrate sometimes on one group, sometimes on another. This will widen your understanding of the complicated geranium and give you more fun, too. And if, as is inevitable, you collect more plants than you can accommodate, you can always pass on the extras to enthusiasts in a less advanced stage of geranium madness.

Zonal Treasures for the Collector

BIRD'S EGG GROUP

'Bode's Coral-Pink Bird's Egg', single
'Bode's Light-Pink Bird's Egg', single
'Lavender-Pink Bird's Egg', double
'Mrs. J. J. Knight', single white to pink
'Rose-Pink Bird's Egg', single

CACTUS-FLOWERED GROUP

'Double Poinsettia', red
'Morning Star', double soft
  salmon
'Noel', double white
'Pink Poinsettia', double pink

'Silver Star', single white
'Starlet', double coral
'Star of Persia', double purple-
  crimson
'Tangerine', single vermilion

CARNATION-FLOWERED GROUP

'Cerise Carnation', double
  cerise
'Fiat King', double salmon-
  coral
'Fiat Queen', double salmon-
  pink
'Jeanne', single salmon-pink

'Madame Thibaut', single
  white bud to pink bloom
'Princess Fiat', double white to
  salmon
'Royal Fiat', double soft
  salmon-coral

NEW LIFE GROUP

'Double New Life', scarlet and white
'New Life', single scarlet and white
'Phlox New Life', single white with coral eye
'Vesuvius' (not 'Black Vesuvius'), single scarlet

PAINTED LADY GROUP—SINGLES WITH LARGE WHITE CENTERS

'Alice of Vincennes', red to
  white
'Ann Sothern', fuchsia-pink to
  veined white
'Apple Blossom', scarlet to
  veined white
'Berkeley Belle', light red to
  white

'Bougainvillea', purple-crimson
  to white
'Cheerio', salmon-coral to white
'Holiday', soft red to white
'Lady of Spain', coral-pink to
  white
'Nouvelle Aurore', orange to
  white

'Painted Lady', cerise to veined
    white

'Souvenir de Mirande', red to
    white

PHLOX GROUP—SINGLES WITH DARK EYES

'Ecstasy', white with light coral-pink
'New Phlox', white with brilliant vermilion
'Phlox New Life', white with pink

ROSEBUD GROUP

'Apple Blossom Rosebud'
'Crimson or Magenta Rosebud'
    (Rosette)

'Pink Rosebud'
'Red or Scarlet Rosebud'

OTHER UNUSUALS

'Fingered Flowers' ('Formosa'), semidouble salmon
'Mr. Wren', single scarlet with white edges

Chapter SIX

Winter-flowering Pot Plants and Their Culture

Geraniums are among the finest of flowering plants for the indoor garden. Kept growing well under good culture, they will indeed bloom the year around as new buds form continuously at the tips of new wood. Geraniums do not require a rest period nor do they have a dormant season unless your own cultural procedures force them to stop growing. Some varieties develop new growth faster and are by their nature more prolific than others, but it is hardly possible to recommend the *best* winter-flowering varieties to you, so varied are results in different parts of the country. My own experience, for instance, is sometimes contrary to that of others.

In general, I'd say for winter color depend on the single zonals, the smaller bushy types of doubles, and the dwarf varieties that are discussed in Chapter 8. Considering their inheritance, we might also expect the Fiat, Irene, Better Times, and Painted Lady groups to put on a good winter show. For me, 'Mrs. E. G. Hill', 'Helen Van

81

Figure 25. Through sunny weeks in a window garden of southern exposure large-flowered zonal geraniums bloom continuously and the foliage of the fancy-leaveds is richly colored. Here the handsome scented Peppermint Geranium, *P. tomentosum,* grows in a great, graceful sweep and a variegated ivy-leaved geranium thrives in a wall bracket. Photo by Genereux.

Pelt Wilson', 'New Phlox', 'Mrs. J. J. Knight', 'Always', 'Magnificent' (admittedly a big one), and 'Apple Blossom Rosebud', among others, have bloomed well. There are good reports, too, of the New Life group, the other Bird's Eggs and Rosebuds, and specifically of 'Souvenir de Mirande'. On the whole, select for winter bloom those the catalogs describe as "free-flowering pot plants."

Light, Temperature, and Humidity

Full light and preferably a flood of sunshine, all a bright south or east window will afford—that is the first requisite for successful geranium culture indoors. And as long as the sun shines there, your plants will keep budding. If dull weeks come along and only a flower appears, be philosophic. Enjoy the pleasing leaf forms and the sturdy green or attractive variation of the foliage. Be understanding about the geranium disposition and under no circumstances start a major repotting or feeding program because you suspect ill health.

Next to full light or sun, geraniums enjoy a somewhat cool location. Even at 45 degrees F, they will bloom a little, but 60 to 70 degrees is preferred, 75 degrees briefly endured, with night temperatures dropping about ten degrees. In my very sunny Plant Room with south and west exposures, I set the thermostat at 55 degrees F at night.

Only a moderate amount of humidity is agreeable, for geraniums are not so dependent on moisture in the air as many other house plants. In fact, they resent excessive humidity, particularly the ivy-leaveds, and are therefore well suited to the conditions of the average home. Relative humidity of 40 to 50 per cent is ideal for geraniums. To measure accurately, depend on a hygrometer, an instrument that I find useful and amusing as I move it around to get readings from different locations in the house. You will find that as the heat goes up the relative humidity goes down. In the fall the early morning reading in the Plant Room is temperature

58 to 62 degrees F, humidity about the same per cent. By the sunny afternoon the temperature may go up above 70 degrees F. Then the humidity falls to about 42 per cent. If you grow geraniums with other plants as I do, you will find that they will not resent the 60 per cent humidity that most of the others prefer.

If a number of plants are grown, a 1- to 2-inch deep galvanized zinc or copper tray placed beneath them and filled with pebbles, vermiculite, or sand is both health insurance and convenience. Your local plumber can readily make this simple contrivance to fit your window sill or plant table. You can buy plastic trays in various convenient sizes and colors. I use both metal and plastic types. Excess moisture drips into the trays when the plants are watered. More water may also be poured there to increase the reservoir of water that steadily evaporates from the trays to agreeably moisten the air. Enough pebbles or other material are spread so that pots rest *above* the water level, since geraniums rarely survive a condition of water standing about their roots. Placing an extra large pebble-filled saucer under each plant is a useful modification of the tray device.

In cities geranium leaves may need dusting almost as often as the furniture. A fine camel's-hair brush does the job quickly. And occasionally tops are lightly syringed to cleanse them. About once a week will suffice for most geraniums, and then on a bright day so that evaporation will be rapid and no moisture will linger to start leaf or stem decay. Let the ivy-leaveds go much longer without misting through most of the winter. If plants are washed at sink or in the shower, they are kept in a light place but out of strong sunlight until leaves are dry. Syringe or shower them early in the day so foliage will dry by nightfall.

Watering

The steadily moist condition of soil that delights an African violet or a calla lily does not suit a geranium. Soil should "approach dryness" as Mary Ellen Ross so nicely puts it, but not dry out between *thorough* waterings. A good plan is to let the *feel* of the soil be a guide. When to the touch it seems barely dry, pour on water until the whole ball of earth is saturated. Then, unless there is a layer of pebbles, pour off excess water from a saucer. Geraniums have too often been damaged by the old dictum to "grow them dry." In general, they need as much water as most other plants in your window garden.

Obviously, the amount of water required will vary according to the size of the pot and the brightness of the weather. Whether plants are in active growth or resting will also be a factor. Daily inspection is good policy. Use water at *room temperature* so as not to retard growth with a chilling immersion of roots in cold water. Never use water from an ion exchange water softener. Preferably use rain or distilled water, especially if you live where the water supply is full of chemicals. Under such conditions, let the water stand overnight. Most additives will be dispersed by that time and furthermore the water will be at room temperature. This is what I try to do.

Under Fluorescent Light

All types of geraniums respond well to the increased irradiation possible with artificial light. Recent tests by Elaine Cherry who is a specialist on this subject and author of "Fluorescent Light Gardening" (published by D. Van Nostrand Company, Inc.) indicate that the needs of the geranium are well satisfied by 850 to 1,200 footcandles on a distance of 1 to 3 inches between top of plant and fluorescent tube, 14 to 18 hours a day.

With so little headroom you will pinch out tops often to keep plants under lights bushy and productive. And if you use the excellent Gro-Lux lamps, you will need to water and fertilize more frequently, perhaps two to five times as often. These good red and blue light rays keep your plants very bushy and for such constant flowering they will need the support of extra moisture and food.

For most of us, it is the dwarf varieties that are most practical to grow under lights. Their smaller size makes it possible to have a number in the limited space of, say, a 50-inch shelf with two 48-inch tubes. Under this setup at the top of my west casement garden, I can have seven or eight 3½-inch pots of dwarfs, without crowding. However, I sometimes put some of my 4- and 5-inch regular zonals up there to encourage budding. Then I bring them down where I can watch them bloom on the lower shelves. The lights are fine for the fancy-leaved geraniums, too, bringing out the brilliance of the foliage of 'Mrs. Henry Cox' and 'Skies of Italy' as natural winter sunshine never does. What you place under the lights depends mainly on your space. You can grow big plants as well as little ones there, start cuttings, or carry seedlings to maturity. Under a cellar or other out-of-sight fixture, you might even hold over tall standards or window-box material you want to keep alive but not have on display all winter. You could grow regals there that won't bloom much anywhere until spring.

Once you discover the marvelous possibilities for geraniums under fluorescents, you will look at the dark corners of your rooms and empty wall spaces as possibilities for window gardening without windows.

Soils and Potting

A rather firm soil slightly on the acid side, say pH 6.0 to 6.5, is good for geraniums with some leeway in either direction acceptable. Average garden soil, if there is such a thing, plus coarse sand to insure good drainage and aeration of roots works well. In other words, soil from a cultivated bed for flowers or vegetables plus sand will do. If you are particular enough to make up an ideal growing medium, combine 3 parts garden loam, 1 part leafmold or humus or peatmoss, and 2 parts sand, but increase the sand if the loam is fairly stiff like the cement mix I once had in Philadelphia. Then add for each bushel basket of your mixture a 5-inch potful of a well-balanced commercial fertilizer; if you are dealing in potfuls, allow 1 teaspoon to each 5-inch pot.

Or take it easy and use a commercial potting soil adding sand, perlite, or, following the excellent recommendation of an "I. G. S. Bulletin", one box of parakeet gravel (from the grocery store) for each 2½-pound bag of mix. I have used several of the commercial mixtures but always with some coarsening additive and also a little charcoal. I have found that mixes "as is" are generally too light and humusy. For geraniums, though perhaps a little expensive on a large scale, the commercial bags of potting soil are most convenient, especially if you have to do any repotting in winter.

Pot Sizes and Potting

When you buy plants by mail order, they usually arrive in 2¼- or 2½-inch pots. Shift plants from these to 3's or 4's, if they are going to be big growers, as soon as they have recovered from travel. Window plants flourish in 4's and then in 5's or 6's for years. Geraniums bloom best with tight potting that checks root growth and conveniently limits size. For outdoor terrace or garden decoration, larger pots or tubs are useful; but indoors, if you can keep plants smaller, you can enjoy more varieties in a given space, and that is what most of us want. Once plants reach the 5- or 6-inch pot size—and let them arrive there gradually, for a shift from a 3-inch to a 6-inch, for instance, is not healthy—you can often repot *in the same size*. When spring comes unpot plants, knock off as much soil as you can from sides and bottom, and scrape off the surface soil to get rid of moss or an accumulation of salts from watering. Then if you can, put the plant back with as much fresh soil as possible into a clean well-scrubbed pot.

When you pot a plant either in clay or plastic container, consider drainage requirements. Put an arching piece of "crockery", which is a bit of broken clay pot, over the drainage hole to retard but not stop the outflow of water. One piece will suffice for a small pot. In 4-inch or larger sizes, arrange a layer of crocking above the single piece, and then spread a thin layer of gravel, small driveway stones, or sphagnum moss if you have it. I save the moss packing that comes with new plants for this purpose. Such an arrangement keeps soil from washing down and clogging the drainage hole, and also prevents an accumulation of excess water that will rot roots.

Next, sprinkle a little soil over the coarse material, center the plant, and fill in with more soil, firming it with a stick, ruler, or piece of lath to get soil in good contact with roots. However, the ideal is not a cemented condition, just a comfortably firm one to encourage sturdy, stocky growth. When soil is too loose or too spongy because of excess humus or inadequate firming, growth often gets soft and sappy and flowering is poor. Try to set the plant just a little deeper than before, and do leave space to receive water at the top, ½ inch in a small pot, 1 inch or more in a large one. Nothing is more aggravating than a plant potted so high that when watering, you have to go back to it several times since so much of each application spills down the sides of the pot.

Sterilizing Soil

Whether soil and added elements, as well as pots and crock, should be sterilized is a question. Some growers recommend it in their catalogs; others say they have never found it necessary. Wilson Brothers feel "that sterilized (partial) soil is a must for growing geraniums commercially. In addition to getting rid of the disease organisms, sterilizing kills the weed seeds. And a commercial grower cannot afford the high labor cost of pulling weeds. . . . We sterilize all our soil with steam." Electricity or hot water can also be used to bring soil to a temperature of 180 degrees for a period of 30 minutes. This will not only kill nematodes and weed seeds but various fungi and bacteria as well.

Some packaged commercial soil mixtures are already sterilized, and I use these. For the amateur, the need for treating the soil probably depends on whether you live in an area where the local type of nematodes bothers geraniums. I am told that in some areas of California there is no nematode trouble. In any case, sterilizing should be only partial, as the Wilsons say, not complete, or soil would be reduced to an inert mass, good only to support roots. If heretofore you have found no reason to use sterilized soil, I certainly do not suggest it now.

If you do wish to prepare soil yourself—and it is a very messy, smelly business—bake moistened soil in your oven for 30 minutes at 180 degrees. Let it cool and then stir to aerate it. Wait about three days before using it. Actually, this is pasteurizing, or partial sterilizing.

Fertilizing

When your geraniums are growing well and the weather is consistently sunny, they will benefit from a regular feeding program that will make it possible for you to grow the fairly large plants you want in relatively small pots. It is not possible to lay down rules for fertilizing. Plants might be benefited by applications every two weeks or once a month, or even less in dull weather.

Let the condition of your plants be your guide. If for a variety, growth seems unusually slow and hard, joints are short, leaves are light-colored *for the variety,* and there are few flowers and they are small, you can be pretty sure your plants are in need of food. Of course, it is to be hoped you will not require them to offer such signs of debilitation before you feed them. On the other hand, overlarge puffy leaves, soft, spindly, long-jointed growth, and flowers of lighter color for a variety, are usually indications that you have overdone the matter of feeding. Although light and temperatures affect leaf color, it is the leaf color that is generally your best guide. If foliage has a pronounced yellow tinge, particularly in the lower leaves, check your watering schedule. Acute dryness followed by sogginess because damaged roots cannot take up the water can produce yellow leaves, as can starvation.

Applications of liquid fertilizer at half or even less the strength recommended on bottle or package are usually the most convenient means of feeding. Over the years, I have successfully used a number of these: Hyponex, Miracle-Gro, Ra-Pid-Gro, Plant Marvel, and Stim-u-Plant. Liquid Ortho-Gro, now in a 12-6-6 formula, is particularly recommended. I have long added Epsom salts to the fertilizing solution for my acid-loving plants, as azaleas and gardenias, and now Holmes Miller suggests it also for geraniums to make up for a possible lack of magnesium—¼ teaspoonful of Epsom salts to 1 gallon of fertilizer solution. In any case, when you fertilize, do a proper job with a generous enough application to saturate the whole earth ball. Some solution should run through the hole in the bottom of the pot. (Incidentally, I hope you are never as absent-minded as I was one morning when I was having breakfast and feeding my geraniums at the same time, a poor combination of activities I admit. Only in the nick of time did I discover that I was about to sip a nice hot cup of Miracle-Gro while my geraniums were to dine on instant coffee.)

A Good Program

Generally speaking, geraniums are easy to keep in health with a sensible day-to-day culture plan. It is wise not to crowd them at the window and they should be turned frequently to keep them shapely. They also need space to develop evenly and they benefit from a good circulation of air around them. They must live in an atmosphere free of any taint of gas, and regular ventilation is essential. Admit fresh air daily, for hours during the warm acclimatizing days of early autumn when plants are first brought inside, and daily for minutes (and then indirectly *through an adjoining room*) when the weather is cold.

Cold drafty window sills do not constitute ideal home life for geraniums, although they are more tolerant of this than most house plants. Even with weather-stripping, it is a good precaution on very cold nights to slip a thickness of newspaper or draw a curtain between the icy window panes and the plants. As the sun warms the glass each morning, remove this extra protection.

If, despite your good intentions and loving care, your geraniums in winter look sickly, if growth is lank and soft instead of fresh and crisp, if the flowers are not well formed and too few, check over these essentials of health for geraniums. Briefly they are sun, coolness, some humidity, sensible watering, tight pots, space to develop, and a fresh atmosphere. Perhaps you have watered them frequently but not thoroughly. Perhaps they have had a spell of drouth. Perhaps the location is much too warm. Although geraniums are not difficult their cultural preferences need to be respected. If they are, geraniums will bloom steadily through all sunny seasons.

Spring Decisions

When in cold climates May and June finally bring frost-free weather, your collection of geraniums is due for decisive inspection. Through the winter some of your choicest varieties, you will see, have outgrown their quarters. Since their decorative value is probably as dear to you as their horticultural interest, you are in a quandry—what to do with these giants?

There are two possibilities. You can cut the largest plants back hard, that is, remove two-thirds of their growth, shake off a considerable amount of earth and repot them. If at all possible, as I have said, use the same size pot filled with well-enriched soil. This treatment will check their stature but preserve their health. It will also delay flowering for some two months. Or you can start all over again by taking cuttings at this time. These, by autumn, will have developed into flowering plants at the 3- or 4-inch pot size or even larger.

Figure 26. The broad gray-stone platform and steps of the entrance to Helen Van Pelt Wilson's Plant Room were designed as vacation quarters for winter geraniums and other house plants. The ivy-leaved 'Charles Turner' tumbles out of a basket suspended beside the door and redwood tubs hold plants of 'Fiat', some colorful fancy-leaved geraniums, and a few rambling species. Photo by Bradbury.

Other specimens, still of desirable size, will also need your attention. Almost all at this season will be benefited by a light pruning to achieve again a shapely contour. Some will need repotting. If examination reveals a ball of earth thickly covered with a network of roots, supply a pot one or two sizes larger in diameter.

Perhaps on examination an ailing specimen will show hard, dry, brown roots. This is your cue to discard or rescue. Rehabilitation involves cutting away perhaps two-thirds of the old root mass and pruning off the same amount of top growth.

Repot the plant, then, in a *smaller* container. Or if it looks awful, it may make better sense to throw it away. If the ailment is physiological and not disease, cuttings may be successful, even though they do not look like good material.

Summer Quarters

If you can, get your geraniums outdoors in summer; otherwise keep windows open and the room cool, insofar as this is possible. Outdoors, there are various possibilities. Most, not all, of my plants are set in fairly full sun on the steps of the entrance terrace (Figure 26). They are exposed to the sun gradually, first spending about a week outdoors in light shade. A few varieties resent full summer sun and these go on a plant stand also on the terrace but against a house wall in open shade. Some plants are plunged nearby in the dooryard garden under the fringe tree. Kept together like this, they are in easy reach of the hose, and in hot dry weather they sometimes have to be watered more than once a day. Container plants outdoors always need lots of water, even if there is some rain, since restricted root systems cannot search for moisture as garden plants can.

If you plunge plants in the garden, spread a layer of small stones under each pot to keep worms from tunneling in and upsetting your careful drainage arrangements. To decorate the garden, some plants are packed in their pots in wooden tubs of peatmoss. So insulated, they are not damaged by full sun but the tubs also need regular watering. A few of the ivy-leaved geraniums are suspended in baskets from the uprights of my east pergola. Here there is good air circulation, a necessity for their health in humid weather, and a deterrent though not a complete check against edema.

Autumn Program

Early in August I go over plants and pinch or prune for shapeliness. This needs doing a good two months before you can have flowers again on cut-back growth, not because the plants are resting, but because they need that long to initiate buds and open flowers again. Geraniums, as I have said, require no rest period. I plan then to bring plants in well before frost. Geraniums can stand 26 degrees F, but your pot plants will not benefit from such a chilling. Here in New England, the end of September is about as late as I let my plants stay out. Although there are lovely warm October days, there are also some quite cold nights and the ever-imminent threat of frost. Late in August my geraniums are thoroughly sprayed with malathion 50. Some white flies may be in evidence on the scented-leaveds then, although I may not have seen any through the summer. On the day plants are to be brought in, pots are scrubbed with a pan-scouring pad, any dubious leaves are removed, and tops are sprayed again. A clean, healthy start and *lots of fresh air day and night* until cold weather are insurance for fine winter flowering. Unless absolutely necessary, repotting is not planned at this season. That was attended to in spring.

If plants develop yellow leaves and stop flowering indoors, it is probably because they resent the greater heat and lower humidity of their new environment. Leave the windows near them open all day and also on the nights when there seems small likelihood of a sharp drop in temperature. And contrary to usual practice, mist them several times a day with your house-plant sprayer. Of course, if you have brought in plants just potted after months in open garden beds or boxes, they will be likely to turn yellow. Cut back tops to compensate for the roots that were cut back to fit pots. Eventually, they will recover, but they may not be very decorative for weeks or even months. Some enormous scented-leaveds that I potted in September because I couldn't bear to resign them to frost did not regain their looks until well into November.

Garden Plants in Fall

The approach of autumn poses another geranium problem if you have a great many plants growing *directly* in garden beds or window boxes. In September these are so lavishly in flower it seems as if they will never give out. But if you have ever potted and then petted them, you know what a disappointment they can be indoors until after the turn of the year.

Drastic disturbance of roots is the cause of check to both growth and flower. If you could bring these geraniums indoors intact, that is, in their boxes, and then provide good conditions of sun and air, they would go right on blooming, but you can rarely do this. These plants must be removed from boxes and open beds and their roots severely trimmed to fit them into pots. This is inevitably shocking. Since tops must always be proportionately reduced when roots are shortened, your summer-flowering geraniums must also, of necessity, be relieved of much bloom-producing wood.

With such outdoor material, you will do better to take slips or cuttings in August, preferably, or in September, and leave the large plants to the mercy of frost. If you take cuttings early enough to get young plants into 4-inch pots by late September or very early October, you will have excellent material for winter flowering. If they don't make the 4-inch size, let them stay in well-filled 3's, but then you may have to shift them by February.

Or you can trim and pot a number of the big ones a few weeks before cold weather. Cut back tops to about three pieces of 3-inch growth. Let plants rest outdoors in shade and then, before frost, bring them inside to a cool sunny window. Here for a time they will appear to stand quite still. They will require little water and, of course, no plant food, but by the new year, or even before, root systems will become readjusted. New leaves will appear, a sign to you to start feeding these held-over plants, and to increase the amount of water. Toward the end of February or early in March, they will flower again and by mid-May be large and flourishing, ready to stage again a brilliant summer pageant.

This is only a salvage program to give you late winter bloom in the window garden and a gay summer outdoors. You can hold onto these large plants only if you are willing to have sunny window space filled with not-too-attractive material from October to January. Perhaps, though, you have suitable attic space or an unused room that they can occupy. However, if your sunny windows are already filled by your diversified collection, you will be wise to let frost have the final word with this bedding and window-box material and perpetuate it only in a small way by cuttings.

In any case, do not try to save geraniums by hanging dry plants upside down from the cellar rafters. Apparently this worked in damp, old-fashioned cellars with dirt floors, but in the modern dry warm basement these tactics result in dead geraniums. However, if your basement is not hot (as mine is), you can try a plan that has worked well for several friends who live here in the country and have cool but not freezing cellars. They dismember their window boxes just before frost is expected and cut back plant tops about half way. Then they tie up the soil-covered roots of each plant in a perforated plastic bag. Through the winter, they sprinkle the bags with water the first week in every month and are exact about timing so as not to forget. Toward mid-April, which in most years is about a month before the last killing frost here, they pot up their salvaged plants, feed and water them well, and set them in a light but fairly cool place for about a week, moving them then to sun and warmth up to 70 degrees F.

For geraniums destined to fill window boxes or fancy pots again, this seems much too much trouble for me, since new plants hardly cost the earth. However, the procedure is worth trying for very large choice plants for which other indoor accommodation is not possible.

Chapter SEVEN

Fancy-Leaved Zonals
for Contrast

It is pleasant that the early twentieth-century dislike of variegation in plants has given way to enthusiastic approval, for plants with striped, mottled, and zoned foliage have the special value of contrast at the window, on the terrace, and in the garden. Among these the fancy-leaved geraniums with their charming blends of green, gold, gray, silver, white, brown, and red are surely preeminent. The greatest number of these are from old zonal strains, but recently several varieties have been derived from the boldly-zoned species, *Pelargonium frutetorum,* and from its mutant form, 'Dark Beauty'. There are also a few variegated scented- and ivy-leaved geraniums.

Records of the fancy-leaved zonals go back to the early eighteenth century. As Holmes Miller reminds us, "A geranium with white-bordered leaves was reported in France as early as 1732, only a few years after the geraniums came into cultivation. There were several of this type known in England in the early 1800s. From these the first silver tricolors were developed about 1850. About this time too, a variety called 'Golden Chain', with yellow-bordered leaves, was common in England. About 1855 Peter Grieve conceived the idea that 'Golden Chain' could be used to breed golden tricolors, and by 1858 had succeeded in producing 'Mrs. Pollock', the most famous of the fancy-leaved geraniums. The gold-leaved and bronze-leaved varieties did not get much attention until the 1860s, but may have existed before then. Hundreds of new fancy-leaved varieties were introduced in England between 1860 and about 1885."

Victorians Loved Them

It was the Victorians, of course, who were so taken by these colored-leaved plants. The same taste that led them to drape their mantelpieces with fringed silk scarves and strew wallpaper and carpets with vivid floral patterns made them delight in the essentially *busy* design of these geraniums. For here was a plant literally dressed to kill. Not only is the foliage frequently gaudy but also the flowers of strident rose and vermilion. Victorian England loved them dearly and hybridized them madly so that some varieties were scarcely to be distinguished from others.

Today only a few of these early fancy-leaved kinds can be found. Of the 130 varieties so delightfully described by Peter Grieve in "A History of Ornamental-Foliaged Pelargoniums" but few names survive in American commerce. Perhaps an adventure in "plant antiquing" in England might reveal in private collections his brilliant namesake with its "Vandyked fiery zone and leaf margins of rich yellow." This won first prize at the Special Pelargonium Show held at South Kensington on the 22nd of May, 1869, as the "best golden tricolor introduced, thirty-four varieties competing for this much-coveted prize." Perhaps somewhere awaits discovery 'Victoria Regina' with "broad golden leaf-margins, and proportionate bright flame-crimson zone" as well as 'Beautiful Forever', 'Princess of

Wales', 'Sunset', and 'Illuminator'. From Peter Grieve's list 'Crystal Palace Gem', 'Lady Cullum', 'Lass O'Gowrie', 'Miss Burdett Coutts', 'Mrs. Pollock' (his own introduction), 'Sophia Dumaresque', 'Yellow Gem' and a few others are known today. And some of these have been so altered by time since their origination in the mid-1800s that they do not appear to be the same plants.

Although that early twentieth-century trend away from variegated plants had much to do with the general disappearance of the brilliantly foliaged zonals, the inherent weakness of many of them is also responsible for loss of enthusiasm. Just what causes variation in leaf color is not yet determined but, as Peter Grieve pointed out, "it has been considered by some intelligent persons as analogous to disease, and it is quite certain that its presence is generally, if not always, accompanied by a considerable amount of debility, or at least, by a diminution of constitutional vigour, which, in some degree furnishes argument of this view of its nature."

Certainly some of the tricolors are fairly difficult to propagate although more vigorous strains of some have been developed recently. Cuttings from those albino shoots that unexpectedly appear on many green-leaved zonals never survive. Lacking chlorophyll, the food-manufacturing substance of plants, they cannot live. On the other hand various silver-leaved kinds, such as 'Madame Salleron', have certainly stood the test of the years.

About 1925, I'd say, variegated plants again came into their own. I know that I enjoy them the year around. In my window gardens, they offer color in winter when flowers are scarce. As the warmth of the sun increases so do their hues. By May when they are transferred outdoors, they have real brilliance, especially the tricolors. I keep them potted and combine them with other geraniums in plant tubs with a packing of peatmoss to conserve moisture. Tubs are placed where there is protection from rain, wind, and midday sun.

I find that these fancy-leaved geraniums lend themselves to

charming groupings with plain-leaved zonals, ivy-leaveds and scented-leaveds. In one tub, there will be the brilliant 'Mrs. Henry Cox'—green, yellow, and brown with zones of scarlet—and 'Prince Bismarck'—yellow-green with rust-red areas in the sun. The zonal 'Dark Red Irene' blooms with these, and the old-fashioned rose geranium, *P. graveolens*, with gray-green leaves completes the picture with its delicate sprays of orchid flowers.

Another tub holds the green-and-white 'Silver Lining' with the red-flowered ivy-leaved geranium 'Mexican Beauty', and for scent there is 'Rober's Lemon Rose' and 'Prince Rupert'. Other tubs hold other pleasing combinations of the fancy-leaveds with an ivy-leaved or zonal for flowers and something fragrant to please the nose.

The smaller tubs are placed on tree stumps, cut to 27 inches high, or tubs are used in pairs beside the stepping-stone path to the terrace. In addition, big redwood tubs planted with the fancy-leaveds and others stand on each side of the front door giving pleasure to all who come.

If you can find some old black-iron cooking vessels, they are just right for geraniums. On the covered terrace I have what I presume was a handled soup kettle planted with the handsome golden tricolor 'Mrs. Pollock', silvery green-and-white 'Wilhelm Langguth', and the pungent, sprawling 'Village Hill Hybrid'. The kettle sets on a wrought-iron table, as a "permanent" bouquet. But I also use the variegateds for arrangements, alone or with other foliages and flowers. For a hot-day summer luncheon, I combined green-and-white 'Flower of Spring' and 'Mountain of Snow' with variegated funkia, pachysandra, and fern fronds, all well-conditioned overnight. My centerpiece was indeed a cooling sight.

For Terrace Stands and Garden Beds

A friend whose terrace is furnished with scrolled, wrought-iron chairs and benches has set against the house wall a Victorian hat-

and-umbrella stand. Painted white and fitted with brackets, it holds fancy-leaved geraniums instead of silk toppers and Malacca canes. Her terrace boxes are similarly planted and include the green-and-white *Nepeta hederacea* with its geranium look.

White varieties of green-leaved zonals such as the double white 'Madonna' and single 'Snowflake' are used on a white wire plant stand by another friend to set off her handsome plants of the silver-leaved 'Hills of Snow' and 'Wilhelm Langguth'. In winter these plants are the charming ornaments of a large and sunny sun-room where standard plants of glowing 'Radio Red' zonals provide cheerful contrast.

As Bedding Plants

The fancy-leaved pelargoniums are also being rediscovered in their old use as bedding plants. One gardener made a delightful, frankly nostalgic, 3-foot border planting of contrasting varieties, six plants each of some one brilliant kind. These sections were effectively separated by ribbon strips of small specimens of the silver-leaved varieties. The whole was edged with 'Madame Salleron'. This one is so amenable that cuttings, taken when May is warm, can be planted outdoors immediately. They soon take hold and grow into a lusty satisfactory binding.

Bedding out was beautifully done at Village Hill where in a sunny courtyard many colored-leaved varieties were combined with plain green, large-flowering zonals, to the enhancement of both. Standard wisteria in the center of each bed offered spring color there before the weather was warm enough to set out tender pot plants. Here the red-flowered kinds were kept together in one bed; the pinks grouped in another. I shall never forget the sunny morning loveliness of this picture.

If you plan such a summer delight or, in California, can arrange permanent plantings of these brilliant-leaved plants, take thought of color values. It is easy enough to arrange and rearrange varieties before you remove plants from pots. Flowers must also be considered in grouping the plants. If only foliage matters, the colored-leaved pelargoniums can be indiscriminately planted. Leaves never clash. So if your pleasure is mainly in these, why not pick off and discard the flower clusters as they form? Bedding out then becomes a simple matter and the whole strength of the plant is directed toward leaf loveliness. Decoratively, this seems to me sound policy. The gorgeous 'Miss Burdett Coutts' and 'Mrs. Henry Cox' I thoroughly enjoy out of bloom. But deck Miss Coutts' rose-shaded leaf with a red flower or put a pink blossom above Mrs. Cox's vermilion foliage and I find the ensemble as unsatisfactory as a colorful flower arrangement in a highly decorated vase. Enough is enough, and to my non-Victorian eyes, flowers on a variegated-leaved plant smack of gilding the lily.

Culture of the Fancy-leaveds

These geraniums require somewhat more care than those with plain green leaves. In fact, the brighter the hues, the weaker the plant may be; yet it is those of strongest coloring that appeal most. The fancy-leaveds require sunshine to bring out the strong variegation but the full summer sun is likely to be too much. Morning sun with afternoon shade works well here.

You will notice that it is the new growth that has the best color so you want to keep this coming along with frequent pinching to induce branching. You will observe also that hard growth on slow growers like 'Golden MacMahon' and 'Miss Burdett Coutts' has better color than the lush foliage of a fast grower like 'Happy Thought'.

All in all, these fancy-leaved varieties are more difficult than many other geraniums, and some are quite challenging, as 'Display', 'Dwarf Gold Leaf', 'Golden MacMahon' and 'Pastel'. Although they have rather light root systems they seem to require proportionately larger pots than would seem indicated. And perfect drainage is essential. Use 4-, 5-, and eventually 6-inch pots for these, with a quarter of the pot filled with drainage material and above that soil that is not overly rich. Take care to fertilize enough to keep growth coming along but not so much that foliage gets pale and lush—a nice balance to work out. Too much moisture or too much plant food reduces color.

If these geraniums come to you rather the worse for their journey, do not be alarmed, they will recover. Also, if the light is dim in winter the silver-leaveds and the tricolors may put out new leaves that are not flat but umbrella-shaped. At one window mine usually do this but when the sun gets around there in late winter, they give up the idea of being parasols.

In the garden, the fancy-leaveds succeed only under certain conditions. If plants are to be taken out of the pots, it is essential that their location be well drained. On questionable sites it is a good idea to raise beds a little above the general garden level.

The greatest deterrent to success outdoors in sections around New York or Philadelphia is the variability of the summer weather. Too often weeks of cold rain are followed by intense heat and high humidity. These are conditions resented by fancy-leaved pelargoniums. They prefer it hot, somewhat dry, and with cool nights. Within limits, however, they prove fairly tolerant outdoors if they are protected from wind by house wall or shrubbery line and are located, as I have said, to receive morning rather than midday or afternoon sun. Porch and terrace pots that may be moved back from heavy pelting rains offer the best conditions.

Collector's Choice

If the fancy-leaved geraniums are the ones that appeal most to you, you may enjoy collecting them either as a whole or in fairly arbitrary classifications. Since there are only about fifty named kinds available today, except for some six dwarfs, perhaps you will have room for one of each.

If you prefer to specialize, you might begin with the very handsome tricolors, sometimes divided into golden and silver groups. Some of these are so brilliant they look like those painted sunsets we are sure never happened until we ourselves actually see an unbelievable one. Glamorous in this class is 'Mrs. Henry Cox'. Typical of the tricolors, it has a green leaf center surrounded by a brilliant vermilion-and-purple zone, margined with yellow. Only a little less colorful, smaller, and perhaps not so easy to grow, is 'Miss Burdett Coutts' with a purple-zoned, rose-splashed leaf, cream-edged. 'Mrs. Pollock' is unevenly zoned in brown-splashed red, while the deep margin is golden yellow. The double form is properly called 'Mrs. Strange'. 'Skies of Italy' with its autumn-tinted maple leaves is another lovely golden tricolor, strong and more colorful as it ages.

The green-and-yellow bicolors or "butterfly geraniums" have an irregular, light central zone suggesting a butterfly form and a wide uneven outer area. 'Happy Thought' with a cream center and a green margin bears scarlet blooms. There is also 'Pink Happy Thought'. 'Crystal Palace Gem' reverses matters. Its butterfly is green, its margin yellow.

Then there is a yellow-and-brown class, the predominant color greenish yellow, the zone dark brown. 'Alpha' is a fairly dwarf member of this group, while 'Jubilee' is a tall grower. 'Prince Bismarck', 'Bronze Beauty', 'Marechal MacMahon', are included here. Green with a black zone describes the aptly named and appealing small 'Distinction' with its neat dark circle close to the crenate leaf edge.

The silver-leaved classification is one of the most fascinating. Perhaps 'Mountain of Snow' is the prettiest. Certainly, though a little difficult, it is charming with the whitest leaf of all the green-and-white bicolors, and a constant succession of single scarlet flowers. 'Hills of Snow', 'Wilhelm Langguth', 'Mrs. Parker', and 'Madame Salleron' are other grayish-green-and-white bicolors in this group, while the foliage of 'Beckwith Pride' (Color Plate VI) is marbled when it does not revert to plain green. Few dealers carry it now for this reason and 'Silver Leaf S. A. Nutt' has been dropped on the same account. Merry Gardens has introduced 'Silver Lining', a sport of 'Wilhelm Langguth', with a wider whiter margin splashing irregularly into a gray-green center. I notice also a pinker cast to the new growth.

Gold-leaved geraniums are still fairly rare. Their foliage varies from bright greenish yellow of the sometimes difficult 'Dwarf Gold Leaf' (not dwarf, but fairly large) to the light gold of the large and easy 'Verona'. The small 'Golden MacMahon', often difficult, is light yellow, sometimes with pink markings. The adaptable 'Yellow Gem' makes a medium-sized bushy plant, and is the easiest and best general-purpose variety. These gold-leaved plants are more telling when contrasted with green-leaved geraniums or with more brilliant varieties of the fancy-leaveds. Used alone they tend to appear pallid.

There are also some interesting dwarf variegated zonals. These are more fully described in Chapter 8. In the Finder's List on page 311 are named and described a number of the fancy-leaved geraniums, and here is a list of twelve favorites that have given me much pleasure.

A FAVORITE DOZEN OF FANCY-LEAVED ZONALS

These are older varieties with a wide range of leaf coloring.

'Bronze Beauty No. 2', yellow-green and bronze

'Crystal Palace Gem', yellow and bright green

'Distinction'

'Flower of Spring', silver green and cream

'Happy Thought'

'Jubilee', yellow-green and red-brown

'Miss Burdett Coutts', silver tricolor

'Mrs. Henry Cox', golden tricolor

'Mrs. Pollock', golden tricolor

'Skies of Italy', golden tricolor

'Wilhelm Langguth', green and white

'Yellow Gem'

The Irresistible Dwarfs

If your enthusiasm for geraniums is great but your space limited, the dwarf zonals are surely for you. As a collector you can have a field day with these in just one big sunny window garden. A dozen or so well-chosen plants will readily give you flowers of many colors and forms. There are fancy-leaved varieties, too, and if you are a patient enthusiast, you can train these dwarfs into the same forms as the big ones—little trees, espaliers, or tiny bonsais.

And how the dwarf geraniums bloom. Some, like 'Black Vesuvius', 'Goblin', 'Imp', 'Minx', 'Perky', and 'Small Fortune' incline to year-round performance; and even do well in rather dull winter weather, not demanding the sunshine essential to most pelargoniums. Even if we do not collect them, we all want some of the dwarfs for the dependable color they offer, and we count on the larger ones among them to decorate our entrances, porches, and terraces in summer.

In winter, with fluorescent lights as the sole source or as a supplement to daylight, they can also be a pretty sight. Mrs. Bruce Crane of Dalton, Massachusetts, who has an extensive collection, gets prodigious blooming in 2½- and 3-inch pots set on a layer of sand and soil under greenhouse benches. She gives 12 to 14 hours of 250 to 300 footcandles supplementary illumination and feeds and waters in accordance with the needs of such hard-working plants. Mrs. Crane also grows many "upstairs" on conventional benches, in her so immaculate greenhouse. There I counted more than 100 varieties—such a fascinating and varied array.

Old and New

Not so long ago 'Black Vesuvius', 'Madame Fournier', 'Kleiner Liebling' ('Little Darling'), and 'Pigmy' were about the only dwarfs available. These are the four pictured in Figure 27. They are all green-leaved zonals.

'Black Vesuvius' now in its seventy-fifth year is the oldest and is still popular with appealing single medium-sized orange-scarlet flowers and very dark foliage. A slow grower, it blooms profusely particularly in winter, and stays quite small. It is one of the few that can be considered truly miniature. So pronounced is the zoning of the deep green leaves that early listings place it among the fancy-leaveds, and most of the newer dark-foliaged types derive from 'Black Vesuvius' and 'Madame Fournier'.

'Madame Fournier' is today considered a semidwarf for it is difficult to keep this sturdy one very small, so fast growing is its habit. It has bright single scarlet flowers and leaves darker than those of many of the new varieties. It is an ancestor of all the Rober dwarfs and of some of Holmes Miller's, too. The flowers are less showy and more sparsely borne than on some of the newer varieties.

'Kleiner Liebling' bears single tiny rose-pink flowers with a little white in the center. Leaves are clear green and zoneless, different from any other. This one is also difficult to keep small; it is bushy and compact, a fast grower and not very showy.

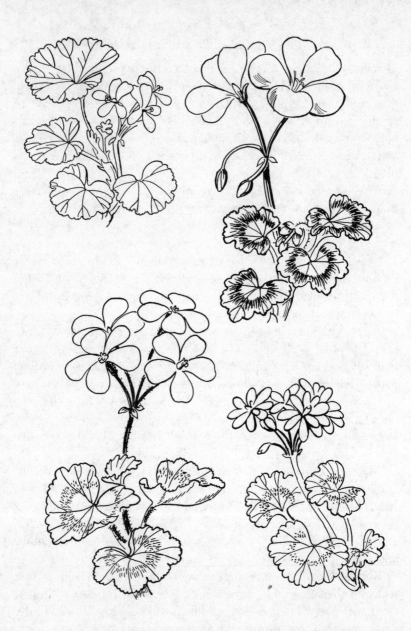

Figure 27. Four dwarf geraniums in review include top left, 'Kleiner Liebling' ('Little Darling'), a rose-pink; top right, 'Black Vesuvius', with bright red flowers and dark olive, zoned leaves; lower left, 'Madame Fournier', a vermilion; lower right, 'Pigmy', a double scarlet.

'Pigmy', called 'Grannie Hewitt' in England, is one of the most popular of all the dwarfs but its origin is not known. 'Pigmy' is so distinct, unique in fact, that it should be easy to trace but has not proved so; being sterile, it is not likely to have rivals. I particularly like 'Pigmy' with its spirit-lifting scarlet flowers because these are in scale with the plant. The light green scalloped leaves are also small, only ¾ of an inch across; all elements are in nice balance. This plant, a moderate grower, blooms steadily through all sunny weather and is ideal for the small window garden. The tiny cuttings are easy to propagate, sometimes taking root in a week. Because plants are self-branching, they need no pinching out to produce bushy growth. However, 'Pigmy' seems to require more water and food than other dwarfs—nearly twice as much. Perhaps in the past, losses of 'Pigmy' have been due to its becoming accidentally dry for the dense growth makes it hard to see the soil.

Today these four green-leaved zonals are far from the whole dwarf story; now there are such fancy-leaved zonal dwarfs as the two sports, 'Variegated Kleiner Liebling' and more recently 'Greengold Kleiner Liebling'; and the interesting, slow-growing hybrids, 'Elf', 'Fairyland', 'Nugget', and 'Sprite'. There are cactus-flowering varieties like 'Red Spider', 'Mischief', and 'More Mischief', all inclined to outgrow dwarf status—if indeed that condition can be defined—and the Rober varieties, mainly of the phlox or eyed-type.

The range of colors, sizes, and habits has been greatly extended since the first edition of this book, and it continues. There are reports from Australia of an 'Apple Blossom Rosebud' miniature, which I have not seen; and of a tiny ivy-leaved geranium, 'Gay Baby', that I find delightful. I hear too of certain smaller scented-leaveds, among them 'Lilliput Lemon', and of so-called miniature regals from England, but these are not our concern here, only the dwarf zonals with their own wonderful possibilities.

•   •   •

Dwarfs from Holmes Miller

It is from Holmes Miller of Los Altos, California, that we have received the greatest number of excellent dwarfs, mainly hybrids obtained by crossings to get new combinations of the old mutations. He considers 'Fairyland' the best of his fancy-leaved dwarfs; 'Imp', 'Perky', and 'Ruffles' the best of the small ones; 'Minx' and 'Small Fortune' of the medium-sized ones; 'Jaunty', 'Keepsake', 'Lyric', and 'Twinkle' the best of the larger dwarfs.

'Elf', 'Fairyland', 'Nugget', and 'Sprite' were produced through planned breeding. Being small and variegated, they are naturally a little difficult at the start, but not so difficult as many suppose. Established plants are hardly more difficult than some of the other dwarfs, but they do have the light root systems characteristic of variegated geraniums, and so are somewhat intolerant of mismanagement. Undoubtedly, they are slow and expensive to propagate. 'Sprite' is the easiest to grow, but harder to maintain as an attractive small plant for a really long time. 'Fairyland' is more difficult to propagate, but established plants are rather easy to keep in good condition for years.

All four bear single flowers. 'Elf' and 'Nugget' are golden tricolors with scarlet and pink shadings, the one with small scarlet, the other with salmon flowers. 'Fairyland' is a silver tricolor also with scarlet blooms. 'Sprite' is silver-leaved with a coral flush in winter and salmon-coral flowers, a slow to moderate grower among these four very slow ones. All are darlings but primarily collector's plants, for they take much patience and great care.

Rober Contributions

The late Ernest Rober also produced a number of dwarf geraniums. According to Mr. Miller, who talked with him several times about his work, Mr. Rober's object was to produce varieties that would quickly grow into compact, bushy, floriferous plants in 3-

or 4-inch pots for florist plants or for border planting. He was not trying to get miniatures. From what I know of his varieties I rate them as just what he intended them to be. Elenore Hamlin, Mr. Rober's daughter, confirms this use of his dwarfs: "Some varieties were tested seven years before they were introduced to the trade. They grew so slowly, he was often discouraged. Some seeds took two years to germinate. 'As slow as orchids,' he complained. He worked with more than a thousand different kinds."

Whether or not the series known as Snow White and the Seven Dwarfs comprise the original Rober varieties is a question. Mr. Miller adds, "I heard Rober state, on several occasions, that he had tentatively selected a Snow White and the Seven Dwarfs. My impression was always that he was staking out a claim to the names, rather than announcing an actual selection of plants. So far as I know, he did not sell any dwarfs under these names during his lifetime, nor release any descriptions."

Mary Ellen Ross has pointed out that while there are existing descriptions of the single white 'Snow White', the single bright-red 'Doc', the single rose-to-white-centered 'Dopey', and cherry-red, white-eyed 'Sneezy', the other four in the series lack definition. She and Mrs. Crane, both of whom grow many of the available Rober dwarfs, have concluded that perhaps 'Bashful' is Rober's 'Lavender' (a choice one, I think), 'Grumpy' is Rober's 'Cerise', 'Happy' is Rober's 'Double Red', and that 'Bumblebee' is an unaccounted-for single red. Whatever the history, these are all excellent free-blooming small plants.

Other Sources

The late David Case produced 'Trinket', a quite small salmon double, and two larger double ones, the dark rose 'Fleurette' and crimson 'Firefly', the very darling 'Snow Baby', a double white . . . "the first pure white double to be offered."

E. H. Eisley gave us the single shrimp-pink 'Pride' and others.

Howard Kerrigan, famous for his regals, introduced one dwarf, the double fire-red 'Goblin', which can be kept quite small for a long time in a small pot.

Wilson Brothers are responsible for introducing 'Emma Hossler' and 'Mr. Everaarts', excellent free-blooming plants among the largest dwarfs. Young plants in small pots are attractive for a while, but these varieties are best if shifted along in the manner of non-dwarf varieties. They can also be used in the garden. Before World War II, Cully Wilson was talked into trying them by a salesman for a Dutch firm. At first they were not considered of much value and were neglected. By the time he realized that they were different and good, the record of the source had been lost. The 1953-54 fall catalog of Wilson Brothers is the earliest to list these varieties. Wilson Brothers have introduced some dwarf originations of their own. 'Robin Hood' is of the 'Emma Hossler' type but larger, with double cherry-red flowers. 'Tu-Tone' and the smaller 'Volcano' are more recent. 'Volcano' is a 1952 cross of 'Black Vesuvius' and 'Mr. Everaarts', similar to 'Black Vesuvius' but more dwarf and the flower a shade darker.

Milton Arndt in New Jersey introduced in the early 1950s a great many dwarf varieties. Some of them are excellent and have stood the test of time, as 'Brooks Barnes', 'Capella', 'Epsilon', 'Salmon Comet', and 'Venus'. All these do particularly well for Eastern growers.

From England have come some interesting imports in this class. 'Timothy Clifford' is a double salmon-rose with black-green leaves, easy to keep small though inclined to legginess. Similar to 'Ruffles', it has perhaps better winter flowers, and not such good summer ones. The double scarlet 'Caligula', single crimson 'Etna', and salmon and pink 'Tiberius' have the same black-green foliage.

Mrs. Crane has been the principal source in this country of these English imports. She has also introduced four dwarfs of her own from strontium 90 radiated seeds of 'Perky'—three singles, the large pink 'Delphin', white 'Tinkerbell', and pink-tinged-white 'Winkie'; and the double white-and-pink 'Nova', all medium-sized growers.

In Australia, the late Ted Both carried on a tremendous breeding program with dwarf types, much of it based on the English narrow-petaled 'Kewense'. Rarest are his miniature Hybrid Staphs, 'Bijou' and 'Bonbon', with dainty starlike blooms. To my knowledge, these are available only from Mrs. Both at Tunia Service in Adelaide (address in Source List). They certainly sound interesting.

What Constitutes a Dwarf

Any zonal geranium *likely* to stay under 12 inches is a small grower in comparison to standard zonals. But dwarfs are more a matter of comparison than of inches. If we could classify them ungrammatically as dwarf, dwarfer, dwarfest, we would be on safer ground. In earlier editions of this book, I tried to set numerical limits proper for dwarfs and semidwarfs. More recently, Mary Ellen Ross, Mrs. Crane, and I, in a sort of informal Eastern conference with hundreds of plants before us at Sugar Hill, attempted to revise my classifications, but further research and experience convince me that classification by inches just won't work. It is impractical because size depends so much on cultural conditions. The varieties that are generally accepted as dwarfs have three distinctive characteristics—small leaves, short internodes, and bushy habit. It is these characteristics that make young plants develop naturally into miniature replicas of the non-dwarf varieties and also make it possible to retard growth enough to retain respectable appearing small plants for a considerable time.

If more definite classifications are required, I like these suggestions:

Miniatures would be varieties that are naturally small and slow

growing, and can be kept reasonably small for a long time with
ordinary dwarf culture.

Dwarfs would be varieties that can be kept small for a considerable time under conditions that restrict growth, but that grow
into compact larger plants if given the chance.

Semidwarf varieties would be those that cannot be kept very
small for long and are best grown as larger plants in larger
pots . . . these make fine, compact, floriferous plants in 4- or
5-inch pots, and stay this way for years with a little pruning
and adequate feeding. So treated, they are superb pot plants.

All this is great common sense. It gets us out of the dilemma
that culture, and perhaps climate, too, have produced. My earlier
comparison of the same varieties grown in New England and in
California indicated that it was easier for us to keep plants tiny
here for some time, one factor being that we have months of little
light and less sun. West Coast plants of smaller varieties started
from hard cuttings that retard early growth, potted in soil of low
fertility, and grown cool in a fairly dry atmosphere will also stay
tiny but hardly below 6 inches. However, it is possible to have a
continuous supply of very small plants, East or West, if cuttings
are started frequently. And this is convenient, for cuttings can be
set in the same 2½- or 3-inch pots and in the same soil in which
they can be maintained for a long time.

The Merry Gardens' list recognizes only two categories, "Miniatures 2 to 3 inches; taller are designated as Semi-Dwarf varieties."
Mrs. Crane indicates three groups but without numbered limits.
Wilson Brothers describe the dwarfs as "Best blooming of all geraniums . . . 8 to 10 inches tall in pot culture, and up to 16 inches
when planted outside." From the English authority, Derek Clifford, we have "mature plants normally less than 8 inches high."
And I consider immediately that England also has its dull months.

It's All Relative

Let us then forget inches and think of the dwarfs as *relatively* small, medium, and larger growers but always of less stature than standard zonals. We can also consider them as relatively slow, moderate, and fast growers and so select them for our various purposes, knowing that culture will not make dwarfs into giants and that some varieties will always be smaller than others. Thus 'Imp' stays smaller than 'Pigmy', and both are exceeded by 'Twinkle'.

If you want tiny plants that will stay *tiny* for a year or longer, there are at least six that are very slow growing. 'Black Vesuvius' and 'Imp' could never be induced to much height. 'Ruffles' makes a fine small plant if started from hard cuttings. The silver tricolor 'Fairyland' is a possibility, but it requires extra care because of the weak root system characteristic of all the fancy-leaveds, big or little. 'Sprite' and 'Variegated Kleiner Liebling' are also silver-leaved little ones.

For a middle-sized group of moderate growers, you could select the variegated 'Frolic' and 'Jaunty', or 'Pigmy', 'Small Fortune', 'Snowbaby', 'Sprite', 'Tempter', 'Trinket', 'Volcano', and 'Whitecap'. The Rober dwarfs might suit also, but they are inclined to grow faster and taller.

Among the fast growers 'Fleurette', 'Firefly', 'Flirt', 'Gypsy Queen', 'Lyric', 'Prince Valiant', and 'Meditation' make fairly big plants. Flowers on the last two, also on 'Dancer', are perhaps the largest produced by the dwarfs, with umbels up to 3 inches.

Then there is a wonderfully useful group, technically dwarfs but inclined to outgrow even 4-inch pots rather quickly. However, as vigorous plants in larger pots, they can well be the choice for enthusiasts to whom *notable* smallness is not so important as continuous color with ease of culture indoors and out. Among these lusty compact growers are 'Bumblebee', 'Dopey', 'Gypsy Gem', 'Emma Hossler', 'Mr. Everaarts', and 'Robin Hood'. There are also

Mr. Miller's three cactus-flowering types, 'Mischief', 'More Mischief', and 'Red Spider'.

Pots for Dwarfs

Pot size is a determining factor in the handling of dwarfs. Outside a greenhouse, plants in 2-inch pots or even the 2½-inch size are difficult, if not impossible, to handle. In a home on a shelf in a window with the full sun that most of them require for flowering, plants in such tiny pots need constant attention. (Of course, a window shelf with sun striking the tiny pots and heating the roots is not ideal, but plants do look pretty there.) In any case, there isn't much soil even in a 2½-inch pot and in bright weather this soon dries out and shallow roots can be damaged. Under such conditions, dwarf geraniums often need water more than once a day. Unless you can always be on the alert, you may want to shift your newcomers immediately to 3-inch pots. I certainly find the larger pots easier because I can leave plants so potted in the care of others for a few days without apprehension or the detailed instructions those 2¼-inchers need. The tiny ones in tiny pots must always be grown with an acute sense of their needs, and somehow you can't write this down.

After one anxious winter of trying to deal with dwarfs—geraniums and others—in 2-inch pots, I shifted them all in spring to 3- and 3½-inch pots, and I still recall my relief. Plants that had been a discipline became a pleasure, and it seemed to me I could sense the gratitude of the plants themselves, no longer required to deny their need for *lebensraum*. Now, as soon as plants recover from travel—and this usually takes 7 to 10 days in the sun after an immediate watering—I keep them on the dry side until they have recovered, for they do not enjoy travel and look it. Then I shift them to 3- or 3½-inch pots.

You can use glazed (best for window shelves), plastic, or clay pots, and it is simpler if you choose one type since culture must necessarily vary with the different kinds. Plants in glazed or plastic containers, for instance, require less water than those in clay; if you are using all three, you must have their varying needs in mind as you water. I prefer clay pots, especially the new nicely designed ones that curve in a little toward the base.

About Soil and Fertilizer

A soil mixture that works well for many people consists of half garden soil, preferably clay loam, and half sand with no organic material added. The sand helps aerate the growing mixture and the soil offers nourishment. Mrs. Crane uses 3 parts top soil, aged two years, 2 parts sphagnum peat, and 1 part coarse vermiculite or perlite, but this comes only in bulk. Success is also reported with certain commercial soil mixtures, which are a great convenience.

In addition to full light for all the dwarfs and sunshine for most of them, if plants are to bloom well they need weak solutions of fertilizer whenever the weather is bright enough for growth and bud production. This is usually year-round in California. From February to mid-November in the East we can be sure of fine flowering, and all through some winters. For a likely twelve months of bloom, the dwarf geraniums have few equals among flowering house plants.

A schedule can hardly be supplied as a guide to fertilizing. It's the look of the plant that tells you. If growth is rank with oversize leaves of dark color for the variety and there is a scarcity of flowers, you are probably feeding too much; if it is hard, abnormally slow, with poor leaf color—the most sensitive indicator—or loss of lower leaves, your plants may be starving. I give a weak solution of one of the complete house-plant fertilizers—Hyponex, Stim-u-Plant or Ra-Pid-Gro—fairly regularly but guided by the "look," and I alternate brands to insure good nutrient balance.

Sometimes plants do not respond to fertilizer. This could be because they have been growing too long in tiny pots and roots are no longer able to absorb fertilizer. The soil may have become poorly aerated or collected an excess of salts with resulting root deterioration. Take a look at those roots. If they look healthy and are hungrily enveloping the earth ball, supply a larger pot; if the roots look gummy or rotted, better wash them off and supply fresh soil but return the plant to the same size pot.

In general, as I have indicated, the 3-inch size pot is tops for the little fellows or they will lose their miniature status. Most of the others, as 'Keepsake', 'Jaunty', 'Lyric', 'Medley', and 'Minx' do well in 2½- to 4-inch pots, which really are not very large. Rober's varieties are also thus adequately accommodated, and this is apparently the use for which they were bred. 'Emma Hossler' and 'Mr. Everaarts' look nice for a time in 4's but need pruning to look well very long. And there is a report of a plant of 'Mr. Everaarts' in an *8-inch pot* taking first prize in the dwarf class in a geranium show. Definitions must have been suspended to permit that award. (But this does suggest the discoveries awaiting the long-term grower.)

The other basic needs of the dwarfs are the same as those for the standard geraniums—good ventilation certainly, and no crowding. It is difficult not to jam in one more plant because you want another variety, but crowding brings real trouble to geraniums. Fresh air is easy, of course, indirectly in cold weather from a window opened part-way in an adjoining room. I grow most of my plants no warmer than 70 degrees F during the day, and at night set the thermostats at 55 degrees in the Plant Room and 60 degrees in the living room. Geraniums can be grown warmer, but they don't like it as well. The dwarfs being naturally bushy require little pinching or pruning to develop well-rounded forms.

Propagation by Cuttings or Seeds

To increase your collection, cuttings are the surest means. Take 1- to 2-inch pieces of tip growth that is not just newly grown but has matured enough to be quite firm. Remove all flower buds, even the tiniest ones. If left on to open, they will weaken the cutting. Prepare flats or pots. Then proceed the way you do for standard varieties, as explained in Chapter 14. Hormone rooting agents are "iffy" for these tiny cuttings and are not recommended since it is difficult not to use too much. Besides, they are not necessary. Almost all varieties root so easily and quickly in practically any material, even in clean, medium-to-coarse sand that you can obtain almost anywhere. Firm the sand well around the base of each cutting.

Apparently all dwarfs root more quickly than non-dwarfs; some are a little faster than others, a negligible factor unless quantities are being produced commercially. 'Pigmy' is very fast; 'Kleiner Liebling' is one of the slowest.

If you grow from seeds, it really takes patience but the process is interesting. Some of the seeds will germinate in two weeks; some will take two months. You can obtain Little Read's Strain of English dwarf seed from the Geo. W. Park Company in this country (address in Source List). Half the resulting seedlings will be standard zonals but half will produce plants that are likely to stay small. Seeds sown early in spring will presumably produce blooming plants in 5 months, which is very quick indeed. Mr. Read reports that some of these "grow very strong, like a telegraph pole, with the leaf nodes set very close together, and they will continue to grow up until they finally make an odd break which usually induces flowering." If you let them go to about 8 inches, you can take cuttings 3 to 4 inches long. "Usually within 6 weeks the new plants will flower. Strangely they never try to run straight up again."

Of course, *varieties* of dwarfs do not come "true" from seed.

Varieties to Consider

With more than 100 dwarf geraniums available at this time—and more to come—it will probably be difficult for you to make first choices. On that account I have prepared these short lists—and I must say I had a terrible time being selective. On page 316, you will find most of these described, and I have given the source of each one when I knew it.

TWELVE DWARFS FOR A START

These include a full range of color and variations in rate of growth; they are suggested only as an interesting start. All are free-blooming.

'Brooks Barnes'	'Pigmy'
'Epsilon'	'Prince Valiant'
'Goblin'	'Small Fortune'
'Lyric'	'Snow Baby'
'Minx'	'Twinkle'
'Perky'	'Whitecap'

SIX VARIEGATED DWARFS FOR THE COLLECTOR

Except for the 'Kleiner Lieblings' these are a challenge, for they are hardly of easy culture.

'Elf'	'Nugget'
'Fairyland'	'Sprite'
'Greengold Kleiner Liebling'	'Variegated Kleiner Liebling'

SIX SLOW-GROWING TINIES FOR THE COLLECTOR

Kept small in 2½ inch pots for two to three years, these require close attention to watering and feeding.

'Black Vesuvius'	'Perky'
'Fairyland'	'Ruffles'
'Imp'	'Small Fortune'

TWELVE FREE-BLOOMING LARGE DWARFS

Most of these, *only technically dwarf,* make excellent house, porch, and terrace plants, easy and colorful to grow in 4- to 6-inch pots; they may also be enjoyed as border plants in the garden.

'Bumblebee'	'Mischief'
'Dancer'	'Mr. Everaarts'
'Dopey'	'Pride'
'Emma Hossler'	'Robin Hood'
'Friesdorf'	'Sorcery'
'Gypsy Gem'	'Sparkle'

Figure 28. A study in scented-leaved geraniums includes, top to bottom, left: *P. glutinosum*, the Pheasant's Foot Geranium; *P. acerifolium*, Maple-leaved; 'Mrs. Taylor'. Center: *P. odoratissimum*, Apple-scented; *P. radens*, Crowfoot Geranium; *P. crispum* 'Gooseberry Leaved'; *P.* × *limoneum* 'Lady Mary'. Right: *P. denticulatum* 'Filicifolium', Fern-leaf Geranium; 'Pretty Polly'; 'Mrs. Kingsley'.

Chapter NINE

The Intimate Appeal
of the Scenteds

The scented-leaved geraniums with their wide range of "sweet" foliages have charmed window gardeners for generations, in fact, ever since these plants were brought to England in the seventeenth century. They have even acquired sentimental meanings. In old books we read that the oak-leaved one signifies true friendship; the rose-scented, preference; the nutmeg-scented, expected meeting; but the lemon-scented means unexpected. This geranium vocabulary is but one of many pleasant aspects.

A Romantic Past

The scented-leaveds were first brought to England about 1632 from the African Cape. By 1795 Dutch and English navigators had imported many kinds for plant lovers in the British Isles were tremendously enthusiastic over these novelties from a distant clime. Scented geraniums were grown everywhere, in cottage windows,

125

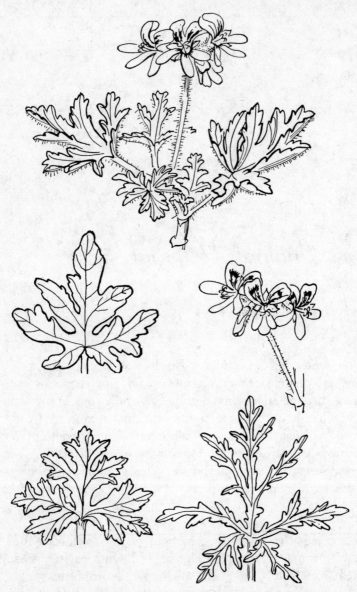

Figure 29. These varieties of the Old-Fashioned Rose Geranium, *P. graveolens*, include: top, *P. graveolens* 'Camphorum', the Camphor-Rose Geranium; left center, *P. graveolens* 'Rober's Lemon Rose'; left lower, *P. graveolens* 'Minor', the Little Leaf Rose Geranium. Middle and lower right, *P. radens* 'Skeleton Rose' ('Dr. Livingston').

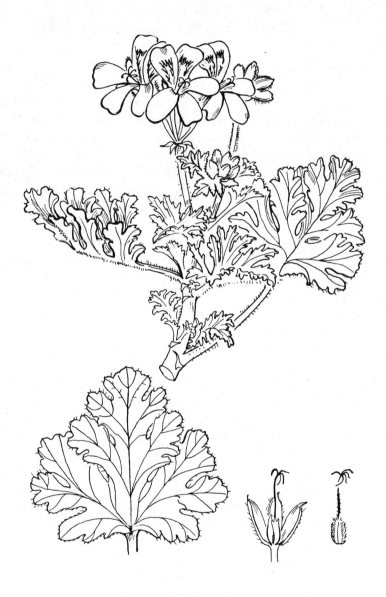

Figure 30. *P. graveolens* 'Red-Flowered Rose' bears cerise flowers with upper petals black-spotted, effective on compact plants with very crinkled young leaves. Detail shows calyx with stigma and at right, style and ovary.

manor halls, and greenhouses. Commercial growers found in their easy propagation a mine of opportunity.

When it was discovered that *P. capitatum* and *P. graveolens* would furnish a substitute for the costly attar of roses, extensive fields were planted in southern France and Turkey. By 1800 geranium oils distilled at Grasse practically replaced the more expensive rose oils. As their economic value was further appreciated, great plantations of scented geraniums were developed by the British in Kenya Colony in Africa. Before the American Revolution, they were brought to this country where they attained popularity in Colonial days that never completely waned.

Today the United States Dispensatory lists a number of rose-scented geraniums grown for perfume. It takes 35 ounces of leaves to produce 2 drachmas of the volatile, crystallizable oil. Dissolved in alcohol in the proportion of 3 ounces to 1 gallon, a delightful preparation called Extract of Rose-leaf Geranium results.

The tremendous general interest in this scented group did not last, perhaps because of over-hybridization and the confusion that arose from the crossing of the various species. So carelessly multiplied were they that no botanist has since bothered to untangle them. Although some species grown today exactly resemble the paintings in Sweet's and Andrews' volumes, many bearing the species names show considerable variation. Doubtless this is sometimes due to outright confusion and the substitution of unrecorded hybrids or sports for originals but also, perhaps, to natural changes wrought in the species themselves through three centuries of varying soils and climates.

However, the scenteds we grow today are much the same as those that were taken to England some two centuries ago. As Derek Clifford points out, "the basis of any collection . . . remains those wild pelargoniums that grow among the scrub on the mountainsides of South Africa." Some of the species are apparently more genetically compatible than others. *P. crispum* and *P. graveolens*

Figure 31. This hybrid of *P. graveolens* is often offered under the incorrect name *P. scabrum;* it is attractive in both flower and foliage.

have kept their identities as the two warm groups, and *P. tomento-sum* and *P. quercifolium* have freely associated with *P. graveolens*, as a glance at a specialist's catalog readily indicates. Some species like *P. abrotanifolium* have produced no cultivars; *P. odoratissimum* (Figures 28, 43) only a few, but this one and *P. × fragrans* have united to give us 'Old Spice' with a subtle aroma of both apple and nutmeg. The nutmeg-scented variety 'Cody' and the 'Variegated Apple' that originated at Village Hill have apparently disappeared from commerce. But from *P. fulgidum* came several of the so-called Uniques—'Old Scarlet Unique' or 'Old Unique', 'Rollisson's Unique', and perhaps several others now in hiding. The quality of their scent, or smell, is certainly in dispute, perhaps it is best considered pungent.

Wide variety of leaf form is also characteristic, with the ferny *P. denticulatum* 'Filicifolium' having the finest foliage, and next the quite threadlike *P. denticulatum*. The free-flowering *P. radens* is also fine-toothed, but the oak-leaved *P. quercifolium* and its varieties are broad and usually coarse.

As I know these plants better, I find it more difficult to be selective, as my crowded window sills plainly indicate. Indeed, anyone who had a garden-minded grandmother recalls sweet-leaved geraniums with pleasant nostalgia. It isn't just the sprig of lemon-scented geranium floating in a finger bowl or the rose-scented leaf firmly set at the base of each glass of apple jelly that we remember, but also the mantel jars of fragrant potpourri where "a wizardry of charms, aromas sweet in tender strife and conflict meet." And some of us remember sachet bags hanging in clothes closets or envelopes of dried leaves that gave to bed linens and blankets a clean refreshing aroma. Mrs. Vandivert writes of an inherited English cupboard that still smells faintly of the lemon-scented geranium her mother kept in it when she was a child.

Although I have always disliked the expression "conversation piece"—it evokes a silent group of desperate guests lighting upon some object and breaking into a wild babble about it—a window sill of scented-leaved geraniums does invite comment. And I enjoy the different personal reactions to a sampling of the various bruised leaves.

Seven Classifications

It is difficult to make classifications among the scenteds, and botanical groupings have proved impossible. Arbitrarily, then, I suggest seven *practical* groupings of Rose, Mint, Lemon, Fruit, Nut, Spice, and Pungent. There are some seventy-five scenteds available to us from the 250 of which there are records. The odor of the slightly bruised or fingered leaf gives the best clue to a classification, although when the sunshine is strong and the day hot, the volatile oils stored in the veins and pits of the leaves may be automatically released to enliven the air with their sharp herbal scents. In winter in full sun, their scent is strong. More often, unless the foliage is touched, it yields no scent, so if you would identify unknowns you must touch each one and then wash your hands before going to the next. Otherwise your fingers soon emit the pleasantly combined fragrance of a spicy bowl of potpourri and you cannot distinguish rose from apple.

Even then your nose won't always know. One day the leaves of 'Clorinda' may bring you the scent of lemon. Another time you will describe it as nutmeg, or it may resemble eucalyptus or pepper. 'Rollisson's Unique', classified as peppery, suggests only mint to me. Uncertainty is due partly to varying conditions of perception but also to the amount of oil released. A plant may emit one perfume from a lightly bruised leaf, another scent from a crushed one. Weather and time of day have an effect, too, and also the inherent strength of scent in different specimens of the same plant and at different stages of growth. In fact, the scent of geranium leaves is not a subject for logic, only a cause of delight.

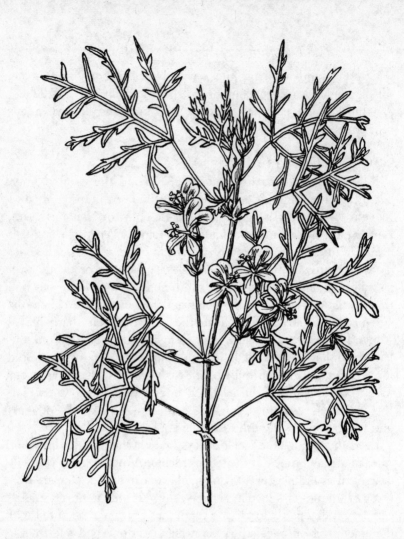

Figure 32. The Crowfoot geranium, *P. radens*, freely produces its small rosy flowers. The new name, *P. radens*, for *Geranium revolutum* was provided by Prof. H. E. Moore in 1955 to transfer this popular plant to its proper place in the genus *Pelargonium*. Prof. Moore found that this plant was often mislabeled *P. denticulatum*, P. 'Skeleton Rose', or P. 'Dr. Livingston'.

Rose Scenteds

The popularity of the rose-scented group has never waned and many varieties are grown today. Leaves are usually broader than long and vary from the deep cutting of 'Skeleton Rose' ('Dr. Livingston') to the scalloped roundness of 'Snowflake'. Who can say which varieties have the strongest rose scent? I check my plants repeatedly and conclude not too firmly that 'Attar of Roses' (at least the plants I now have) and *P. graveolens,* the Old Fashioned Rose Geranium, seem the most roselike. Mary Ellen Ross puts 'Rober's Lemon Rose' first, 'Attar of Roses' second, and *P. graveolens* third. And so it goes, person by person. I always pause with pleasure over *P. graveolens* 'Camphorum'; and 'Variegated Mint Rose' invariably appeals to me. From Merry Gardens I have recently received this pretty thing, a form of *P. graveolens* with a finely divided white-edged green leaf and a good rose scent.

The Rose Geranium of history, if one dare extract it from a mass of nomenclature, is probably *P. graveolens,* the name meaning "heavily scented," and the quality of its fragrance unmistakably rose, as we know this in the Damask Rose whose scent most of us identify as the true rose one. For quality of flower, more cerise than scarlet, pleasing fragrance, but not so strongly rose as some, and fine gray-green foliage, you might select 'Red Flowered Rose'. It blooms well all summer and in winter provides welcome flowers from late January on. The silvery 'Grey Lady Plymouth' and white-flecked 'Snowflake' offer attractive foliage variation but only faint scent. 'Variegated Mint Rose' has the lightest foliage color of the scenteds and its cream-edged gray-green leaf is a redolent combination of both mint and rose. You will grow 'Little Gem' for its flowers, the scent being more pungent than roselike; but the also small Little-leaf Rose Geranium (*P. graveolens* 'Minor') for both convenient size and unmistakable rose fragrance.

Figure 33.   The Peppermint Geranium, *P. tomentosum*, has velvety "grape" leaves and is a procumbent grower with a refreshing mint fragrance.

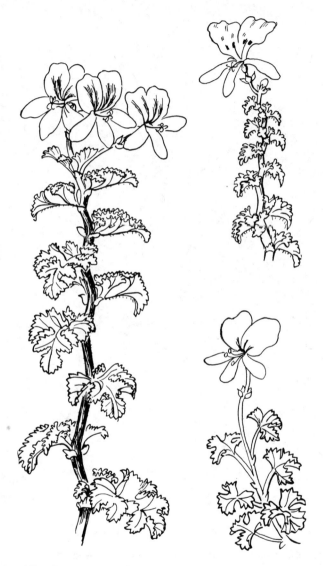

Figure 34. The Lemon-scented Geranium, *P. crispum*, has various forms: left, *P. crispum* 'Prince Rupert' has the largest leaves of the *crispum* group; upper right, *P. crispum* 'Minor' is the old-fashioned Finger-bowl Geranium with tiniest leaves and citronella scent; lower right, the flowers of *P. crispum* have long petioles.

Figure 35. *Geranium citriodorum* is now considered a synonym for *Pelargonium acerifolium*, with a pungent, spicy odor from the maplelike leaves.

Mint Scenteds

The mint-scenteds are indeed favorites, and if I could have but one of the scenteds I would certainly select *P. tomentosum*, the Peppermint-scented Geranium, with its refreshing odor (Figures 25, 33). The great downy grapelike leaf and horizontal-to-pendant manner of growth, also tolerance for light shade, make it an excellent plant to tumble over the side of a window box or to float down from a window bracket. 'Pungent Peppermint' has a fine penetrating but less pure aroma of mint and the leaves are also downy but smaller. This offers a profusion of small white flowers, carmine-brushed. The cross of mint and rose scents, 'Joy Lucille', bears inconspicuous pink flowers and is a big-leafed rangy grower with a strong predominantly minty scent.

Lemon and Other Citrus Scenteds

From the leaves of this group we enjoy in miniature the wonderful heady fragrance of a citrus orchard in bloom. Everyone must have at least one of the tiny-leaved fresh lemon-scented *crispum* varieties. Their curled leaves are perky as fresh parsley and the plants look like small upright yew trees. *P. crispum* 'Minor' is the Finger-Bowl Geranium, named for the custom of floating sprigs of it in finger bowls for the refreshment of guests after dining. This one has the tiniest leaves of the crispums and a strong pleasing citronella scent. I enjoy it on a high-up glass window shelf where it departs from tradition to send out stiff side shoots and so serves there as a vine. 'Prince Rupert' has the largest leaves of the crispums, pretty lavender flowers, the same sturdy upright growth, and a strong pleasant lemon scent. The white-to-yellow edged 'Prince Rupert Variegated', sometimes called 'French Lace', has somewhat finer growth and the lemon scent is less pronounced.

In the Lemon-scented Geranium, *P.* × *limoneum*, a citronella overtone is again noticeable in the fine-toothed, fan-shaped leaves.

Figure 36. The Lime-scented Geranium, *P.* ✕ *nervosum*, has sharp-toothed pleasantly fragrant leaves that cover the compact plant of this century-old hybrid, and darkly marked lavender flowers.

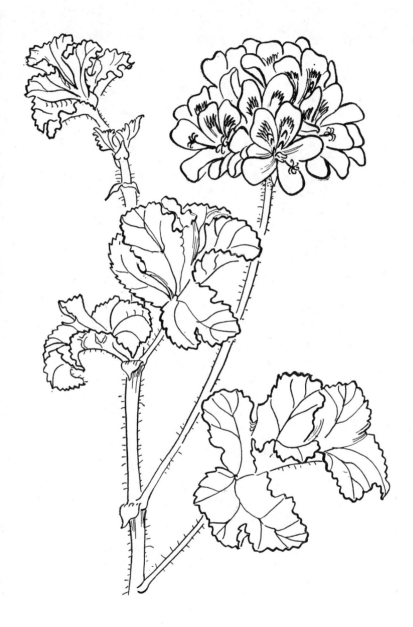

Figure 37. Mint-scented 'Rollisson's Unique' is a rangy grower that in spring is gloriously covered with brilliant magenta flowers.

Figure 38. *P. grossularioides*, the Coconut-scented Geranium, has clusters of tiny magenta flowers.

'Lady Mary' makes a handsome, free-flowering specimen with effective magenta blooms but the lemon scent is slight. 'Prince of Orange' has showy flowers and the true orange scent in its small leaves. This one makes a large plant. The Lime-scented Geranium, *P.* × *nervosum,* has a fine astringent quality and quite large lavender flowers. I am also very fond of *P.* × *melissinum,* the Lemon Balm Geranium, with its soothing fragrance. It makes a big shrub, fine for the summer garden or terrace but somewhat overwhelming in a window garden.

Fruit, Nut, and Spice Scenteds

Some of the attributions to fruit in this group tend to be pretty fanciful. *P. odoratissimum,* the Apple-scented Geranium, with its soft round ruffled leaves and vinelike flower branches, does smell of apple but hardly of the crisp fresh fruit. The nutmeg-scented *P.* × *fragrans* is indeed spicy and sometimes I do think it is like nutmeg. It's a plant I dote on, and I let it ramble considerably. Growth is open and airy and the small, pleated-edged gray leaves are spaced out and the plant is nice for basket or bracket. 'Old Spice' is a white-marked cross of these two; and 'Snowy Nutmeg' is also a variegated with white-edged bright green leaves.

Perhaps 'Rollisson's Unique', one of the most handsome of all geraniums, may also smell spicy to you rather than minty or eucalyptus-like, as is often claimed. This plant produces cerise flowers of true magnificence to adorn a greenhouse wall or cover a stalwart trellis thrust into the back of a pot, for 'Rollisson's Unique' has a definite penchant for climbing. In a sunroom with hydrangea-blue walls it provides a heady color scheme. Because the foliage is sometimes considered pepper-scented, it is included here to the special glory of this spicy class.

Apricot, coconut, ginger, pine, or strawberry are other scented possibilities, which you may or may not detect. Anyway it is fun to try, and almost all the scents in this group seem delightful to me.

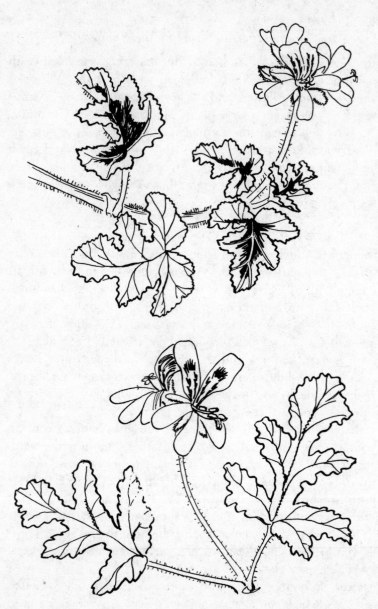

Figure 39. Here are two hybrids of *P. quercifolium*: above, the low spreading *P. quercifolium* 'Prostratum', the Prostrate Oak Geranium, has an excellent pungent scent and small lavender flowers with purple-veined leaves; below, *P. quercifolium* 'Village Hill Hybrid' is pleasantly pungent and also has attractive lavender flowers.

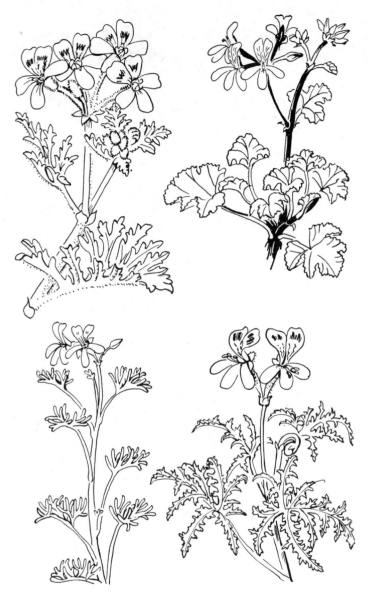

Figure 40. Upper left, P. × *Blandfordianum* has pungent gray leaves and white flowers; lower left, P. *abrotanifolium,* the Southernwood-leaved Geranium, bears carmine-dotted flowers and silvery leaves; upper right, P. × *fragrans,* Nutmeg Geranium, has gray foliage and red-lined white flowers; lower right, P. *denticulatum* is rose-scented with carmine-brushed lavender flowers and filmy foliage.

Figure 41. *P. quercifolium* 'Giganteum', the Giant Oak Geranium, is a coarse, tall grower, adaptable for standards, with a variable 3- to 5-lobed leaf form, small rose flowers, and a pungent scent.

Pungent Scenteds

These incline to rank growth and heavy texture, often with more smell than scent since a number emit a heavy oily odor. Others are pleasant and aromatic. Here belong the *P. quercifolium* or oak-leaved varieties, the gawky though brilliant 'Old Scarlet Unique', the beautiful bright red 'Mrs. Taylor', *P.* × *Blandfordianum*, and *P. abrotanifolium*. Handsomest of all is the stunning, bright rose 'Clorinda' with blossoms to rival the best of the garden zonals. In this class *P. glutinosum*, the Pheasant's Foot Geranium, is also noteworthy for its contrasting foliage of finer texture. The name came from the resemblance of the leaf to the bird's footprint in the snow. And I also enjoy my 'Village Hill Hybrid'.

Lore and Fact

It is around these scented varieties that geranium lore has so richly collected. Grown and loved by ardent gardeners for many years, these appealing plants have received many common names. Although these are descriptive and often amusing, they are confusing to those of us who would prefer to mean what we say when we call one of the scenteds by name. We are therefore appreciative of the 1955 work of Prof. Harold E. Moore, Jr., at the Bailey Hortorium of Cornell University. A number of illustrations from his "Pelargoniums in Cultivation," ("Baileya" Vol. 3 1955) are reproduced here through the courtesy of the Hortorium. For further descriptions of scented-leaved varieties, see the Finder's List on page 320.

Here are some selections to help you choose scenteds for some special purposes.

A DOZEN SCENTEDS WITH FINE SCENT

Or select a half-dozen if space is limited and you want variety of form with a selection of scents.

P. crispum, lemon
P. × fragrans, nutmeg
P. graveolens, rose
P. graveolens 'Camphorum', camphor
P. × limoneum, lemon
P. × nervosum, lime

P. odoratissimum, apple
'Prince of Orange', orange
P. radens 'Skeleton Rose' ('Dr. Livingston'), lemon-rose
P. × rutaceum, rue
P. tomentosum, peppermint
'Variegated Mint Rose'

VARIEGATED-LEAVED SCENTEDS

P. crispum, Gooseberry-leaved, lemon
P. graveolens 'Lady Plymouth', rose
P. odoratissimum, apple

'Prince Rupert Variegated', lemon
'Snowflake', rose
'Variegated Mint Rose'

TALLEST SCENTEDS

P. graveolens group, rose
P. × melissinum, lemon balm
P. quercifolium, oak-leaved

RAMBLING OR PROSTRATE SCENTEDS

P. × fragrans, nutmeg
'Godfrey's Pride', mint
P. grossularioides, coconut
'Joy Lucille', mint
P. quercifolium 'Beauty', pungent

P. quercifolium 'Skelton's Unique', pungent
'Rollisson's Unique', pepper
P. tomentosum, peppermint

COMPACT SCENTEDS

'Clorinda', eucalyptus

P. *crispum* 'Prince Rupert', lemon

P. *crispum* 'Prince Rupert Variegated', lemon

P. *crispum* 'Minor', citronella

P. *graveolens* 'Lady Plymouth', rose

P. *graveolens* 'Little Gem', pungent

P. *graveolens* 'Red Flowered Rose', rose

P. × *limoneum* 'Lady Mary', lemon

P. *odoratissimum*, apple

'Prince of Orange', orange

P. × *Scarboroviae* 'Countess of Scarborough', strawberry

'Shottesham Pet', filbert

Chapter TEN

Culture and Use of the Scenteds

In areas where winters are cold, the scenteds are enjoyed as pot plants in spacious window gardens, or collections are moved to a greenhouse. The plants do need plenty of room for they soon reach considerable size. An October-acquired nursery plant of a rose-scented or oak-leaved variety in a 2½-inch pot—and after only one repotting—can easily be 18 inches high by April, and the nutmeg-scented readily spreads as far. Except for 'Brilliant', 'Shrubland Rose', 'Clorinda', and a few others with large flowers, the scenteds are plants to choose for foliage rather than blooms. However, in a cool room, that is, not above 70 degrees F, and with higher humidity than other geraniums enjoy, or in a greenhouse, they produce some intermittent bloom, and from March on through the summer quite a lot. They are the only geraniums on which I frequently use the mist sprayer and, of course, the same pebble-filled trays as for all my house plants. Scenteds need frequent turning in the window

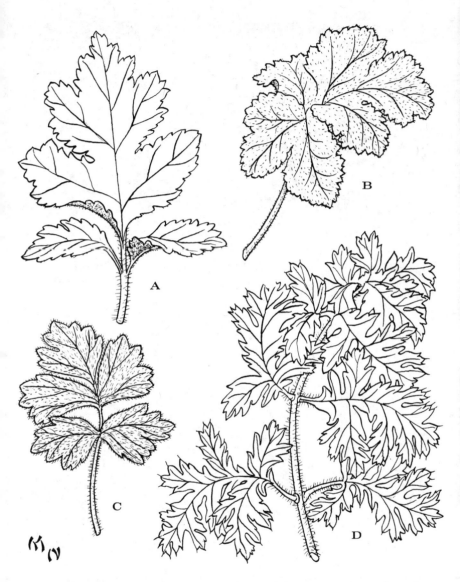

Figure 42.   These are hybrid and species leaf variations: A, *Pelargonium* × *glaucifolium* leaves 3-lobed but not pinnate; B, leaves of *P. bicolor*, the Two-colored Cranesbill, are not lobed so far as the midrib; C, the divided leaf of *P. fulgidum*, the Celandine-leaved Storksbill; D, bi-pinnate leaf of *P.* × *rutaceum*, the Rue-scented Storksbill.

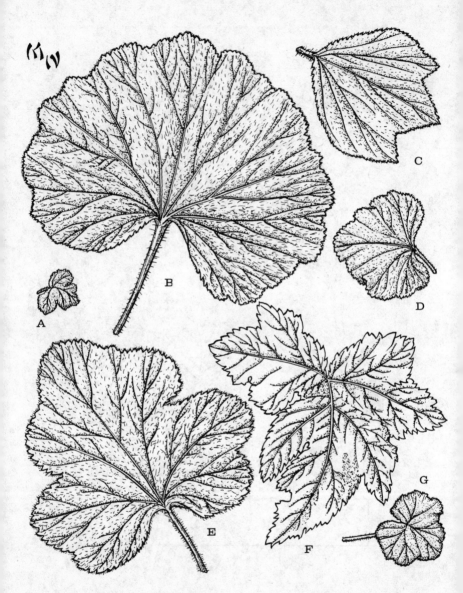

Figure 43. Typical Pelargonium leaves. A, *P. crispum,* the Lemon-scented Geranium; B, *P. cucullatum,* Hooded Cranesbill; C, *P. angulosum,* Marshmallow-leaved Cranesbill; D, *P. australe*; E, *P. vitifolium,* Balm-scented Cranesbill; F, *P. glutinosum,* Pheasant's Foot Geranium; G, *P. odoratissimum,* Apple-scented Geranium.

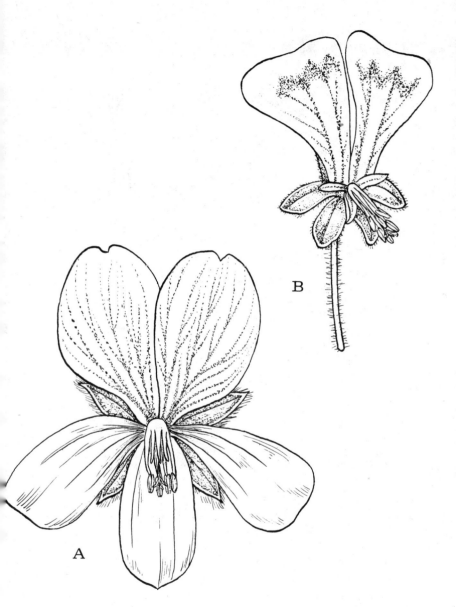

Figure 44. A, red flowers with deeper red veins of *P. cucullatum*, Hooded Cranesbill; B, lower petals of *P. papilionaceum*, Butterfly Cranesbill, are shorter than the sepals, contrasting with the much larger upper petals, pink in color, splotched with purple.

Figure 45. 'Old Scarlet Unique' is a handsome pungent geranium with grayish, wooly leaves and impressive scarlet flowers strikingly marked black. It is probably a *P. fulgidum* hybrid.

to avoid one-sided growth and some pinching out or even cutting back to make them bushy. I use the cuttings for lovely little bouquets in a small amethyst jug for the breakfast table, and they are charming with cut flowers. I wonder why florists do not grow them more often just for this pleasing purpose.

Summer Care

In summer the scenteds that are to have a future as house plants are kept in pots, and these are either sunk in garden beds or grouped in tubs, boxes, or kettles with a peatmoss packing. Except for *P. tomentosum*—which thrives in light shade and adorns my porch in summer and a kitchen bracket in winter—the scenteds thrive in full summer sun. To have them shapely, pinch them back as needed. Left to roam in a garden bed, they will spread to 3 feet or more and flower profusely.

Toward summer's end some of your potted plants will look too big for a window garden again, but the scenteds are so easy to root, you can start a sturdy fresh crop from cuttings. Do this in August. About the same time, repot plants that need it. Keep to as small pots as possible for indoors. Sometimes you can knock off enough soil to get room for some fresh mixture and return plants to the same pots; otherwise, provide pots just one size larger.

Avoid fertilizer high in nitrogen since the scenteds hardly need encouragement to produce foliage. The standard 5-10-5 suits them with its high phosphorus content for flowers. The scenteds are not particular about soil and do well in whatever you are using for your geraniums in general, a commercial mix perhaps with half sand or perlite added. Or use half garden soil and half sand.

Some Problems

I have never had to deal with disease or aphids on the scenteds, but I have found them susceptible to white flies. One winter I think they got these from a standard lantana or from heliotrope,

Figure 46. The loss of an ancient elm beside the author's brook is some-what mitigated when, in summer, the broad stump serves as base for a great tub of the two fancy-leaved geraniums, 'Mrs. Henry Cox' and 'Prince Bis-marck', with *P. graveolens,* 'Dark Red Irene', and the sprawling *P. reniforme.* In the ground tub are *P. crispum* 'Prince Rupert', 'Silver Lining', *P. grave-olens* 'Rober's Lemon Rose', and the ivy-leaved geranium 'Mexican Beauty' —all in pots packed in peatmoss. Photo by Bradbury.

which I should never have allowed in the same room with them. White fly is a big bother to treat in the house for it takes strong measures repeatedly applied until you get rid of the infestation.

I moved all my plants to the garage and gave them a thorough spraying with malathion 50, carefully reaching the undersides of leaves. I repeated the treatment in two weeks—what a job—and you might have to repeat sooner. It depends on the speed of white fly multiplication, which could be in five days. I did get my plants clean again and so vigorous I could hardly wait till frost danger was past to put them outside where they could spread out as they apparently yearned so intensely to do.

For Outdoor Decoration

Outdoors these sweet-leaved geraniums with their mimicry of scents grow even better than zonals, being more tolerant of heat, humidity, and heavy rain. Cuttings inserted in a garden and kept watered become bedding plants in a couple of weeks. Selected according to type, large plants are attractive on stoop, terrace, and porch, or placed importantly about a patio. When a number of my cherished elms succumbed to blight and had to be removed, I had one cut at a 3-foot height to serve as a table on which to place a big wooden tub of the scenteds.

When roots are confined special attention must be given to watering. In clay pots evaporation is rapid. If these are set in jardinieres or tubs or if glazed pots are used, less water is needed. Take care, particularly after a rain, that water does not collect in saucer or jardiniere. Such neglect is likely to kill plants by damaging roots.

Imaginative collectors have used scented geraniums in many ways—for accent on each side of an entrance, at the end of a walk, or in contrasting groups beside a greenhouse or around the garden. Utilizing half-height kegs for tubs, Virginia Vandivert of New Jersey places rose-scented geraniums at each side of her kitchen

Figure 47. In the scented-leaved Geranium Terrace at Village Hill grew seventy-five species and varieties in a small area. 'Beauty' and 'Mrs. Taylor' rambled out of the long bed of mint, spice, and fruit-scented geraniums. Nearby, *P. quercifolium* and *P. graveolens* were pleasantly aromatic. Photo by Cushing-Gellatly.

entrance, "handy for butcher, baker and milkman who snip off leaves all summer long." In mid-October the tubs are carried to a cool light cellar where the plants sojourn healthfully until it is time to bring them out in spring. Then when warm weather comes again, they are moved back to the kitchen door. Or she places three plants of *P. tomentosum* or four of a *graveolens* type in a tub, or she plants a single oak-leaved variety in the center with small plants of *P. quercifolium* 'Beauty' near the edge. Sometimes a large *P. graveolens* is surrounded by smaller plants of an oak-leaved variety, or *P × limoneum* 'Lady Mary' is bordered by apple-scented *P. odoratissimum,* or 'Mrs. Taylor' grows regally in the midst of the nutmeg-scented *P. × fragrans* with plants of tradescantia often used "to fill out and bind into a unified picture. With plenty of water these fulfill every expectation long before summer is over."

Dorcas Brigham at Village Hill in Massachusetts used to fill ancient black kettles supported on tripods with luxuriant plants of *P. quercifolium* 'Prostratum' and *P. tomentosum.* One of these stood at the top of a little flight of stone steps that led to the Scented-leaved Geranium Terrace. This entire triangular area with its southeast exposure measured only 10 by 30 feet but here were displayed the gamut of the scenteds at their most interesting, Eastern best. On a warm summer morning this was indeed a pleasant spot for the aroma here was tantalizing and pleasant. A sunny pathway edged with rose- and mint-scented varieties also afforded the passerby who lightly brushed the plants or crushed a leaf as he stepped along, a delightfully tonic aroma.

A bit of the Lemon Balm Geranium *P. × melissinum,* a branch of almond-scented 'Pretty Polly', or a sprig of *P. crispum* "tucked into the belt, through the buttonhole, or carried in the hand on a warm day enlivens and refreshes one amazingly," as that connoisseur of fragrance, Louise Beebe Wilder, once observed. She made other delightful suggestions for the enjoyment of the scented-leaved geraniums. "Nasturtium and rose geranium also make a stimulating nosegay. Once no bouquet was deemed complete without a bit of this fragrant foliage and far from detracting from the sweetness of other flowers it has the faculty of enhancing it. The large much-cut leaves make a delightful frill for a nosegay of sweet peas or stock, and, of course, they are invaluable for use with flowers that have no scent of their own. White pinks and Lemon geranium are delicious together, and if you want a nosegay that is altogether 'different,' try rose geranium and a few sprigs of mock orange."

As Standard Plants

The scenteds make handsome standards which in the East are not too difficult to carry over in a cool *but not freezing* garage, attic, or basement with some light. In year-round mild California, Robert T. Warner of Manhattan Supply developed for his garden some 6-foot specimens of 'Rober's Lemon Rose', 'Joy Lucille', *P. quercifolium,* and *P. graveolens*—a nice combination of scents with good contrast in foliage. In his account of this project in "Geraniums Around the World" he wrote:

"Plants were started about four years ago as slips in 2½-inch pots. They were not topped but merely given side pinching to discourage branching. After root systems completely filled the pots, plants were moved on into 4-inch pots and staked for the first time with bamboo. When they were about a year old and 30 inches tall, they were shifted again, this time to 6-inch pots, and supported with quarter-inch redwood stakes. The second year they were shifted again—to 12-inch redwood tubs—and staked with 1-inch redwood stakes. The third year, all except 'Joy Lucille' were shifted to their present 18-inch redwood tubs. 'Joy Lucille' is still in the 12-inch tub. Each is now more than 6 feet tall."

Recipe for Potpourri

And then there is the fragrance of the dried foliage in winter.

Who, indeed, is not refreshed by a whiff of potpourri made from geranium leaves? This is the way it is prepared:

On a dry morning, before the sun is high and after several days of dry weather, pick leaves of your best scented *graveolens* varieties. Add a quantity of *P.* × *limoneum* and *P. crispum,* a very small amount of *P. tomentosum* or other mint-scented leaves, with a few leaves from other geraniums with pleasing aromas. Spread these out thinly to dry on pieces of cardboard, newspaper, or on window screens covered with tissue paper. A warm dry well-ventilated room without sunshine is best. Shake the leaves daily to turn them so they will dry evenly. Usually in a week they are ready for your potpourri jars.

Next, select some fixative agent to absorb the oils and scents and so preserve them—orris root, 1 ounce to 1 quart of petals, or substitute calamus gum, benzoin, or storax. For an attractive container, select glass pears or apples with pressed flowers pasted on the inside of the glass as decorative substitutes for old ginger jars. But if you have these, or the real Chinese potpourri jars, look no further. They are by far the nicest, although I have liked using my black gold-etched antique sugar bowl for potpourri.

Place the dried petals with the proper amount of fixative in the containers and add the spices at the rate of 1 tablespoonful for 1 quart of leaves. Cloves, cinnamon, allspice, mace, and powdered nutmeg may all be blended to your purpose. Fill jars only two-thirds full to permit stirring.

Shake up the materials well to combine petals, fixative, and spices. Then cover tightly and let stand to mellow for six weeks. During this time tilt the crock every few days or remove the lid long enough to stir the contents. After that it will be time to enjoy. You will find then, every time you uncover your jar of potpourri that a pungent spicy smell, predominantly geranium, will pervade the room, reminding you of the beauty of your scented plants in the sunny summer garden.

Finally, in order to select and use to advantage,
"genteel Geranium,
With a leaf for all that come,"
it helps to know the type of growth of each kind and the distinctive qualities each offers. The Finder's List on page 320 more fully describes these delectable scented varieties.

Chapter ELEVEN

The Elegant Ivy-leaveds

Surely there is no more beautiful plant than the ivy-leaved geranium, *Pelargonium peltatum,* and its popularity increases year by year. At flower shows, great baskets of pink, rose, lavender, purple, cerise, and white-tinted blooms command long attention, and in the greenhouse suspended from the ridge pole they are a lovely sight. As hanging plants, ivy-leaved geraniums are unsurpassed, and as pot plants in the home they are also a pleasant sight. I have them in Mexican baskets, for basketry and geraniums have a natural affinity, suspended before a long east window, also in open brass cage containers in the kitchen, and in the Plant Room on lamp brackets beside the casement that faces west.

The ivy-leaved geranium is so called for the resemblance of the leaf to the true ivy, *Hedera Helix.* You will notice that the brittle, dark green glossy leaves have what I think of as a pleasant "green" odor, of cucumber some say. The botanical name, *peltatum,* means

161

shield-shaped and refers to the way the petiole is usually fastened to the leaf, not as with most plants at the margin, but underneath in the center in the manner of a warrior supporting his shield.

These geraniums supply the lovely lavenders and purples that the zonals lack; the near-whites among them have a mauve cast. Pinks and cherry-reds or cerise are common but there are few salmon tones. As with the zonals, upper petals are larger, and there is often attractive feathering or dotting. No matter where you live, you will be sure to enjoy the ivy-leaved geranium, as pot or garden plant or, in California, as a lawn if you wish.

Indoors in Winter

Whenever there is sun and coolness indoors the ivy-leaveds bloom through the winter months. They are not put off by a dry atmosphere, only by heat, and they will take less of that than the zonals. For winter success, they need to be grown below 70 degrees F in the daytime and at 55 to 60 degrees F at night. Even so, they are likely to be only handsome green vines without much color from mid-November to mid-February if the winter is dull with few really sunny days. During this stretch, your ivy-leaveds will be unlikely to benefit from extra feeding. This is the time for growing rather dry and for severe pinching out of healthy plants. This can be done now without later loss of bloom. In fact, early in spring stocky pinched plants will send up many shoots from the crown and buds will appear weeks ahead of bloom on plants that have been allowed to go their straggly winter way. As the spring urge develops, your ivy-leaveds will require comparatively more water than the zonals and more plant food, too. In full sun, when they are putting forth new growth, don't be afraid to fertilize liberally, even every week if they are large, established plants in pots that have to be watered every day or two.

Figure 48. Glorious ivy-leaved geraniums grown in standard or tree form dramatize the setbacks in a high garden wall of soft red brick. Photo by Roche.

Outdoors in Summer

In the East, the ivy-leaveds stay in their pots in summer, and from June to October are handsome indeed except in areas of extreme heat and humidity. These they do not enjoy and when they do fail under these conditions, it is usually because they have been weakened and have become prey to a fungus attack. Spraying with a fungicide will help and if brown patches appear on the foliage and leaves dry up, plants will usually recover with cooler weather if you can pull them through. In New England where I live near the Sound, we have excessive heat only for short periods, so the ivy-leaveds can take it. Around Philadelphia, Washington, and New Orleans they have a harder time, but even there a variety like 'Pink Rampant' performs well.

I find the best location is not in full sun for the whole day but in full light with a few hours of preferably morning sun. I hang baskets at the end of a screened terrace where plants get only partial sun and I place pots in wooden tubs in a packing of peatmoss to keep roots cool. If you have a broad tree stump with a flat top, put a big tub or iron kettle of the ivy-leaveds on it and they will be most decorative provided they are in a fully-light, not heavily tree-shaded, location.

They are lovely in window boxes that are placed in east and west locations rather than south. They can be slipped into decorative iron brackets and fastened against a house wall or fence adjacent to garden or terrace. Most ivy-leaveds, as 'Jeanne d'Arc', 'Santa Paula', and 'Apricot Queen', often sold on trellises, can also be trained into espaliers. Again, if you value them for winter, *keep them potted* and adequately watered as well as fertilized. The roots of potted plants cannot go foraging for moisture, so don't forget to water them. In a peatmoss packing, however, your task will be less arduous. Ivy-leaveds can also use generous amounts of fertilizer in summer *when they are performing well*. Avoid feeding them in a very hot spell.

Repotting and Health Insurance

Repot them as they require, preferably in June when you take them outside or in early September a few weeks before they must be brought in as it gets cold and frost threatens. Pinching out stem-ends means, of course, no bloom on that branch for some eight weeks, so be mindful of this when you prune in fall. However, shapeliness is desirable and some pruning and even removal of crowded growth may be indicated.

Ivy-leaved geraniums have a few disadvantages. The singles, like the single zonals, do shatter indoors so there is a fair amount of cleaning up after them. The doubles are less troublesome in this respect. However, some singles like Bob Warner's new 'Lady Lavender' do not seem to shatter. This is a pretty vivid light-violet with well-zoned foliage in the class of medium trailers. It has been fun to give this one an Eastern tryout.

I have found edema and spider mites the worst hazards. These are discussed in full horror in Chapter 20. But 'Joseph Warren', which is supposed to be mite-prone and gave me such a bad time one winter, next door at my daughter's flourished like the proverbial green bay tree, probably because she grew her plants drier than I did. Knowing how mite spreads, I never went near her plants without washing my hands. On occasion white flies have been bothersome on my plants but I have never had aphids or mealy bugs.

It is good mite-insurance, especially if you grow your ivy-leaved geraniums with other house plants as I do, to spray them thoroughly with malathion before you bring them indoors in fall, and then to insert a systemic like Sel-Kap in the soil. This is an easy and usually quite certain mite-deterrent on plants kept healthy and growing. If trouble develops in winter, you can spray tops with a house-plant aerosol bomb (which may do the job; it didn't for me), or take plants to the garage and spray with malathion, which did work. Usually you have to spray more than once. And if malathion does not give control, spray with a specific miticide like Kelthane. Our hope lies in the new systemics that I am told will some day be mixed in potting soils and "protect the plant for its pot-life." It has also been discovered that plants produce their own systemic protection if they are healthy and not suffering from malnutrition. The experience of Mary Ellen Ross supports this. She found that it was the heavily-fed plants in her greenhouse that showed the least evidence of edema.

In the Midwest

Because she has had notable success with the ivy-leaveds in Wisconsin, I asked Mrs. West about culture there. She grows them "rather dry" with full sun in winter but with morning sun and afternoon shade in summer. "If exposed to full sun outdoors, plants stand still, leaves curl and the few blossoms are half size. If the ivy geraniums hang free over a wall or cascade from a pot so that air can go through the vines, they are easily grown but not as ground covers here; planted directly in soil, they get soft and rot and are a prey to fungus diseases. Ivies grow better down than up and, if they get out of hand they can be pruned just like roses; in three weeks new bloom shoots will carry on."

Mrs. West selects only those varieties "that bloom in California in the short-day period. These do well in the greenhouse [in Wisconsin] in winter with a 55-degree F setting and, if 'short day' is translated to 'half shade' in summer, they bloom well then, too." She writes, "I have found no pure reds nor whites that I can recommend. I like the full doubles because they do not shatter. Favorites include: the lavender 'La France', dark pink 'Charles Turner', rose-pink 'Sybil Holmes', the two lovely cerise-pinks, 'Beauty of Eastbourne' and 'New Dawn', and the cerise-red 'Charles Monselet', which is tops."

To avoid edema, Mrs. West cuts back stock plants to the ground each autumn and propagates only clean shoots in pure sand. Some-

Figure 49. Lawns and terraces covered with ivy-leaved geraniums are a lovely sight in southern California. The kinds most commonly used are 'Cesar Franck' (rose), 'Intensity' (red), 'Comtesse de Grey' (light pink), 'Jeanne d'Arc' (lilac), 'Mrs. Banks' (white), and 'Joseph Warren' (light purple). Photo by Max Tatch.

times cuttings that she buys show this trouble until she "can grow them out of it." So whatever the cause, she avoids edema on new plants.

For Indiana, W. Howard Wilson reports a tremendous increase in sales of the ivy-leaved geraniums for outdoor growing. These are the favorites: 'Charles Turner', 'Intensity', 'Joseph Warren', 'Mrs. Banks', and 'Sybil Holmes'.

In the Lucky West

In California, the ivy-leaved geranium is quite something else from the delicate and carefully nurtured pot plant of the East. To one who long knew its limited value here only in window gardens, its use as an acre-beautifying ground cover at La Jolla was awe-inspiring. Indeed, through weeks of observation in California I simply never grew used to it but kept walking backwards or leaning perilously out of cars or crossing streets unheedingly because I was sure the eyes that saw ivy-leaved geraniums climbing up palm trees in Los Angeles, trailing over walls in Berkeley, and glorifying wide parkings in San Francisco were simply deceiving me.

Where it is hardy, the ivy-leaved geranium is a magnificent, adaptable and a most easily grown pelargonium. At Pasadena on a slope I saw the double pink variety 'Galilee' riotously combined with the luxurious blue of *Plumbago capensis*. And frequently the various pink ivy-leaved geraniums are planted with lavender lantana. I had a feeling that the path of learning was somehow smoother in a high school whose long approach was colorfully bordered by 3-foot beds richly filled with the dwarf lavender lantana on the walk side and pink ivy-leaveds spilling over onto the grass on the lawn side. I loved, too, the rich unsubtle combination of yellow and white marguerites in yellow urns from which that brightest of scarlet ivy-leaveds, 'Intensity', flowed out in extravagant brilliance.

When climate permits, there is no end to the imaginative use of these ivy-leaveds or their garden values in both sun and partial shade. Let them alone and they will not be disappointing. Train them carefully as basket plants suspended from tree branches or at regular intervals from the beams of a pergola and they will repay you with bountiful interest for every jug of water carried and every moment spent in feeding, pruning, and training. Tie them in the way they should go on division fences of wire or wood and they will make delightful low walls for your intimate garden rooms. Brighter than a green demarcation, they require little more than an occasional vigorous going over with the hedge shears to keep them flat and proper and not so bulky as would result from unchecked exuberance.

I recall in Hillsborough, Iva Newman's garden where ivy-leaveds were used on a fence to divide herbs from flowers. Branches of the variety 'Mrs. Banks', the color of a clean blue-white well-done washing, were loosely tied with cotton string. This does not cut as certain wire gadgets might and eventually drops off to leave a stalwart vine safely enmeshed in the wire fencing. Elsewhere a 3-foot gray retaining wall with great bushes of forsythia above it and clumps of 'Inglescomb Yellow' tulips at the base formed a background for plants of the double soft pink 'Comtesse de Grey' ivy-leaved geranium. This spread out and down covering the surface of the wall with a rose-splashed green blanket in less than a year. Here in spring appeared an harmonious enchantment of pink and gold while summer was always gay with the light green of the forsythia foliage and the pleasing pink of the flowers of the ivy-leaveds. These two geraniums are useful for their strong, leggy type of growth and their tendency to bloom practically every week in the year with heavy masses of flowers during spring, summer, and fall. Another long trailer, 'Jeanne d'Arc', puts out such regular pale lavender flowers that they look almost artificial and pinned on.

In Mrs. Newman's garden, ivy-leaveds were not permitted just to grow. Watered, trained, draped, pinned, and fed during their ten

Figure 50. At Piedmont, California, superb plants of pink, white, and lavender ivy-leaved geraniums cascade in loveliness over a stone wall. Photo by Alma Lavenson.

months of development, they were cut back to 12 inches each September. Then old or damaged wood was pruned out and plants grown too bushy to conform to the intended design were carefully thinned. Bare spots in the wall planting were covered by placing hanging branches over them and stapling these to the soil with pieces of bent wire. This program regularly insured a timely spring florescence.

Culture in the West

Ivy-leaved geraniums, like well-bred guests, seem always willing to pursue an obliging course. You can depend on them to travel down gracefully from urn, basket, or balcony or, with a little guidance, to travel up a wall, bank or tree trunk. They will even wander through the base of shrubs and then among the lower branches.

For support, you can combine ivy-leaved geraniums with true ivy, where ivy will cling by its aerial roots but the geranium alone cannot. Or you can plant together a red ivy-leaved like 'Carlos Uhden' with a red rose like 'Paul Scarlet'. When the two are in bloom in spring the difference at a little distance will be indistinguishable and the color effect doubled. Later the geranium will carry on alone bringing brightness to an otherwise green area.

When extensive wall space is to be adorned with ivy-leaved geranium, you will find it convenient to trellis it first with wide mesh wire through which you can work and tie the young shoots until the whole surface is smoothly covered. If low retaining walls are protecting some choice trees on your property, you will find potted ivy-leaved geraniums just the plants to blend the protective contrivance inconspicuously into the garden picture. And, finally, have you ever considered bedding that little welcoming avenue of white rose trees before your front door with pink 'Galilee' ivy-leaved geraniums, or going South American-gay and planting 'Scarlet Beauty' beneath yellow roses? Where these pelargoniums are hardy, it seems imaginations are strong, so in California the ivy-leaved geranium has a rich and varied existence and rarely fails to live up to its many delightful possibilities.

Planting time in the West may go on at any time in frost-free areas; otherwise when danger of frost is over, with early April preferred so that plants can get the benefit of the last of the rainy season to get started. Since type of growth varies it is wise in selecting plants for a definite purpose to have your eye set for more than color and beauty of bloom, ever the most appealing characteristics. For pots and baskets, choose fairly compact growers. Grace and free-blooming qualities are essential and good health, too, since undue sensitivity to heat and cold (as in 'Alliance') or attractiveness to spider mite (as in 'Victorville') are hardly assets. But what marvelous assets the fine ivy-leaveds have in the fantastic blooming qualities of 'El Gaucho', 'Jester', 'The Duchess', and 'Valencia', which do not ever require pinching back to develop their shapely growth. In larger baskets 'Apricot Queen', 'Santa Paula'—such a handsome plant for me, too—and any of the Galilee varieties can also go unchecked.

Ivy-leaveds in Mexico

When you travel in Mexico, particularly the western part and also around Baja California, where big farms are being broken up, you will be touched by the affection the people have for the ivy-leaveds as well as for the zonal geraniums. The workers—or more likely their wives—depend on geraniums to soften the stark newness of their adobe-block houses that are often but 10 by 12 feet at the start. Before there is a door, while only a curtain conceals the sparkling white-washed interior, a little garden of geraniums—red, purple, white, and pink—is planted. In one of these small plots in the village of Santa Maria south of Baja California, Frances Hartsook discovered a new purple ivy-leaved geranium somewhat like 'Joseph Warren' but so strong it was trained 6 feet up a wall. It is now in trial but some day we may hear of this giant, under the appropriate name of "Santa Maria."

In other areas like Morelos where the architecture is predominantly modernistic, patios on the flat roofs are outlined with planter boxes of two ivy-leaveds, 'Mexican Beauty' and 'Comtesse de Grey'. Plants hang down 6 to 8 feet and the combination of intense dark red and violet-marked pink is exciting—if you don't see it too often.

In Obregon where houses are raised 8 feet above the ground, planter boxes are used around the line of the floor level. These are filled with a variety of long-trailing ivy-leaveds. Hanging down 4 to 6 feet they act as transition plantings for these houses raised on stilts.

Variegated Ivy-leaves and Others

Now which of the ivy-leaveds shall we choose? From Australia come some interesting fancy-leaved varieties hybridized by the late Ted Both. 'White Mesh' and 'Crocodile' have been introduced here by Fred Bode with the statement that the "meshing" or brilliantly veined effect is due to a "non-spreading" virus. 'L'Elegante' (by whatever name!) is also a suspected virus variegation, and this kind of thing occurs in other plants and in other pelargoniums. For instance, there is a beautiful meshed form of 'Dark Red Irene' that hase been named 'Mrs. Sarah Pell' by Jake Shields of Shields Greenhouse in Dalton, Georgia. 'White Mesh' is a fancy-leaved version of 'Comtesse de Grey', with veins outlined in white or yellow, and the same soft pink semi-double free-flowering habit; 'Crocodile' is similar but the leaf pattern is even more complicated and turns red in winter. Mrs. Crane has grown it into a handsome basket specimen. Flowers are pink and single. Foliage of both fades to solid green when plants are not in growth. In the "Journal" of the Australian Geranium Society another fine-veined unnamed variety is reported with a more rounded leaf than 'Crocodile' and with double red flowers.

Figure 51. The variegated ivy-leaved geranium with lilac-white flowers, often called 'L'Elegante', has thick, green-and-white foliage, often pink-tinted.

Two trailing varieties from the same Australian source, not true ivy-leaveds but hybrids of the old *P. frutetorum,* are 'Magic Lantern' with quite brown leaves zoned in red, yellow, and light green, and a single salmon flower; and 'Mosaic', free-blooming, also with single but larger salmon flowers, and with dark foliage splashed light green. These *frutetorum* varieties, although not ivy-leaveds, are mentioned here because they make interesting basket plants. They are discussed in Chapter 2.

Not for all that famous tea in China would I again enter the controversy, sometimes acrimonious, on the correct designations for the old and popular 'L'Elegante' and 'Duke of Edinburgh', of 'Madame Margot' and 'Sunset'. William Schmidt has made a practical recommendation that amalgamates history. He considers the four names interchangeable, as indeed they often are in usage. We then come out with two understandable and descriptive terms:

Variegated Ivy-leaved, Lilac-white Flower

Variegated Ivy-leaved, Pink Flower

Records of the lilac-white one go back almost a century. Derek Clifford lists a 'L'Elegante' with "flowers white with reddish purple feathering very free." He states that this was introduced by Cannell and Sons of Swanley in 1868. Habit is "dwarf, leaves small, margined white, changes to pink mauve when grown hard." And we have seen that under certain conditions the foliage coloring of any of these could qualify as 'Sunset'. I myself have seen silver-leaved and yellow-leaved forms and also an all-green reversion with pink flowers; sometimes all three types of branches on the same plant. When catalogs of older firms list 'L'Elegante', they refer to the variegated ivy-leaved with lilac-white flowers, in Figure 51.

Other Fine Ivy-leaved Geraniums

Three other ivy-leaveds, not variegated but of hybrid origin, sometimes with the blood of *Pelargonium acetosum,* and long enjoyed as basket plants, are the crimson-spotted lilac 'Alliance', 'Pink

Alliance', and the handsome double 'E. H. Trego' with enormous red flower heads. (These three are unfortunately subject to mites; if mites are controlled the plants are indeed beautiful; they are wonderful but lots of work.) Then there is the reliable (since 1898) 'Scarlet Beauty' ('Corden's Glory') with clear red semidouble flowers abundantly produced. This geranium is close to the true ivy plant in appearance. With its reliable and profuse bloom, it is considered by some to be the best of all basket ivy-leaveds. 'Forest Maid' from Germany is a lovely pink and one of the latest ivy-leaved hybrids.

In past years, William Schmidt has concerned himself with hybridizing ivy-leaveds as well as zonals and regals, for which he is famous. We have him to thank for some of today's most beautiful and free-flowering varieties as 'Bridesmaid', 'The Duchess', 'Jester', 'Valencia', 'El Gaucho', 'Neon', and 'Old Mexico'. Mr. Schmidt has also introduced, among others from England, two doubles, the incomparable 'La France' with big flowers of deep lavender, one of my great favorites, and 'Beauty of Eastbourne', a handsome cerise. This one is an excellent variety for outdoors in California. You may have seen a beautiful planting of it at the Tappenier growing grounds in Santa Barbara. It was planted at the top of a low bank, next to a glasshouse, and it spilled down the bank in a solid profusion of rich color.

Worth growing among double peltatums are four charming rosebud types. 'Jean Roseleur', a brilliant cerise, flourishes at my window. 'Snowdrift', almost pure white is lovely but slow growing and a little difficult. 'The Blush' is its pink version, and 'Sybil Holmes', a Rober variety, with rose-pink rosettes has a white reverse to give a two-tone effect. This has indeed stood the test of time. It is a compact grower, always full of color. All four are better for pots and baskets than in the open ground where rosebud types do not flourish.

'Princess Victoria' ('Enchantress') used to be known as 'Pepper-

Figure 52. Ivy-leaved geraniums with red and bright-pink flowers make a colorful ground cover along a sandy beach beside the sea on Palos Verdes Peninsula, California. Photo by Hort-Pix.

mint Stick'; it requires special comment. It is one of the loveliest, white to pale lavender, rose-feathered. I admire it but it is far from reliable. Plants are often of slow weak growth and leaves tend to cup badly, evidence of virus. Also they often revert to 'Salmon Enchantress' or 'Rose Enchantress', a rose-pink variant but the reversion is charming. Perhaps a more dependable strain of this lovely thing will be developed. 'Carnival' is another of these unstable sports. Like 'Princess Victoria', it needs constant watching when it is being propagated and only the most highly-colored flowering branches should be used. Otherwise it will soon resemble 'Leopard' from which it sported. As compared to a reliable like 'Jester', these two are hardly to be considered by the average gardener.

For Flower Shows

Ivy-leaved geraniums grown in special ways appeal to judges, and many an award has been bestowed on 'Apricot Queen', 'Charles Turner', or 'Santa Paula' trained to a trellis and often pruned to espalier form, or grown on a totem. 'Santa Paula' makes a nice round basket also, with one, two, or three plants putting on a fine display. 'Carlos Uhden' is another variety you can trust to be in bloom. 'Sybil Holmes' makes an attractive medium-sized basket and is also pretty for a wall pocket, and 'Old Mexico' in a pocket against a white wall is always a good entry. "Variegated Ivy-leaved, Lilac-white Flower" usually gets a prize even if the plant is only reasonably good, for the public dotes on this one by any name, 'L'Elegante' or otherwise, and it has a nice natural growth for a basket division. For a very big basket plant, 'Estelle Doheny' is stunning, well grown it produces flower clusters 5 and 6 inches across; 'Crocodile' and 'White Mist' are so different looking they command sure attention in any exhibit, as did Mrs. Crane's plants at the 1964 International Flower Show in New York.

In California, shows recently have been glorified with what appear to be great baskets of multicolor ivy-leaveds. Actually, these baskets are planted with three varieties of different hues. Started, say, three months ahead, the plants blend both growth and colors. Good combinations can be planned with any of the 'Galilee' and 'Barbara Wirth' varieties plus 'Cliff House' and 'Barbary Coast'. Or, 'Mrs. Banks', 'Comtesse de Grey', and 'Mexican Beauty' can be assembled. If 'Mexican Beauty' seems to you too dominant a color, substitute almost any of the semidouble long trailers, but 'Mexican Beauty' is a spirited color that almost everybody likes. The list of pot and basket plants at the end of this chapter may give you other ideas for exhibiting.

Another possibility is 'Gay Baby', the pretty little lilac-tinted, violet-striped miniature, planted in a jewel box or a crib, as the Harry Mays did for their award. 'Gay Baby' makes a unique exhibit, since few other miniature ivy-leaveds are known.

Peltatums for a Purpose

There are no precise classifications among the ivy-leaveds, but I find it convenient to group them according to use, as for Pots and Baskets, for Small Ground Areas (these also good to grow over stumps), and for Lawns and Terraces. I have listed them accordingly at the end of this chapter, and described most of them in the Finder's List on page 329. Some plants are suited to more than one purpose, and most of the long trailers make good pot plants for Eastern use. When young, they are fine for the same purpose in the West.

For narrow spaces, as between curb and walk, or house walls and walk, select ivy-leaveds that are medium trailers and easily kept bushy by an *occasional* nipping back close to the crown. I think of these as limited ground covers and suggest varieties without the range, say, of 'Charles Turner'. Most of the more compact varieties suggested for pot plants would also be suitable.

Very vigorous growth is an asset if you want to cover a large retaining wall with ivy-leaved geraniums or plant one of those astounding lawns we so admire in southern California. The six starred (*) varieties in the list below are favorites for this purpose. They are grown by specialists in bedding geraniums and are offered quite inexpensively by color, not name, but the six are practically *always* the same. Thus "Rose" is always 'Cesar Franck', "Red" is 'Intensity', "Light Pink" is 'Comtesse de Grey', "Lilac" is 'Jeanne d'Arc', "White" is 'Mrs. Banks', and "Purple" is 'Joseph Warren'. The last is the only one not mite-resistant and so it often disappears after a few years while the other five keep health and looks almost indefinitely, even if they are neglected.

Fred Bode writes of a groundcover planting of 'Jeanne d'Arc' untended at Palos Verdes Estates near San Pedro that has survived and put on a wonderful show every year for twenty years to his knowledge. And, incidentally, if you want a geranium that will climb a tree or make a good espalier, try 'Jeanne d'Arc'. Fred reports a plant that has climbed to the top of a 25-foot tree. He has also told me about a red zonal, unnamed, that is known to be thirty-nine years old and "has survived the burning of the building that supported it, being twice chopped down, and the construction of a new concrete building within 2 feet of it." What constitutions these geraniums have!

To return to the ivy-geranium lawns. If you live in the East, you must actually see these plantings to believe them. If you live in the West, I do hope you never get so used to them you take them for granted. They are truly magnificent.

Here are some lists of ivy-leaved geraniums for special uses. These are necessarily arbitrary, really only suggestions. As I have said, most in the Pots and Baskets list could be used for Small Ground Areas, and vice versa. In youth the Long Trailers accommodate themselves to more limited uses. Some enthusiasts in areas with periods of extreme heat—South, Midwest, and Florida—have reported as satisfactory the varieties on the Hot Climate list.

FOR POTS AND BASKETS

'Apricot Queen'
'Barbara Wirth'
'Carlos Uhden'
'Charles Turner'
'Comtesse de Grey'
'Corona del Mar'
'Double Lilac White'
'Galilee'
'Giant Salmon'
'Hummel's Monselet'

'Jean Roseleur'
'Jester'
'Joseph Warren'
'La France'
'Mexican Beauty'
'Santa Paula'
'Sybil Holmes'
Variegated Ivy-leaved, Lilac-
    white Flowers

FOR SMALL LAWN OR GARDEN AREAS

'Apricot Queen'
'El Gaucho'
'Galilee'
'La France'

'Santa Paula'
'Scarlet Beauty'
'The Duchess'
'Valencia'

LONG TRAILING FOR LAWNS AND TERRACES

* Varieties usually grown by specialists as bedding geraniums;
the first two are identical.

*'Cesar Franck'
*'Charles Turner'
*'Comtesse de Grey'
 'Corona del Mar'

*'Intensity'
*'Jeanne d'Arc'
*'Joseph Warren'
 'Mrs. Banks'

FOR HOT CLIMATES

'Alliance'
'Cliff House'
'Comtesse de Grey'
'Galilee'

'Mexican Beauty'
'Pink Rampant'
'Santa Paula'
'Scarlet Beauty'

$\mathcal{D}$istinguished $\mathcal{R}$egals for
$\mathcal{E}$ast and $\mathcal{W}$est

The regals are plants of many virtues, and unlike the other geranium groups are usually called pelargoniums. They are also called Lady or Martha Washingtons, show pelargoniums—for the obvious reason that they make excellent exhibition plants—and most commonly today, regals. This name, regals, is a suitable designation for plants of such distinction and superiority. Botanically, *Pelargonium* $\times$ *domesticum* is the proper name. Both size and beauty are attributes since cuttings within two years may grow into specimens more than 3 feet in diameter while adorning themselves for months with quantities of glowing, velvet-textured flowers 3 and occasionally 4 inches across.

This is the geranium of marvelous two- and three-color blendings, of transluscent whites tinged with pink and lavender, of glowing reds and soft pinks. It is the plant that brings the mauves and deep purples to the pelargonium world through inheritance from *P. cucullatum*. Flowers are also quite unlike those of zonals in petal and grouping, harking back to the original Storksbill. The rough, plain green, somewhat cupped and pointed leaves are quite different from the succulent zonal foliage, and hybridizers are working toward further differentiation. Some of the newer varieties like 'Confetti' have soft hairy foliage and leaves that suggest the maple. Commercially, foliage and plant seem as important as bloom since the regals, where they are hardy, are handsome shrubs indeed, and they are the glory of California gardens.

The regals have long been popular in England and were fully described in Robert Sweet's Volume V. It was in Germany, however, that hybridizers started them on the road to glory that they are now traveling in California. Faiss, Richter, and Burgers changed the old small-flowered type with its short period of spring bloom to the large-flowering, long-blooming varieties we enjoy today. So excellent was their work that such German varieties as 'Marie Vogel', 'Grossmama Fischer', and 'Mackensen' are still grown, although they came to this country before 1925.

Hybridizers

Hybridizers in the United States have also introduced many handsome cultivars. Bode, Brown, Cassidy, Diener, Evans, Howard, Jarrett, Kerrigan, Outwater, and Rober are names associated with many of the finest plants. Today, Harry and Clara May and William Schmidt are the foremost hybridizers of regals. Mr. and Mrs. May's 'White Chiffon', 'May Magic' and 'Roulette' are recent offerings; Mr. Schmidt's 'Autumn Haze', 'Chiquita', 'Circus Day', 'Grand Slam', 'Joy', 'La Paloma', and 'Lavender Grand Slam' are popular here and have also won commendations and awards from the Royal Horticultural Society in England where they perform particularly well in that cooler climate. Among English hybridizers, Ayton, Cannell, Case, Clifton, Cole, and Telston are well known, and such varieties as 'Carisbrooke' (considered England's best),

'Irene Burton' (named for Lady Burton whose family have collected geraniums for generations), 'Machioness de Bute', 'Mount Macedon', 'Telston's Prima', as well as such old favorites as 'Victoria Regina' (1910) and 'Princess of Wales' (1877), are grown with pleasure there and many of them in this country as well.

The present trend of hybridizing is toward everblooming varieties, for wherever regals are used the quality of re-bloom is an asset. Newer varieties such as the lovely, very ruffled white-centered pink 'Applause', 'Aztec', 'Country Girl', 'Halo', 'Lavender Gibson Girl', 'May Magic', 'Vin Rouge', and 'White Chiffon' are judged for extended performance as well as for beauty, since handsome flowers are almost a commonplace among regals. Varieties of good re-bloom habit include 'Amour', 'Chorus Girl', 'Confetti', 'Destiny', 'Easter Greeting' (long famous for this quality), 'Dubonnet' (such a fine hue), 'Josephine' (most dependable), 'Melissa', 'Mood Indigo' (so marvelously named), and 'White Cloud'. Breeders are also concerned with producing pure whites since this "color" is now in high favor with gardeners. Among the finest are 'April', 'Destiny', 'La Paloma', 'Moon Rapture', 'Mrs. Mary Bard', 'Snowbank', 'White Cloud', 'White Sails', and 'White Swan'. Excellent near-whites include 'Clown', 'Gardener's Joy', 'Gay Nineties', and the English 'Victoria Regina'.

For Hobby or Show

The regals offer an area of delightful, even somewhat controlled, emphasis for the collector. Unlike many plants—I think first of African violets—there is a chance of "keeping up" with the regals since improvements are limited to a few yearly introductions that are completely new or real improvements. These can be easily acquired to keep a collection up to date and interesting.

As for shows and exhibits, here the regal comes into its own. In a general flower show or specialized geranium exhibit at Chelsea, New York, or Santa Barbara, well-grown plants of *Pelargonium* ×

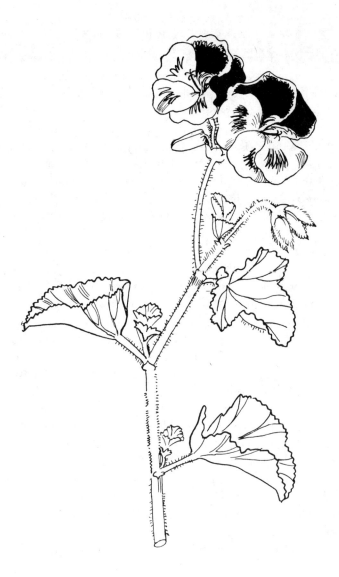

Figure 53.　The Pansy Geranium, 'Madame Layal', is an old favorite, particularly as a pot plant. This small-flowering P. × *domesticum* hybrid is a blend of purple, rose, and white.

domesticum are always outstanding as large potted specimens, tree forms, trailers for baskets, or in collections. In England, Lady Irene Burton has received every possible honor at the Royal Horticultural Society shows for pots of 'Grand Slam'. And in Australia, 'Corsage' and 'Mood Indigo' have rewarded the "tender, loving care" of their exhibitors. In California the James Minah's have won prizes with a gorgeous tree of 'Holiday', its 3-foot crown richly covered with bloom. The Harry May's at Long Beach won a first-class ribbon with a 12-inch redwood basket of 'Melissa', a variety most happy to indulge its natural propensity for wide-spreading growth.

'Black Lace', 'Flower Basket', and 'Santa Cruz' make fine hanging-basket plants. And there is considerable satisfaction in developing a pretty basket of regals for home or show. Plants need a little pinching and pruning to make them bushy and to prevent crowded growth. Training is about the same as for cascade chrysanthemums. Furthermore, a well-developed basketful goes on improving for at least three years before any drastic replanting is required.

The pansy geraniums—'Madame Layal' is the familiar one—always appeal to flower-show visitors. Recently hybridizers have turned their attention to altering the color (to mainly white in 'Seeley's Pansy'); doubling the flower size (as in 'Salina'); and making the plant smaller (as in 'Tiny Tim'). However, my plants in the pansy group seem very like each other and since they do not re-bloom, the value is only as a spring-flowering florist plant, but one easily held over from year to year by the home gardener. The pansy varieties are also fine for baskets or hangers. A couple of plants of 'Tiny Tim' in an 8- or 10-inch redwood hanger suspended against a light-colored wall is bound to catch a judge's eye.

Care of Gift Plants in East and Midwest

In general, aside from the pansy types, regals are not much

known outside California or the Midwest, and those in the East
who receive a gift plant usually admire it curiously and discard it
promptly after a somewhat languishing sojourn in their homes.
Many of us feel this is not getting nearly enough out of a big expensive pot plant, and experiment has indeed proved it often has
further possibilities. I have had particular success with the pink-
and-white 'Josephine', which has bloomed to a degree for me both
winter and summer, and 'Chorus Girl' has been reported as practically continuous in Iowa, also 'Dubonnet'. In propitious seasons
any of the good re-bloomers already mentioned may well go on
flowering intermittently for us into the fall, whether in a pot on the
terrace or planted directly in a garden bed, but in partial shade in
either location. The trouble is the regal is just as allergic to pro-
longed stretches of day-and-night heat and continuous wet weather
as we are. And in some years, all of us suffer.

If your gift plant arrives with many open flowers, place it in a
light rather than sunny window so as to prevent fast fading. And
grow it cool. A temperature of 55 to 60 degrees F is preferred,
although 65 degrees will be tolerated. However, if you have a cool
landing window or a not-too-well-heated sunroom, or a cool Plant
Room like mine, put your pelargonium there in preference to the
living room. Give it a good soaking each time the soil feels a little
dry, but never let excess water collect in the plant saucer unless
there is a layer of pebbles there to receive it. Once a week spray
the foliage vigorously with water from below to deter the lurking
enemy, the white fly.

When frost danger is past and summer seems a fair certainty,
plunge your pelargoniums in a bed with only 2 to 3 hours of, preferably, morning sun and where there is room for them to develop.
Before plunging a pot, spread a layer of cinders or small stones
under it to insure good drainage. Water daily unless there is a
dependable shower to moisten more than the upper inch of soil.

Give a little extra plant food early in June and again in late July and, if you want to try your luck at starting some new plants, take slips in August. Well before frost lift the pots from the garden bed, scrub them, and check the drainage arrangements. Then prune your pelargonium back to 3 to 5 pieces of growth, each 3 to 5 inches long. If roots have gone through the pot and spread out in the ground, you will have to cut them off, or sometimes actually break a pot apart to lift your plant, and then repot. When this occurs, trim roots sharply so as to leave no torn pieces. You can place plants for the winter in a cool spot, 40 to 50 degrees F, where there is light and, if possible, sun, or in your window garden if it is fairly cool there. I grow mine with my other geraniums, jasmines, and ivies. Water the resting plants sparingly, only when the top soil feels quite dry.

About the first of February, loosen topsoil carefully with a fork and work in some prepared plant food, only about a teaspoonful to a 4- or 5-inch pot, and a little lime to keep up the pH. Water generously and bring resting plants to a sunny 60-degree F or so location. As growth develops, a little pruning may be necessary for shapeliness, but no more or flowering will be checked. The ideal free-blooming plant is stocky, low, and branching. In mid-February and again on March 1, give an extra feeding of 5-10-5 or something similar and again transfer plants to the garden after frost danger is over.

Indoors, be on the watch for white flies. Segregate any affected plant and spray every week until the flies disappear. Dusts or sprays containing malathion (I use malathion 50) give good control or when repeated, a thorough cleanup.

Uses in the West

In California and the Northwest, this occasional Eastern pot plant becomes a grand and glorious garden subject, filling beds and covering banks, tumbling from baskets, or growing in splendid isolation as carefully nurtured patio and terrace ornaments. Anything more beautiful cannot be imagined than a fine regal well-tended in a California garden.

And regals are lovely for bouquets, too. Indeed, I shall never forget the great rosy bunch presented to me some years ago on my first day in San Francisco. It seemed too valuable to leave by itself in my hotel room. But then I thought, having read a great deal about applying liquid glue to the center of the flowers, the blossoms will shatter by night. Such was not the case at all. The regals make excellent, long-lasting cut flowers. They are also fine for corsages, as I discovered on another day, when I wore a charming arrangement of the white variety 'Shasta', which has now been superseded by better whites, as 'Snowbank'. 'Joy' is excellent for cutting, too, and the English 'Caprice' and 'Carisbrooke'. The regals also make handsome leis. It takes 100 to 150 flowers and these are strung cone inside cone, rather than sidewise as with other flowers.

While mixed plantings may be interesting to you as a collector, the self-controlled use of one variety will do more for the pictorial beauty of your garden. How attractive in a California garden is a brilliant bordering of a walk or foundation with one outstanding variety of regal. A little pinching back of taller kinds will keep them low and bushy. And if faded flowers are picked, many varieties will bloom long, and from April through September offer a gay procession of color.

The regals are also pleasing trained against a bright patio wall or on a redwood fence. Taller growing types such as 'Carmen', 'Circus Day', 'Edith North', 'Mary Elizabeth', 'Marie Rober', and 'Ruth Eleanore', look particularly fine when permitted to reach up according to their natural inclination. They may also be used as background for other plants, as long as color harmonies are considered. Some pruning will be necessary to keep them flat and in hand.

A rock wall in semishade is another possibility for this adaptable pelargonium provided there is sun some part of the day. An unusual effect is possible if plants are set at the top of a low wall, carefully pruned after the blooming season, and then the new shoots trained persistently down so as to hang over the rocks. All varieties are not suited to this purpose, but the rosy-red 'Azalea' and ruffled, white-throated, pink 'Springtime' have proved amenable to such treatment.

Regals at my Window

I'd like to suggest also a use of regals I have enjoyed—that of temporary and eventually disposable pot plants. From a mail-order house you can obtain regals early in spring in 2½-inch pots but with full-sized buds and blooms. These are inexpensive, and a half-dozen or so are wonderfully effective indoors, particularly if yours is a predominantly green indoor garden they will transform it into a colorful bower. In full light without sun every bud will open to give you four to six weeks of pleasing color. Then with good conscience you can discard the plants as you do poinsettias, primroses, and others that you buy from a florist or receive as gifts.

To help you make selections from this almost-too-alluring category of pelargoniums, I have made these lists. You will find the varieties described in the Finder's List on page 333.

EARLY REGALS FOR GREENHOUSE OR FLORIST

'Amour'	'Fire Dancer'
'Aztec'	'Grossmama Fischer'
'Carmen'	'Grand Slam'
'Chorus Girl'	'Holiday'
'Conspicuous'	'Josephine'
'Corsage'	'King Midas'
'Country Girl'	'Lavender Grand Slam'
'Destiny'	'Mackensen'
'Dubonnet'	'Melissa'
'Easter Greetings'	'Mrs. Mary Bard'

'Madame Layal'   'Rapture'
'Our Frances'   'Waltztime'
'Pink Gardener's Joy'

FOR THE CALIFORNIA COLLECTOR

These are selected primarily for the great beauty of their blooms.

'Aztec'	'Holiday'
'Chorus Girl'	'Joy'
'Confetti'	'Lavender Grand Slam'
'Destiny'	'Melissa'
'Dubonnet'	'Parisienne'
'Grand Slam'	'Rapture'

FOR BASKETS OR HANGERS

'Black Lace'	'Melissa'
'Flower Basket'	'Prime Minister Menzies'
'Madame Layal'	'Santa Cruz'
'Mrs. Mary Bard'	'Tiny Tim'

FOR CUTTING, CORSAGES, AND LEIS

'Applause'	'Joy'
'Caprice'	'Lucy Ann Leslie'
'Carisbrooke'	'Snowbank'
'Corsage'	

Chapter THIRTEEN

Care in California

In this land of the luxurious geranium, cultural rules are hardly necessary; all of you might well follow this advice for successful pelargonium culture in the West: "Move to southern California and throw your geraniums in vacant lots. Don't cover with soil or water and the lot will be covered with geraniums." Any traveler to Los Angeles or San Diego knows how very near to complete truth this is.

The flaw is that while all kinds of common varieties will flourish when so casually dealt with, the finer ones won't. Furthermore, though culture is never exacting in the Golden State either north or south, super results are possible only with super efforts. Even California has its cultural problems, though none seems very serious. Mostly they are concerned with frost possibilities in certain sections, with watering during the long dry months, and with wise pruning practices. Here nature does not check growth for definite periods as it does in most of the other states so man must exercise the necessary control.

Cold Tolerance

Within very small sections in California, temperature varies considerably and the plant that is safe from frost in the thermal belt of the Los Altos hills may be tender at Palo Alto, only five miles away, so each gardener must be observant of his own local conditions. Records of the International Geranium Society indicate that "P. × *domesticum* is in danger at temperatures of 28 degrees F or lower, and the P. × *hortorum* and P. *peltatum* groups at 25 degrees F or lower. Although P. × *hortorum* is hardier than P. × *domesticum*, it is liable to be the more severely damaged in very cold winters. This is because of its greater succulence, P. × *hortorum* usually not developing woody stems at the base as does P. × *domesticum*."

As for the fancy-leaved zonals, one California grower finds that they will stand as much frost as other zonals, but, when damaged, may not recover so well, partly because of their susceptibility to botrytis and other rots, partly because of rather weak root systems, especially in tricolors.

"With the scenteds, there is much variability. Coconut [P. *grossularioides*] will stand 20 degrees or lower. Peppermint [P. *tomentosum*] and 'Schottesham Pet' are very tender. Most will stand a little more cold than Lady Washington varieties, a little less than zonals. Many make good recovery even after much damage, notably rose-scented types, even when frozen to the ground, but if these are variegated they will often come up all-green. Any apparent differences in hardiness among zonals are more likely due to differences in condition of plants or to small local variations in temperature than to inherent characteristics."

Generally speaking, well-hardened and practically dormant plants are considerably more resistant than actively growing ones. Yet in

Figure 54. The easy gradations of an outside stairway in California are attractively marked with potted pelargoniums. Photo courtesy *Sunset Magazine*.

a climate where winters are, on the whole, mild, it is almost impossible to maintain complete dormancy. Dry plants, of course, withstand more cold than wet ones but the soaking winter rains occur just at the time of lowest temperatures.

Often "lost" plants come up again from the roots, so don't be hasty about discarding. About the top pruning of these frosted plants there are two schools of thought. One maintains it is best to cut back to sound wood at once. The other believes that it is wiser to wait until there is definite new growth visible.

Possible Precautions

There is a choice of precautions for those growing geraniums where frost is a rare thing, as in the higher elevations of Hillsborough or Berkeley, or a fair certainty as at Sacramento or in the Sierra foothills. When sundown is accompanied by alarming signs of cold, the potted plants, if not too numerous, can be whisked into the basement, garage, or laundry. And under the same conditions garden pelargoniums may be protected with a covering of burlap or newspapers. Of course, these are temporary emergency measures since pelargoniums require light for survival and could not for extended periods endure such conditions. For longer sojourns they would have to be placed, as they are in the East in winter, in some light, preferably sunny, window or sunroom. Here they are grown fairly cool and watered sparingly.

Outdoors in California a mulch of coarse sand, mounded six inches high around each plunged pot plant or each garden-growing specimen will save it even in a cold winter. It will not bring the top through but the geranium will remain root-hardy and produce new branches toward spring. Other mulching materials such as soil, leaves, peatmoss, and sawdust may be used. But because they may absorb and hold considerable moisture and so keep the plant base in a sort of wet compress, they are not nearly so safe.

Coldframe protection is another possibility. Potted plants may be plunged deeply or set on top of the ground and surrounded by a rectangular board box. The sides of this should be somewhat deeper than the height of the plants and the box large enough to hold them without unhealthy crowding that inevitably results in leggy plants and pest-ridden growth. On this wooden frame a lath screen is set to support a frostproof covering through the cold weather. This covering, consisting of boards, newspapers, building paper, carton paper, canvas, or burlap, weighted down with pieces of wood to prevent its blowing away, can be removed on warm bright days or left off entirely during a favorable week. It is an inexpensive makeshift for the usual sunken coldframe of the East with its glass sash. On the whole, it is better suited to warmer, variable California.

For choice rare pelargoniums, a flat of fall cuttings is a good safety measure. They can be grown on the dry side in the same box of sand from September to February in a light, frostfree place and pinched back once or twice to prevent leggy development. Don't crowd your "insurance" cuttings and don't expect very fine plants unless you shift the new plants to pots. This is just a means of holding on to valuable material in case you need it.

Watering

Watering is a California necessity except along the coast where a bath of cool fog refreshes plants each night. There a thorough soaking of soil once in two weeks suffices as long as the fog rolls in regularly. In the interior valleys and other dry places, garden-grown plants of any value will require watering weekly, or oftener.

Soil and location are contributing factors. If plants are set in the sand of the Monterey peninsula, they will grow fairly well but they will need a great deal more water than if the beds containing them have been prepared with some moisture-holding material, such as compost or rotted manure to about a fifth of the soil bulk. And if, in the hottest sections, pelargoniums are planted so as to

Figure 55. Where climate favors a long growing period, the zonal geranium readily develops sturdy, vinelike growth to decorate a balcony. Photo by Gabriel Moulin.

receive afternoon shade or are set under open-branched trees, they will not need so much water as in all-day, sun-drenched spots.

Pot plants require daily attention unless specimens are very large. This is something to consider if you are decorating an upstairs balcony or an outside window shelf. If plants here suffer drought, they will not beautify your home, as you intend, so arrange for no more than you can adequately attend.

In the garden, plants in glazed pots need less water—and grow quite as well, if not better—than those in clay pots from which moisture evaporates not only from the soil surface but from the sides of the pots as well. In exposed locations, to reduce the high and inconvenient rate of evaporation it is a good idea to place each pot in another pot, one or two sizes larger, with or without a filler of peatmoss or sawdust between the walls of the two pots. The outer pot protects the inner one from wind and sun, while a packing between is good insulation. With such an arrangement, you can safely skip a day or two of watering if you want a weekend away from home without enlisting the horticultural aid of neighbors.

Pruning

Whenever and however pruning is managed, keep in mind that flowers are produced from the tips of new growth; if you cut this off, it usually takes about two months for buds to develop again. But all pelargoniums need a more-or-less severe cutting back each year, and more-or-less light but continuous pruning through the growing season. This will keep them shapely, prevent that elongated bare-stemmed look they attain so easily, and stimulate the development of new flowering wood. Pruning can never be by rote but rather by purpose. Think what you want to achieve and proceed accordingly. The specimen plant in a pot needs but three main stems. The bedding plant must be kept extra low and bushy. The ivy-leaved geranium cannot be left to its own devices if it is

Figure 56. Potted geraniums on a stand and zonals and regals in beds decorate a California terrace that is charming both from within and without. Photo courtesy *Better Homes and Gardens*.

to cover a walk adequately or mount a trellis. Hedge plants need plenty of determined shearing and also some removal of big stems at the ground line.

Pelargoniums you want to grow tall for the side of a balcony must be relieved regularly of side growth. Those of bedding destination will be benefited by some pinching out at the base and perhaps by the removal of a center branch to let the flower-producing sunshine into the heart of the plant.

These are general considerations to guide you in ruling your pelargoniums. Your plants may be moved by certain dynamic impulses not at all in line with the decorative role you intend for them. Guide and train them, therefore, according to your design, not theirs. You will find more specific suggestions for training included under each pelargonium classification.

However, I'd like to mention that regal geraniums must be pruned in fall if they are to produce properly and early enough the next year, but that zonals seem to benefit from spring pruning. Excess growth left on over the winter affords a measure of protection to the center and lower parts of the plant. Furthermore, spring weather is more favorable for rapid recovery than fall, and the loss of geranium color less noticeable then, when a California garden is brilliant with many other flowers. In autumn, geraniums, nearly at their best, make a marvelous showing; in many places they go on blooming for a good part of the winter so it's a pity to recondition them with hard pruning at this time, unless there is some special reason for it, as ungainly growth of noticeable unattractiveness.

Feeding

As for fertilizing, let the *look* of your plants be your guide. Foliage that is paler than usual, growth that is woodier and with shorter nodes, and flowers that are smaller than usual generally indicate hunger.

Geraniums in garden beds, as a rule, need very little fertilizing in California, but plants in pots do. Many satisfactory complete brands of fertilizer are available. Give *quite a little less than the manufacturer suggests* since geraniums do better when not too richly fed. Vigoro is good but just ½ teaspoon to a 5-inch pot, and not oftener than once a month. You may prefer a fertilizer in solution as Hyponex, Ra-Pid-Gro, Spoonit, or Liquid Ortho-Gro. The Ortho one is 12-6-6 with some trace elements and a chelating agent added. The nitrogen is derived from fish but has been processed so that it is immediately available and quick-acting like the inorganic fertilizers, and there is little insoluble residue to build up excess salts. I also very occasionally use Atlas Fish Emulsion, applying it on a Sunday before church. The smell usually disappears before I get home if I am careful not to let a lot of excess run down into the pebble trays or pot saucers where the "fragrance" will linger on. Fish fertilizers are not recommended except for special purposes, as for sales or shows.

Even in a California garden there may be some need for spraying for pest and disease. New multi-purpose sprays are being offered all the time. Isotox Garden Spray is excellent and for minor attacks of this and that or for prevention on pot plants, you can use the aerosol bombs prepared for house plants. There is more on this unpleasant subject in Chapter 20.

I can't end a chapter on Care in California on such a note, for the need for care there seems slight. It's geranium enjoyment, par excellence, that you who live there know.

Chapter FOURTEEN

New Plants from Cuttings

The amenable disposition of the geranium is never more in evidence than when slips are started from a friend's plants or cuttings made from our own. We who love geraniums and are ever on the alert to add a new species or variety to our hobby collection value this ease of propagation. We enjoy dealing with cuttings that are sizable enough for convenient handling and speedy enough not to tax our patience by a long growing period before bloom.

When to Start Geranium Cuttings

Although you can successfully start cuttings in any month in the year, it is a good plan to take them in August or September if your aim is a fulsome lot of spring- and summer-flowering plants. Make cuttings in late May or June if your intention is a colorful winter window garden. Flowering from these spring cuttings will then be in fairly constant succession from September on during all

202

Figure 57.   HOW TO GROW PLANTS FROM CUTTINGS. Top, a 4-inch tip is cut from a mature geranium plant; lower left, most of the leaves are removed; lower right, cuttings are inserted in a pot-in-pan device.

stretches of sunny weather. July and August are also preferred times for starting regal cuttings.

In most cases allow two to three weeks for cuttings to strike root, and look for the first flower bud in about ten weeks if the weather is bright and conditions are favorable. Expect some species and varieties to be less obliging. I have known cuttings of 'Countess of Scarborough' to take five months to strike root. In this time they did not wilt or die. They simply developed at their own natural convenience and scorned human haste. *Pelargonium crispum* 'Minor' is often slow to root. Much depends on the condition of the wood, the time of year, and the locality of the plants.

Easy Way to Root Cuttings

If you are dealing with only an occasional slip or cutting, it is no trick at all to get it to root by removing the lower leaves and placing it in a glass of water in a light but not sunny window. Or you can pack a small wad of damp sand or unmilled sphagnum moss around the cut end and insert it in the soil at the side of one of your mature geraniums. In less than a month it will be self-supporting and ready for a life of its own in a 2½- or 3-inch pot. Another simple method is to insert each cutting into a 3-inch pot of sterilized geranium soil. Results are excellent, and first transplanting is not necessary for several months.

When your ambitions lead to a half-dozen or so new plants, try the pot-in-pan method. Obtain a shallow flower pot, termed a bulb or azalea pan, in a large size, 8-inch diameter or bigger. Place in the center of this a corked 3-inch flower pot filled with water. Pack the space between small pot and large pan with clean, sharp builder's sand (not beach sand) or a half-and-half mixture of sand and peatmoss, as in Figure 57.

Take your cuttings from vigorous plants. If the parent or stock plants are weak or diseased, failure with cuttings is almost certain. The end or terminal growth of a healthy plant is so full of vitality that the progeny are a chipper lot right from the start. No matter how rare a geranium is, you risk dire problems with disease if you try to salvage tip cuttings from a plant that is suffering from bacterial stem-rot or other disease.

Select tips of firm but not woody growth. A geranium stem is prime for cutting if, when bent, it snaps but does not break through entirely, a few fibers holding. This is a good way to test its condition but the desired number of cuttings are taken with a sharp knife. Make a clean, straight cut just below one of the small joints or nodes on the stem. Let each piece contain two or three of these nodes, and select, if you can, short-jointed growth that will be only 2 or 3 inches long. (Some growers prefer cuttings 4 to 5 inches long but the plants from these too often get off to a spindly start.)

Avoid bruising as you cut. Snip off the lower leaves and all flower buds. Remove also the little wings or stipules you find along the stems. These incline to rot if they remain on cuttings. The aim is to reduce the top growth so that cuttings will not wilt or die before they have developed a root system to supply them with moisture. Allow some leaves to remain, about two to a cutting, since these are needed to manufacture food for the infant plant. Dip the cut ends in hydrated lime to prevent decay.

Then, insert the stems deeply enough in the sand to support the cuttings and hold them erect when they are watered. Firm the sand securely around each one. Place them so that lower leaves do not touch the sand surface. The sand will keep evenly and constantly moist from the seepage of water through the walls of the small water-filled pot you placed in the center of the bulb pan.

Indoor cuttings taken in fall or winter for summer flowering are kept at 60 degrees F, but shaded the first few days with a sheet of newspaper spread over them. When cuttings are made in warm weather, you can set the planted pan in any fairly light but not sunny spot outdoors.

As evaporation and seepage slowly empty the small center pot, add more water. In two or three weeks, carefully dig out one cutting to judge progress. Usually, ¾-inch roots will have formed. At this stage the cuttings, actually plants now, are ready for separate 2½-inch pots. These are filled with the usual soil mixture but no fertilizer or manure is added beyond what may have originally gone into the compost.

By September (for May cuttings) and January (for August ones), when examination indicates a mass of roots cramped by the 2½-inch containers, shift the plants on to 3- or 3½-inch pots, later to 4's. This can be the final useful size for first-year flowering. If you want large specimens, shift again to 5½-inch pots, as growth indicates.

It may be necessary to pinch out the centers of young plants at the time of the first potting. This induces the formation of side growth, desirable in both pot and bedding plants. Short stocky cuttings, however, usually will not require pinching. It all depends on how they develop. Keep in mind that a tall, one-stemmed geranium with a single bloom at the tip is not your aim. You are trying to produce low, well-branched growth on plants with about three stems apiece. To promote even development, turn plants at the window or on the porch about once a week, but not if a flower stem is strongly pointed in one direction. Let the umbel mature before redirecting growth.

Rooting Cuttings Outdoors

If you want a great many new plants the pot-in-pan method will be inadequate. As soon as frostfree conditions prevail in your locality, you can raise a bumper, fall-flowering crop (or in August a grand midwinter one), by preparing in a sunny place outdoors a board-bound bed of clean sand. Soak the sand well before inserting the cuttings in rows. Protect them while they root, and thereafter during the hottest sunny hours, with a cloth screen. This is easily made by tacking lengths of muslin or pieces of an old sheet to a frame made of lath, reinforced at the corners with short extra pieces, and the whole raised on blocks of wood. These serve as legs to support the screen sufficiently above the cuttings to allow some ventilation. A convenient size for the board-bound bed and its makeshift awning is 3 by 4 feet. An open coldframe with a slat shade is likewise a good place to root cuttings outdoors.

Where there is a greenhouse, it is a simple matter in cold weather to start a batch of cuttings either in a propagating bench or in a flat of moist sand. Covered with a single thickness of newspaper during early days of rooting, the cuttings come along rapidly, particularly if they are placed where there is a little heat from pipes below the bench. The daytime temperature of the greenhouse can average about 65 degrees F with a 10- to 15-degree drop at night.

Started preferably in September and shifted two or three times to pots, they will be in prime condition for setting out in beds in May or June. A dozen plants of some choice fancy-leaved variety like 'Happy Thought' are lovely to have for May bedding-out in a sunny garden. Or perhaps you would prefer a corner planting of the colorful 'Jeanne'. Even a tiny greenhouse makes possible such thorough geranium indulgence.

Commercial growers proceed somewhat differently in the matter of shading and watering. Because he is so successful, I want to outline here the way one geranium specialist handles thousands of cuttings in his big greenhouse that aims primarily at flowering plants for Mother's Day late in May. In October the propagating bed is prepared with clean sand, watered well, and then pounded hard with a brick. The sand is then soaked again. Next, cuttings are inserted and firmed with the index finger and watered to settle the sand disturbed by their insertion. Although many cuttings wilt during the first 48 hours, they absorb enough moisture after that to freshen up. They are not shaded nor sprayed with water, nor is the sand moistened again until it shows signs of becoming definitely dry. The ideal in this procedure is for cuttings not to need watering at all until roots have formed.

About Root Growth Stimulants

Opinions vary on the use of root-growth substances. According to trials by the Eastern originators of 'Picardy', they are beneficial for geranium cuttings only when temperatures are low, as in fall and winter. If hormone-dipped cuttings are grown above 60 degrees F they incline to rot since too much of the rooting substance is drawn up into the cutting when the temperature is high. Hormone substances hasten the action of autumn cuttings of most varieties.

Western growers hold various opinions about the value of rooting aids, and also about the use of fungicides on cuttings. One California grower reports: "Although I used rooting hormone powders for several years, I finally decided that they were not worth the trouble. At best, they save only a few days' rooting time. They do not decrease losses under any reasonable conditions, and on some varieties, if used carelessly, will increase losses. There is much variability in susceptibility. Rooting powders should not be used on 'Pigmy' or on most dwarfs. 'Miss Burdett Coutts' is also susceptible to damage. I believe that, in general, better plants can be produced without hormone powders. Furthermore, with clean cuttings and clean rooting medium, there is no need for fungicidal treatment. If fungus diseases cause trouble, the best solution is better sanitation."

Fred Bode gives this advice in his catalog. He is writing for other commercial growers but in your greenhouse you may want to exercise this caution:

"Cuttings that turn black from the base upward to about the level of the sand and appear all right above the sand are usually the victims of a rooting powder that is too strong but cuttings killed by rooting powders look exactly like those killed by bacteria or fungus. . . . However, extra-mild rooting powders are available . . . and should be used when possible. Geranium stems are hairy, and excess powder should be tapped off with the hand. Never dip geranium cuttings in water before powdering."

Mr. Bode recommends for Zonal geraniums Cutstart 1-X, Hormex 1, or a similar extra-mild powder, mixed four or five parts to one part of Parzate (available at garden centers and farm-supply houses). Mr. Bode writes, "Parzate is desirable as a fungicide, and we use it in preference to equally good fungicides because it, in itself, is a good rooting-aid. Cutting-ends can be dipped into the powder by hand, but we find that if one of the small hand-dusters (we use a Hudson) is used to blow the mixed powder onto the stem-ends, sufficient powder will blow up into the stems and further protect the cutting from lesions which commonly appear at the sand-surface level."

Apparently the trick with the rooting hormones is to use only extra-mild types, and to use only enough to coat *lightly* the cut surface. A dipping of the lower inch of the stem, as is usually recommended, causes too much wild cell growth when only a proper stimulation of the cut area is desired.

Here, then, is a simple and a complex *how* of geranium propagation. Anyone with a big plant can develop a number of small ones. It is just a question of selecting the method best suited to your own facilities and then attacking this delightful business at your earliest convenience.

Chapter FIFTEEN

New Plants from Seed, Cross, and Mutation

Growing geraniums from hybrid seed is an unpredictable adventure. Usually seed produces delightful plants within a certain class, as zonals, regals, or dwarfs, but you will not know exactly what plants you have until the seedlings mature and bloom. The seeds of hybrid plants, whether the plants have been self-pollinated or crossed with a species or another hybrid, produce plants whose identity cannot be predetermined. (The only sure way to perpetuate a hybrid geranium is to propagate it by cuttings, as discussed in Chapter 14.)

Species plants perpetuate their own kind from seeds, but few commercial seedsmen offer seeds of species. The apple-scented geranium, *P. odoratissimum,* sets an abundant seed crop. Gathered in late summer and stored over winter for sowing in May, the seed germinates in two weeks and produces fine little flowering plants in about four months.

Geranium seedlings require a considerable amount of time and space, so it is only sensible to start with high-quality seeds. Purchasing these from a reliable grower or seedsman is one way to insure against wasting a great deal of your time on nonentities.

Commercial growers usually produce bedding-plant geraniums from cuttings of stock plants. To avoid the transmission of disease, an attempt has been made to produce hybrid geraniums that come true from seeds. 'Nittany Lion Red', co-developed at Pennsylvania State University by Dr. Richard Craig and Dr. D. E. Walker, is an example, and seeds of this hybrid are now available. 'Nittany Lion Red' blooms in 100 to 110 days from seeds. The flowers are single, bright red above vigorous foliage that is marked by a distinctive, bold bronze zone. This is a most satisfactory way to grow an abundance of bedding plants for small cost.

How to Start Geraniums from Seed

A geranium seed is about ³⁄₁₆ of an inch long (about the same size as salvia seed)—large when compared to the seeds of other common bedding plants, as those of petunia or snapdragon. A husk with a feathery appendage encloses a geranium seed. The seed, easily shucked from the husk, usually has a hard, smooth, shiny brown seed coat that is practically impermeable to water. Because the hard seed coat is a barrier to the moisture needed for germination, sprouting is generally slow and sporadic.

Dr. Craig and Dr. Walker reported in 1959 that seed scarification—chipping, filing, or piercing the seedcoat—greatly increased the germination of geranium seeds, and shortened the germination time from about three weeks to one week or less. Their tests were made under laboratory conditions, but it would seem safe to conclude that scarification enhances germination of geranium seed. Scarification is accomplished by holding the seed with tweezers and removing a section of the hard seed coat by chipping with a small scalpel, or by filing, or by any method that will not injure the living embryo but will allow moisture to enter the seed. (At least one dealer already offers scarified geranium seed.)

Geranium seeds can be sown at any time. Plant the seeds no more than ¼-inch deep in a mixture of equal parts of sand, leaf-mold, and loam. Set the seed pot or pan in a container of water until water has been drawn to the surface of the soil, and repeat watering by this method as it is required. Soil should not dry out, nor should it be kept in a soggy state. The best temperature for germination of geranium seed is 55 to 60 degrees F.

When seedlings are large enough to handle and before they become crowded, the geraniums intended for pot culture are planted in individual 2-inch pots, and shifted to larger pots according to their rate of growth and root-room requirements. Seedlings destined for bedding plants may be transferred from the seedbed to individual peat pots. Plants can grow in these until weather conditions permit peat pot and plant to go into the ground. The use of peat pots prevents the disturbance of roots that often retards growth.

Hybridizing Geraniums

If you are a geranium enthusiast, you will at some time want to have a fling at hybridizing and the production of your own geranium seed. Perhaps the brilliant zonal variety 'Olympic Red' will be your inspiration. Or perhaps with an interest in leaf forms and fragrance, you will become an aspiring hybridizer among the scented-leaveds. The charming 'Village Hill Hybrid' was produced by crossing *P. × jatrophaefolium* with *P. graveolens,* the Old Fashioned Rose Geranium. The spicy *P. × fragrans* 'Old Spice' was developed at Danielson, Connecticut, by crossing the apple-scented *P. odoratissimum* and the nutmeg-scented *P. × fragrans.*

Have a definite goal in mind when you select the parent plants. If you are adventurous and feel a yellow geranium, for example, would be desirable, you will probably start working crosses involving *P. gibbosum* with its yellow-green flowers, or *P. × rutaceum*

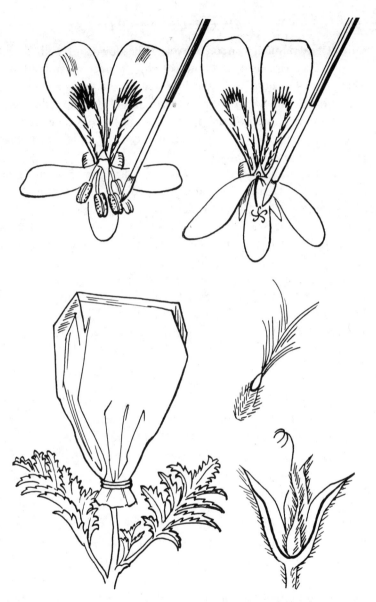

Figure 58.   How to Hybridize. Top left and right, paint brush conveys pollen from opened anthers of male parent to ripe stigma of female flower, from which anthers have been removed. Lower left, fertilized seed parent is bagged to prevent pollination by bees. Detail lower right of pistillate flowers; upper right, ripe seed.

with yellow-rimmed maroon flowers. The flowers of both of these have, besides the elusive yellow coloring, a trace of fragrance, another trait we would welcome in modern geraniums.

There are among existing varieties few that could not be improved. As you experiment, try to breed *in* the desirable characteristics of the parents and breed *out* the faults. The field of hybridizing is wide open.

Do not be discouraged if you discover that your favorite hybrids are sterile. Alas, they often are. Just consider that Joseph Pernet, who developed the great Pernetiana class of yellow roses, made thousands of crosses over a period of ten years before he finally obtained *two seeds,* from one of which came the now famous 'Soleil d'Or'.

If you succeed in producing something good, watch it for three or four years. Often sports or mutations develop from new varieties. These sports frequently are much better than the plants from which they sport. The old favorite 'Picardy' was a sport that Herbert C. Schneider of Max Miller's discovered on 'Salmon Ideal', which was a cross of 'Jean Viaud' and 'Beaute Poitevine'.

How to Pollinate

The method of hybridizing is simple but timing is an important factor, and recognizing the best possible moment is a matter requiring some experience. May and early June are usually good months. Earlier, the atmosphere inclines to too much dampness, while hot weather later on is seldom propitious.

To produce according to specifications and avoid self-fertilization, before the pollen is ripe remove the anthers from the flowers you want for seed bearers. You will discover the anthers, or sacs, carried by tiny bristles, surrounding the more prominent stigma or pistil in the center of each flower.

When this stigma is ripe, or sticky, put on the pollen from the other selected parent. Usually a paint brush is used (sterilized in

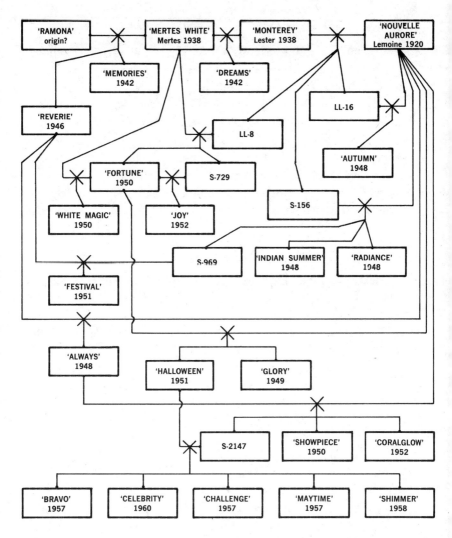

Figure 59.   Family Tree of Zonal Varieties from Holmes Miller.

alcohol between different crosses). Old hands at this may remove the whole anther with tweezers and dust the pollen directly from it onto the stigma of the seed parent.

The seeds that subsequently develop may or may not contain qualities of greatness. If from the ensuing sowing even one first-quality plant develops, it will be a miracle to be thereafter perpetuated by cuttings. The second generation sowing of hand-pollinated seed, even from a beautiful parent, usually produces only another ordinary mixture. Perhaps not a single one of the offspring will equal the distinguished grandparent—if, indeed, that one first cross did produce distinction.

Family Tree of Holmes Miller Varieties

Here you can see (Figure 59) the charted history of four famous hortorums—'Ramona', 'Mertes White', 'Monterey' and 'Nouvelle Aurore'—as they were used in a hybridizing program by Holmes Miller. This family tree began about 1940, and progressed to the introduction of 'Celebrity' in 1960. Before stock of any new variety was offered to the public it was checked for general worth by two more years of propagation by cuttings. Thus at least one sensation of 1960 was patiently begun about twenty years before.

The World of Mutations

Since mutations or sports that have occurred in cultivation have given us some of today's finest varieties, hybridizers and geneticists have sought to increase the rate at which these occur. One means is by the use of the chemical colchicine, derived from the autumn-flowering crocus. Radiation is also effective in producing sports, and since 1952, the U. S. Atomic Energy Commission, working through institutions like Brookhaven National Laboratory on Long Island, has carried on an active program aimed at plant improvement.

Dr. Seymour Shapiro who worked on this project reported ". . . a single radiation treatment will produce genetic instabilities that cause mutations to appear for a very considerable length of time after treatment. For example, I have in my laboratory plants that were irradiated five and six years ago. They are still showing new mutations that stem from this original mutation. I have one plant that displays on different branches five different types of flowers. It thus appears that small islands of mutated tissue are produced at the time of treatment. These mutant areas are carried along and may not work their way into a flower bud for months or even years. When they are successful in becoming incorporated into new buds they will then, for the first time, display the change."

Whether a mutation or sport occurs naturally or by artificial inducement, if it shows desirable characteristics, the next step is to root a tip cutting of the variant branch. Generally the favored traits will become stabilized in the new plant and it is suitable for vegetative propagation, or for use in a hybridizing program.

Chapter SIXTEEN

$\mathcal{T}$ree $\mathcal{F}$orms, $\mathcal{B}$askets, $\mathcal{B}$onsai, and $\mathcal{E}$spaliers

Standards—plants trained to tree form with one stem and a large head—have style. Introduce to the proper places tree-form geraniums, roses, heliotrope, lantana, or wisteria and immediately your garden has an air. The small plot in which are planted a pair of standards at once appears distinguished; the formal garden with corners or elevations so accented achieves an indefinable elegance.

Old World gardeners knew this. They had not our passion for diversity but were willing to make drastic selection of their material. Then they grew it superbly and displayed it wisely. With standards for accent and bedding plants for power, they planted restricted gardens of great charm.

Sometimes these had a simple beauty, as in the tiny walled gardens of France where straight pebbled paths accentuated a design of white rose trees and red everblooming begonias. Or in the superb undeviating green of an English lawn, with a gray wall for

218

background, set like a jewel was a form garden of scented, purple heliotrope trees rising above the constant color of pink and lavender petunias.

Today our gardens could often be lovelier if we would but re-discover the charm of standard or tree-form material. And for this type of development, no plant lends itself more readily than the geranium. It offers many new and interesting possibilities whether you garden in the East or West.

Consider now: if you live in a cold-winter section, how attractive would be even a 2 by 4 garden in the sun with early yellow tulips followed by bedding plants of that enchanting rosebud-type gera-nium, 'Apple Blossom', with standards of white 'Madonna' gera-niums for taller beauty in each corner.

If yours is a California garden where no winter storage problems occur, imagine garden beds containing an engaging procession of bright 'Olympic Red' or 'Orange Ricard' standard geraniums march-ing above broad drifts of single, white 'Marguerite de Layre'. Such an effect would be brilliant and, in this country, refreshingly new.

On open sunny terraces, East or West, and in patios or beside garden pools, the geranium standard also has exciting decorative possibilities. Perhaps you have been saving two handsome jar-dinieres from Spain for just such worthy denizens. Or perhaps the French windows in your dining room open onto a small sunny terrace that would be ideal for two tubbed, salmon-pink 'Picardy' standards. Maybe the entrance of your house requires a duet of 'Masure's Beauty' to extend a perfect welcome.

Scented-leaved as well as zonal geraniums can be grown to standard form. Eleanor Sinclair Rohde, an English gardener, writes in "The Scented Garden" of the sweet-scented standards she saw at Aldenham House. "One could easily spend two hours looking at that wonderful array, and nowhere else have I seen standards quite ten years old and measuring roughly five feet around." A trio of rose-scented, oak-leaved, and mint-scented geranium standards

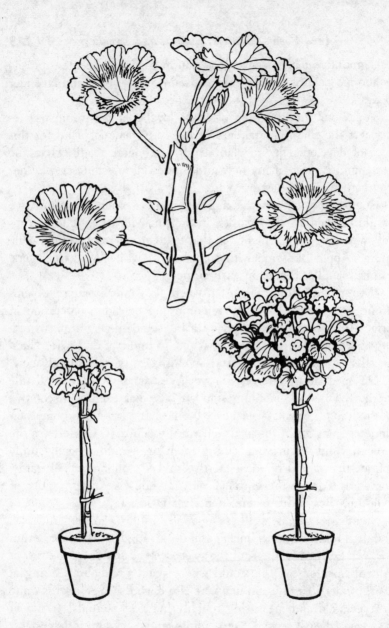

Figure 60.   How to Make a Standard or Tree Geranium. Top, a long-jointed cutting is selected; lower left, growing plant in a 5-inch pot is staked and relieved of side growth; right, flowering head is permitted to develop at 30- or 36-inch height.

would be charming all winter long in a sunroom. Robert Warner at Manhattan Garden Supply, Manhattan Beach, California, has had excellent success in training *P. graveolens* 'Rober's Lemon Rose', 'Joy Lucille', the oak-leaf *P. quercifolium,* and the Old Fashioned Rose Geranium, *P. graveolens* as standards. Development from rooted cuttings to specimens 6 feet tall in 12- to 18-inch tubs requires about four years. Mr. Warner describes his method in Chapter 10.

Wherever you live and however you garden, do let me tempt you with this delightful plant form. Start mildly, perhaps, with just a pair of standards but grow them from slip to crowning glory all by yourself. Then the excitement of creation and the pride of exquisite and unusual accomplishment will be yours.

How to Train a Standard

Proceed in this way. About the middle of February take about a dozen 4- to 5-inch cuttings of some favorite and sturdy variety. A long cutting will be better than the short ones you selected for bedding plants but short ones will do. Figure 60 shows the method.

Many of the single and double zonals make fine standards, especially those of the French type. Scarlet 'Flame', 'Lavender Ricard', rosy-red 'Masure's Beauty', scarlet 'Missouri', 'Orange Ricard', soft red 'Prize', 'Salmon Supreme', white 'Summer Cloud', and purple-crimson 'Will Rogers' are all good possibilities for such training.

In mid-March when the February slips are well rooted, select four or five for your venture. Take a few more than you will need. This will allow for possible mishap. Select on the basis of straightness and vigor. Plant each rooted cutting in a 2½-inch pot. Do not pinch out the tops—you want a tall plant, not a wide one.

As soon as the slips are established and growing in these first small pots, fertilize lightly. About May 1, or just as soon as root development permits, shift the plants to 4-inch pots; then about

June 15 to 5½-inch containers. It is possible to reach the desired 8-inch pan or azalea pot by September.

As growth proceeds, pinch off all side shoots, forcing activity to the tip. When the plant is 9 or 10 inches high, provide the support of a 15-inch bamboo stake. Insert it deeply and firmly in the soil, but carefully so as not to injure roots, and tie the geranium stem to it with a piece of pliable plastic plant tie or raffia.

As height develops and the would-be standard reaches the 5-inch-pot size, replace the 15-inch stake with a 30- or 36-inch stake, depending on the ultimate height you desire. Geranium standards are usually stopped at 30 or 36 inches, though 4- and 5-foot plants are possible. Firm staking and adequate tying are essential to success. A gust of wind can so quickly snap a tall, brittle geranium stem and in a moment destroy a year of careful training.

Fertilize the developing standard more than you do other young plants destined for flowering. You are now interested in promoting vegetative growth. Every other week sprinkle plant food lightly over the soil surface and water it in well. It is important to make the transfer to 7- or 8-inch pan some weeks before frost, while outdoor growing is still possible.

The 7- or 8-inch pan can be the final one, although 10- up to 14-inch tubs are possible. Usually some ornamental container awaits the final perfection. This is a healthful procedure, provided the container is not too large. Overpotted geranium trees become water-logged and fail both in health and beauty.

By the first of September allow branches to develop at the tip. As the nights in the East turn cool, you will notice signs of accelerated activity as if the plants knew that the best growing weather was soon to end. The head will now grow quickly with 4- to 8-inch branches by October 1.

Stop feeding by mid-September and well before frost place these amazing specimens (that early last spring were naught but cuttings) in your greenhouse or at a sunny window. Continue to watch your standards for stem shoots. If the tree form is to be maintained, all branches appearing below the head must be removed promptly, and preferably while small enough to rub off with your fingers.

In March and April of the second year will come a great delight, for as spring advances these standards so faithfully tended from babyhood will begin to deck themselves with colorful blooms. At the start there will be only a few but when transfer is made to the open garden, the whole top will be bright with color. Since a natural break takes place from an eye behind every flower head, little pruning will now be necessary, although faded blooms must be removed promptly. Any non-flowering shoots should be pinched back to stimulate the development of blossoming wood.

In southern California, growing standards is an even simpler matter. As they reach full development their first autumn, they are encouraged to continue with no winter rest such as the colder Eastern climate requires. And soon they begin to flower. Where temperatures of 28 to 35 degrees F occur, it is wise to set the plants indoors at night.

Standards are never planted directly in garden beds. They are grown in pots and either plunged or set in ornamental jardinieres or tubs about the garden, according to their most beautiful advantage. Whatever their location, they must be safely out of the wind and the stake that supports them, while inconspicuous, must be reliably strong.

Calendar for a Geranium Standard

February 15. Take cutting.

March 15. Plant in 2½-inch pot. From now on pinch off stem branches.

April 1. Start fertilizing. Continue fortnightly.

May 1. Shift to 4-inch pot. Supply a 15-inch stake.

June 15. Shift to 5½-inch pot.

August 15. Shift to 8-inch pan. Supply 36-inch stake.

September 1. Allow head to develop.

September 7. Fertilize for last time in sections where frost comes soon; otherwise continue at monthly intervals only.

September 15 to 30. Bring indoors to avoid frost.

February 15 (second year). Pinch back branches of head; thereafter enjoy!

GERANIUMS FOR BASKETS

Baskets of geraniums suspended in a window garden, a greenhouse, or outdoors from the overhang of roof, porch, pergola or lath-house are a lovely sight, and when a number of large specimens are grown to perfection as in Mrs. Crane's greenhouse, they are astoundingly beautiful. At flower shows the basket geraniums always draw an admiring crowd.

Probably no other plant family can equal the geraniums in kinds and colors suited to basket gardening. Consider first the ivy-leaveds. All are suitable for basket culture, and while some varieties may do better than others in your climate, in the beginning make your selection on the basis of plant habit and flower color. Where space is at a premium, as in a window garden or small greenhouse, chances are you will choose a compact variety like 'Santa Paula' or 'Sybil Holmes' and not a long-trailer like 'Mrs. Banks'. The hybrid ivy-leaveds also have candidates for baskets, including 'Alliance', 'Irma', 'Pink Alliance', and 'Scarlet Beauty'.

Among the regals, there are a number of outstanding varieties that look well grown in baskets. These include 'Black Lace', 'Flower Basket', 'Madame Layal', 'Mary Bard', 'Melissa', and 'Prime Minister Menzies'.

'Forest Maid', a newcomer from Germany where it is one of the most popular varieties, makes a superb basket plant covered with

Figure 61. How to Prepare a Hanging Basket. Start with three ivy-leaved geraniums in 3-inch pots. Line wire basket with moist sphagnum, sheet moss, or with polyethylene plastic (double thickness of a dry-cleaning bag) in which holes are punched for drainage. Remove plants from pots and arrange in basket. Fill in around roots with soil or course sphagnum moss. Water well. Under good growing conditions, plants are soon covered with flowers and the vines cascade from the basket.

masses of fully double, ball-shaped dark rose-colored flowers. At first this zonal makes a low, upright plant, but with age it begins to cascade, and as the heavy flower heads bend downward, the effect is delightful.

Varieties of *P. frutetorum* are also excellent for basket gardening. 'Magic Lantern' is the standout of the group with brown-zoned leaves with tones of red, yellow and light green. Also consider 'Dark Beauty', 'Mosaic', and 'Royal'.

As your interest in geraniums grows, you will try other kinds— perhaps some species or scented varieties as apple, coconut, nutmeg, coriander-leaved, 'Beauty', 'Joy Lucille', 'Fair Ellen', 'Rollisson's Unique', and 'Old Spice'.

How to Plant a Basket

For one geranium, use a wire or redwood basket at least 8 inches in diameter and 4 to 5 inches deep as in Figure 61. For three plants of the same variety, or a combination planting, select an appropriately larger basket. Next line the basket with moist sheet moss or unshredded sphagnum moss. Put plants in place working your favorite geranium soil around the roots and filling the basket to within an inch of the top. There is increasing use today of unmilled sphagnum moss alone as the growing medium for hanging baskets. This is highly moisture retentive, yet the weight of a basket planted with moss is far less than when soil is used. Since sphagnum moss is sterile, regular feedings with a liquid fertilizer are necessary.

Success with geranium baskets depends on careful attention to watering. If drainage from the basket is likely to damage the floor, carry the basket to sink or tub returning it only after the drip has stopped. Try to keep the growing medium moist at all times but not too wet, especially for ivy-leaved geraniums, or edema may show up. Outside where evaporation is rapid you must also be careful not to let plants dry out.

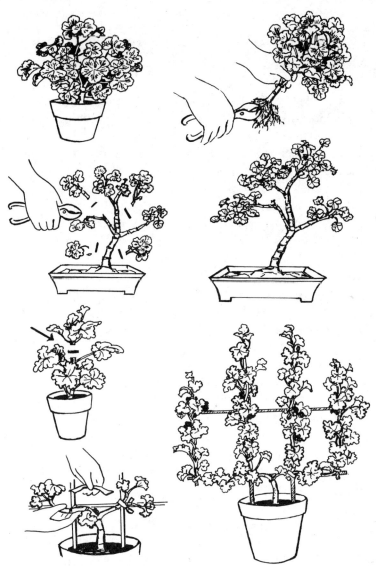

Figure 62. Above, How to Develop a Bonsai. Select a sturdy, well-branched specimen. Remove the pot and reduce roots by pruning. Set plant in soil in a bonsai container. Prune into a bonsai form. Cover soil with sheet moss if you wish. Below, How to Train an Espalier. Select a young plant with one strong stem. The candelabra model is 'Rollisson's Unique'. Pinch out growing tip. As new branches develop from the point where growth was stopped, tie them with soft plastic onto a frame of bamboo stakes or redwood. Other designs are described in Chapter 16.

BONSAI FORMS

The Japanese art of growing trees and shrubs in containers, shaping them to decorative sculptured form, or maintaining their natural habit—but always in miniature—has become a popular hobby in this country. Heretofore only hardy woody plants have been selected but these can be kept inside only for a few hours at a time.

Now those who enjoy plants indoors in winter are applying the techniques of bonsai to tender materials, and various types of geraniums are proving ideal. Their framework is sufficiently woody, and even in pots and not specially trained, they often take on the gnarled look so desired in bonsai. The slowest-growing dwarf varieties, like 'Black Vesuvius', 'Imp', and 'Small Fortune', make good *mame* or baby bonsai which even in age are kept to about 2½ inches. For average bonsai—if there is an average—plants are allowed to reach 24 to 30 inches in height and about the same width. The tops are pruned regularly, perhaps to look like a miniature tree, as these are seen in the forest, perhaps to one of the five basic bonsai styles: formal upright, informal upright, slanting, semi-cascading, or full cascading. Meanwhile roots are restricted in the special bonsai container which is always designed with a foot so that air can flow under the root area. Furthermore, to limit growth and obtain the desired ancient look, plants are fed diluted fertilizer periodically and not over-watered, in order to keep the leaf size small in scale with the stems.

It takes experience to manage the cultural niceties that retard growth without harming the plant. When planting, spread coarse sandy material over the bottom of the container with your preferred geranium soil on top. For an attractive finish, a layer of moss is spread over the top soil or some tiny creeping thyme grown there.

Geranium varieties with small leaves make the most attractive bonsai, the foliage thus in good proportion to the plant size. Many dwarf and semidwarf varieties qualify and many of the scented-leaveds. My friends who are bonsai enthusiasts have looked so covetously upon my plants of *P. crispum* and *P. crispum* 'Minor' that I have lost all these to their bonsai experiments. *P. abrotani-folium* and *P. reniforme* are good possibilities and my 'Variegated Mint Rose' would make a charming bonsai subject with its attractive green-and-white but quite small leaves. On the other hand, the peppermint-scenteds and the various *graveolens* varieties have too-large leaves. Some of the oddities like *P. gibbosum* and *P. tetra-gonum* would be interesting to work with but these do have a dormant period. With the larger dwarfs like 'Mischief' and 'Tu-Tone' you could in time get flowering specimens comparable to the handsome azalea bonsais I have seen.

These remarks on bonsai are made simply to suggest the possibilities. Very likely exhibitions at flower shows will soon include bonsai geraniums. You will have fun training such plants for your own pleasure; it is certainly not necessary to produce a perfect stylized specimen, but if the art of bonsai appeals to you, that is just what you will want to do. And you will need to know much more about it. At your library, you will find a number of books on the subject, and from the Bonsai Society of Greater New York (c/o The New York Botanical Gardens, Bronx, New York 10458) you can obtain for $1.00 the Society's excellent handbook, "Art of Bonsai for Beginners."

GERANIUMS AS ESPALIERS

Geraniums can also be trained as espaliers or wall plants, again in prescribed forms or in designs of your own devising. Plants then become two-dimensional having only height and width and relatively no depth. Modern architecture with broad expanses of unadorned wall, has opened the way for an unprecedented interest in the espaliering of ornamentals. Gardeners everywhere see the design possibilities and also recognize the value of plants grown flat to fit a space that could not provide room for a natural plant form.

Actually, geraniums have been trained as wall plants for many years. In old books it is interesting to notice how often *Pelargonium acetosum, P. gibbosum, P. scandens, P. tetragonum,* and 'Skelton's Unique' have been called "climbing," or "excellent for training on a wall," yet the more appropriate term, espalier, has not been applied.

Also good for espalier work are 'Mrs. Pollock', 'Skies of Italy', 'Happy Thought', and 'Rollisson's Unique'. These lend themselves to informal designs and are also excellent for training to classical espalier patterns, as three-armed palmette, double-U, horizontal-T, palmette oblique, arcure, Belgian fence, and fan. In climates where the ivy-leaveds grow easily, they may also be used as espaliers although the generally scandent stems need more frequent tying to frame or trellis.

In frost-free climates geranium espaliers can be planted directly in the ground in front of the walls on which they will be trained. Allow about 6 inches between plant and wall to permit free air circulation. You can support a wall espalier by means of stand-off screws with shanks several inches long set at strategic points to hold the design. Or attach a sturdy redwood framework to the wall and tie the plant to the support with plastic plant-tie material but not the kind that has a wire inside. I have used such a frame satisfactorily for pyracantha espaliers. I have also fastened espalier plants with Francis wall nails directly to the clapboards. Both look well. Of course in this cold climate standard and espaliers are kept potted and are wintered inside.

To espalier a potted geranium, insert into the soil a framework or trellis made of small pieces of redwood in the design you wish to develop. Bamboo stakes make good temporary supports, but they rot after a year or two and require replacement. This is difficult and usually involves breaking some of the branches so it is wise to set in a permanent framework at the start.

There are two ways to develop a geranium espalier. You can take a well-started clambering specimen and maneuver existing branches into a pleasing design. The plant of 'Rollisson's Unique' in Figure 62 was about one year old from a rooted cutting at the time it was removed from the shelf of a home greenhouse and turned into a stylized candelabra shape. By gently persuading stems to assume a new shape, it was possible to create this striking form in less than an hour; only two small branches did not fit and they were pruned off. Aside from routine culture, maintenance of an "instant" espalier like this amounts only to the removal of any growth that disturbs the design.

The other way to grow a geranium espalier is to start with a vigorous young rooted cutting. When you transfer to a pot place the framework on which branches are to be trained. Nip out the growing tip at the point where you wish side branches to develop. As growth expands, train it into position. This is tricky business. Be prepared to mourn the breakage of some branches as you attempt to tie them into shape. Sometimes it is necessary to tie only partially into position; a few days later you can tighten the plastic tie, letting intuition guide you as to whether the branch can then stand being pulled all the way into place.

Figure 63. For a summer cottage in the mountains, pink and white geraniums planted in a hollowed-out log or railroad tie can make an instant flower garden. Photo by Roche.

Chapter SEVENTEEN

For Urns, Tubs, Planters, and Window Boxes

Plants in containers have become increasingly popular as our pleasure in outdoor living has increased, and we have more opportunity to enjoy our gardens and plants from the closer view. And for container growing there is no plant more diversified, attractive, and adaptable than the geranium. It has always been the favorite for window boxes but now it is grown in many types of planter boxes, set along the edge of terrace or patio, on the top of a wall, in the angle of a plank walk at the seashore, in the areaway to a city house.

Geraniums are probably the most colorful of all plants for tubs or urns that offer hospitality beside the entrance of country or town house. In terra-cotta pots they make fine accents for the steps of a garden; in handsome stone containers, they gracefully emphasize the termination of a wall. The ivy-leaved geraniums are particularly lovely for this use. Hanging in wicker baskets or redwood

233

boxes from the cross pieces or uprights of pergola or arbor they are also decorative. If pots of geraniums are slipped into metal-ring supports, they can be fastened to a fence to transform this bare type of garden division into a flowery background.

IN CONTAINERS IN SUMMER

I enjoy container geraniums in so many ways in summer. The finer kinds are always left in pots, these slipped into ceramic covers and grouped along the entrance steps of the Plant Room or arranged in a wire stand set against the wall of the platform outside. As I have said, I delight in plant tubs of mixed kinds—zonal, fancy-leaved, scented-leaved, and ivy-leaved. If pots are packed in peat-moss or unmilled sphagnum, they are not hard to keep watered and they make such pleasing path accents for the Round Garden or the Doorway Gardens beside the porch.

Planted in soil the basket geraniums are heavy and require strong supports. I suspend them from double birdcage hangers. If the ivy-leaveds are grown in sphagnum, pots are much lighter. Either way, I do enjoy a graceful plant hung at the corner of the house and always in pleasant view from the breakfast-room window. Beside the front door, a basket of ivy-leaved geraniums is invariably welcoming. And for window boxes, the ivy-leaveds make a more interesting edging than the ubiquitous periwinkle. However, they will not prosper in all locations. Only where there is shade for part of the day are the ivy-leaved geraniums good outdoor container plants. Morning sun with afternoon shade is ideal.

The fancy-leaved geraniums must also be used cautiously. In a hot climate in strong sun they lose their good coloring. I set tubs of them in protected fully light rather than sunny locations. In fall they come indoors with brighter leaves than they went out with in spring.

Scented-leaved geraniums thrive mightly in pots and boxes in summer. There they reveal their ancestry as strong shrubs so that

Figure 64. This well-built window box is one of four at the Commodore Restaurant in Beverly, Massachusetts. Here pale pink zonal geraniums are combined with blue lobelia, a greenish form of iresine, and white sweet alyssum. In the others (not shown): pink geraniums with dark red coleus and alyssum; 'Madame Langguth' with yellow coleus and purple alyssum; bright red geraniums with single white petunias. Photo by Taloumis.

Figure 65. At the seashore, a box of flowering geraniums makes a bright accent in the angle of an exposed plank walk. Photo by Roche.

by September, I often view their exuberance with dismay. They are so big they have outgrown my accommodations. Sometimes I find room somehow, as for a handsome *P. tomentosum* in an iron kettle that requires a 3- by 3-foot space on its own table. True I could take a cutting but a new little plant of peppermint does not compare decoratively with this fine rambling specimen that is in no wise deterred by winter weeks of fairly dim west light.

FOR WINDOW BOXES

Today geraniums are used with new associates in window boxes. I think of the four boxes that decorate the Commodore Restaurant in Beverly, Massachusetts. George Taloumis in "Outdoor Gardening in Pots and Boxes" shows these in color. In Figure 64, you can see one of the boxes with pale pink geraniums, iresine, blue lobelia, and trailing white sweet alyssum. In the other boxes, geraniums are always the important plant but they are used with dark red coleus, white petunias, and purple sweet alyssum.

Mr. Taloumis shows geraniums in other imaginative uses as in boxes on the Chapel Bridge in Lucerne, in concrete tubs in the streets of Stockholm, and in baskets hanging from lamp posts in Victoria in Canada. In New York City, geraniums often fill the big urns on Fifth Avenue, and the traveler through the little towns of Switzerland and Germany is enthralled by the constant colorful sight of geraniums in boxes decorating every story of the houses. In London, boxes and baskets of geraniums decorate banks and department stores.

In the United States we see window boxes of geraniums used with every possible style of architecture. They are a natural decoration for the cottage, good as floor porch-planters for houses of contemporary design, and nice in front of the living-room windows of Victorian city houses, provided these get sun.

You could use rosebud geraniums or other fine kinds in a box in a protected location where plants are sure to get regular care,

Figure 66. White geraniums in a verdigris urn are a suitably elegant orna-
ment for the doorway of a handsome city residence. Photo by Genereux.

Figure 67.   A sunny areaway on a city street becomes a garden with boxes of zonal and scented-leaved geraniums with a few white petunias. Photo by Genereux.

but, generally speaking, the geraniums typed as "commercial" are a better choice. Commercial simply indicates varieties of wide appeal and capable of good spring and summer performance under a variety of climatic conditions. Howard Wilson defines commercial varieties this way: "They have large flowers that will not burn or shatter; they bloom profusely and continuously; make nice compact plants; are disease-resistant; and usually red!" But as reliable as reds like 'Blaze' and 'Olympic Red' undoubtedly are, geraniums in other colors are also dependable and often preferred, as 'Apple Blossom', 'Irene', 'Orange Ricard', 'Penny Irene', 'Pink Cloud', 'Salmon', 'Springtime,' and perhaps 'Snowball' among whites.

A Word on Window Boxes

The boxes themselves are the better for simple designs that are really practical, and good construction. Often boxes are too long. Three to 4 feet is enough. And usually they are too small. Inside dimensions of 12-inch top width, 9-inch bottom, and a 6- to 8-inch depth are ideal (the greater depth for hot dry locations). Preferably built with 1-inch boards (thickness gives insulation as well as durability) of No. 2 cypress or redwood. And use brass screws in preference to nails for fastening. It won't be funny, at least to you, if your window box bursts apart some broiling July day.

It is better not to paint the inside of the box, especially with creosote or a phenolic wood preservative. Plants dislike them. Instead line with polyethylene plastic sheeting, the kind obtainable from a lumber dealer. On the outside go to town with three coats of paint, and don't assume they have to be green and white. Brown boxes or blue ones look much better on some houses. And I have seen dark red ones, too, that indicated the good taste of the owner.

How To Plant Boxes

When it comes to soil, summon your energy. So much depends on a moisture-retentive growing medium. You can use unmilled

Figure 68. Ivy-leaved geraniums in a handsome Italian stone basket accent the end of a stone wall in a New England garden. Here they thrive in morning sun and afternoon shade. Photo by Taloumis.

Figure 69. A dark purple old-fashioned lilac at the corner and pink geraniums with trailing tradescantia in the window box of a colonial cottage offer a succession of spring and summer color. Photo by Molly Adams.

sphagnum moss alone and fortify it with weekly feedings of a liquid fertilizer. Or rely on the conventional mixture of two parts garden soil, one part of sand, and one part compost, humus, or peatmoss (soak this first). To every bushel of the mixture, add a 3-inch potful of some quick-acting fertilizer, or a potful of steamed bone meal and sheep manure combined.

Over each drainage hole in the box (bored ½ inch across and at 6-inch intervals), place a piece of crock. Then spread a 1-inch layer of broken crock, roofer's gravel, or other rough material through which excess moisture can drain. Now fill in soil to within 1½ inches of the top. You need that much space to receive water.

Finally, set the root balls of the plants 8 inches apart. Geraniums are lusty and need plenty of space for summer growing. Set them ½ inch deeper than their previous planting. Hollow out a generous cavity for each specimen and, after locating it, fill up the hole halfway with water. After this drains down, firm the soil around the plant. When all is finished, spread a generous ½ inch of mulching material—buckwheat or cocoa hulls. They give an attractive finish to the planting and prevent surface drying.

Keep in mind that a window box—or other container garden—to look well needs regular care. It is essential to water usually daily at least, and to snip off faded flowers and leaves. Also pinch plants back occasionally to keep them shapely.

Instead of direct soil planting you can fill boxes, tubs, or planters with peatmoss or unmilled sphagnum moss and plunge your potted pelargoniums. The moss, well-soaked, provides good insulation. Even so, these potted plants require more frequent watering than those planted right in the soil.

CONTAINER GERANIUMS IN CALIFORNIA

If you live in the West you are probably acquainted with the use of window shelves instead of window boxes. To me these are one of the most decorative aspects of California houses, and the idea is spreading eastward. Sometimes only a braced and painted board runs the length of the window and on this the plants in colorful pots are nicely displayed. Occasionally the shelf is perforated and each plant, held by its rim, rests in a circular opening instead of on top of the shelf. At its best, the window shelf has a well-designed bracket and apron and a little rim to prevent dislocation by strong winds.

In the brilliant atmosphere of California, containers and plants in mixed colors look gay and attractive. On one small white dwelling with a yellow door I saw a long yellow shelf that ran part way across the front and then around the corner of the house where the modern-type windows joined. The shelf held a bright display of glazed red, cobalt blue, and yellow pots and these were planted with geraniums of vermilion, orange, and crimson. More restrained but lovely against pale gray shingles was a white shelf adorned with white pots of the pink pelargonium, 'Honeymoon'.

Balconies also offer opportunity for pelargoniums of all kinds in pots, regals as well as others. Sometimes plants are set many feet below and trained up to an iron grille or redwood trellis. 'Rollisson's Unique', 'Mrs. Pollock', 'Skies of Italy', and 'Happy Thought' are excellent for this purpose. Or a second-story balcony contains ivy-leaved varieties with some growth trained up over the rail and the rest cascading between the railings and down over the house wall. Regals also adorn these wide window spaces and offer their owner pleasure both within and without. A collection of scented-leaveds in interesting containers makes an unusually attractive group for a balcony off a bedroom or guest suite.

Figure 70. Pink-flowered ivy-leaved geraniums offer a bright greeting to the home of Mr. and Mrs. Edward B. Potter, Beverly Farms, Massachusetts, during daylight hours and in the lamplight after dark. Photo by Taloumis.

Figure 71. Salmon, pale lavender, and white ivy-leaved and zonal geraniums fill to overflowing a sturdy window box delightful to see from within or without. Photo by Max Tatch.

Chapter EIGHTEEN

How To Succeed in Business With a Little Trying

If you grow a number of geraniums successfully in your home or greenhouse sooner or later you may wonder whether an expansion of your delightful hobby could become a profitable business. So many commercial growers started this way that today some of them can't recall just when they ceased to be amateurs. If you are serious about growing geraniums commercially, you will find in this chapter the guidelines you need. They reflect the know-how of this country's most successful wholesale and retail growers.

The Ideal Geranium Business

Several old-time growers admit that, were they again to start in business, they would be specialists, offering trade-leaders for the garden, collector's plants for the hobbyist; they would grow quality attractions—hanging baskets, tree geraniums, handsome specimens in decorative pots, also espaliers. While such a specialist prices his plants only slightly higher than the retail stands, net profits are greater and, if he is properly organized, he finds time for hybridizing, grafting, collecting, or photographing—the many pursuits connected with being a specialist.

Most hobbyists start their own businesses with a general retail line of geraniums in the more popular pot sizes and in hanging baskets. They add a line of garden supplies—pots, insecticides, fertilizers. They soon discover, through normal business demands, which items are most popular. At the same time, they build up profitable services, refilling window boxes, urns, and baskets.

The Wholesale Approach

Size has nothing to do with wholesale growing. For many years a woman in San Antonio, Texas, has grown two hundred 5-inch-pot geraniums each year for one retail nursery. Her space and energy are limited, her profits excellent, and she is satisfied to grow this exact number.

Many wholesale concerns are operated by former hobbyists who are semiretired or who have short work-hours. One postal employee in Oregon grows and wholesales thirty-eight thousand 4-inch-pot geraniums. Since a single large concern may grow up to a million and a half plants each year, you can see that this industry is unlimited.

Few commercial growers trust a large part of their crop to the difficult 'Mrs. Henry Cox'; yet three semiprofessionals in Los Angeles—a fireman and two housewives—specialize in this one fancy-leaved variety in their back-yard nurseries and practically at their own price they wholesale these hard-to-grow beauties to retail nurseries.

In Portland, Oregon, Mrs. Anna Heide, originator of 'Heide's White', is a keen hobbyist and an active member in the Oregon Geranium Society. When Mrs. Heide decided to turn professional, her assets were an attractive home yard and two small greenhouses. She was experienced with dwarf geraniums, and her two greenhouses were large enough to hold many pots of these little gems. Portland is a city big enough to support such a modest specialty, and Mrs. Heide is known far and wide for her dwarf geraniums.

First Decisions About Your Business

Several factors control the type of business you choose, among them your personality and your location. If you like to work quietly without interruptions, wholesaling is the answer. If you prefer to work in spurts—with breaks of diverting conversation—you will enjoy retail. If letter-writing appeals, go into mail order.

The kinds of geraniums you like to grow are also a consideration. For instance, if you want to specialize in scented-leaveds, you must offer them by mail to realize sufficient volume. Conversely, trade-leader zonals can be bought in every hamlet and, although they can be important in mail order, it is the unusual, the new, the rare zonals that will be more in demand. At the opposite end of the trade, if you wholesale to supermarkets, you will probably limit your selection to one variety of each color of zonal and just a few varieties of other classes, say two fancy-leaved, three ivy-leaved, and mixed trays of regals.

Location also affects your choice. If your home is in a city with good rail service, mail order will be fine. If you are in a moderate-sized city with a large farm area to supply, retail is excellent, and this is often coupled with mail order—not by catalog, but through ads in local Sunday papers, a highly successful medium in many areas.

Most large wholesalers are located at least fifty miles from metropolitan areas. Usually such concerns were once retailers who wanted to expand beyond the limits of retail possibilities. Labor in such areas is usually ample and excellent, and overhead costs are often quite low.

Whether you go retail or wholesale, local or mail order, or combine some of these, chances are you will grow geraniums with one or more other specialties as begonias, fuchsias, orchids, petunias, or pansies. Maybe your other crop will be more mundane—at least three large concerns in Kansas and Illinois grow geraniums in winter and from 60 to 120 acres of cabbage in summer.

The Law and Your Business

When you plan to go into business, find out about zoning. In a residential district a business is usually restricted to selling what is grown on the premises; ordinarily you are not permitted to sell such items as pots and fertilizer. Sometimes all sales are forbidden, and you must limit yourself to wholesaling and delivering your own plants—or to selling by mail order. Unzoned areas may later become restricted and, although you can continue as before, expansion is prohibited. If possible, do locate on commercially-zoned property.

Fire and structure laws are also a consideration. In some crowded commercial areas, polyethylene plastic houses are not allowed, while glasshouses are permitted. Polyethylene has been a boon to growers in recent years because of low first cost and low taxes. Polyethylene is often permitted for growing areas, but forbidden by fire laws in sales areas. Also, greenhouses to which the public is admitted must be of sturdier materials than non-public growing-houses.

A talk with your fire inspector and your building-code department will save you a lot of problems later.

Floor Plan for a Retail Business

A retail sales area should be pleasant, compact, and neat, with only the most attractive plants displayed. Make all paths full-circulating so that customers do not have to back out. Divide this sales area from the growing area by a gate, or other well-marked entrance so that customers won't stray into the growing area. Buildings there need not be constructed for the public, and while they must be kept clean, they need not be kept quite so orderly as your sales area. Furthermore, you will have display and stock plants there you won't wish to be pressured into selling. And you will need a rehabilitation area for damaged or shopworn specimens.

Organizing for Success

An important asset of a business is a good organizational plan. Make out a schedule for each day of the year; put down every necessary job. List the daily jobs as well as jobs that must be done for particular times, as filling out tax returns, ordering fall stock, preparing for shows, and a multitude of other special jobs. This planning is easiest done on calendars marked with 3-inch squares for each date.

Another necessity is your notebook. Many a famous horticulturist can credit his fame to a careful notebook. Date each entry, and try to record everything you will need for future reference. Some growers simply keep a running account; others divide their notes into sections. Anyway keep your notebook in easy reach of your work area. If someone gives you a new variety, record it. If you think you are two weeks late or early with your crop—or in obtaining stock, for example—make a note of it. Do the same with any crosses you make; otherwise you are bound to forget the parents.

You cannot imagine how valuable this daily log will become in the operation of your business.

Stocking a Geranium Business

Finding sources of supply can be difficult while establishing a new business. You soon find you must adjust inventory or lose sales. While some growers propagate all or most of their stock, the greatest number buy most of it as cuttings or as 2¼-inch-pot geraniums, and an increasing number start over each year with all new stock purchased from propagating specialists.

A profitable source of pots, hangers, baskets, sprays, fertilizers, and other items is almost impossible to locate without a constant flow of information. You need to read trade magazines. Retailers should also try to keep up with home-garden magazines so they will be prepared to meet demands brought about by feature articles on geraniums.

Do not attempt to grow all your own stock. This is a problem even for large concerns who raise their own stock and handle that of no other grower. The wholesaler of 2¼'s offers a valuable service to other wholesalers, especially to growers who produce and sell geraniums in 4's.

To guarantee a good booking with a reliable concern, commercial growers place orders for their propagating stock in summer or early fall. They find they no more than get stock potted up than new winter or spring varieties are announced. You will get telephone calls for these from, say, a customer who always plants both sides of her driveway with geraniums. This year she doesn't want "that old-fashioned pink, but a bright lavender or a softer red," or whatever "lovely new variety" she has just read about. To fill such an order, and probably more of the same kind, you need to be able to rebalance your inventory quickly from a wholesaler of 2¼-inch-pot plants. Maybe later the same spring, a garden magazine will come out with a beautiful color picture of fancy-leaveds, a patio hung with baskets of the ivy-leaveds. Again you will need fast help, and you will turn to the producer of 2¼-inch-pot geraniums.

Wholesalers who supply retail concerns are as varied as the retailers themselves. Some wholesalers ship, others do not. Some carry a limited number of varieties, others list a wide selection. There are even wholesalers who grow just one type, as the man in Burlington, Wisconsin, who supplies a single specialty—almost all the serrated-petal Fiats for the United States.

In any case, as a retailer, you need to know the wholesale value of 2¼-inch-pot geraniums. Even if you propagate most of your own stock, the pricing of your finished plants should be based upon the wholesale cost of 2¼-inch-pot geraniums. Judgment in this area can mean overall profit or loss, success or failure.

About a quarter of the geraniums sold in the United States are grown from cuttings shipped direct from California growers.

Geraniums are also started from cuttings that are taken from your own greenhouse stock-plants; these were probably originally grown from cuttings you bought. Thousands of plants are started from cuttings taken from 2¼-inch-pot geraniums that get too tall. Whatever your source of propagating stock, quality—in every case—depends upon the history and development of strains as well as on the cultural procedures of the grower. At one time, greenhouses often had stock-plant areas that were maintained over the years. Now the more profitable practice is to get cuttings from California or from stock-plants that are replanted there each year. Where the stock-plant method is used, wholesalers take cuttings and produce 2¼-inch-pot geraniums for their wholesale trade through fall and winter. The last batch of cuttings is reserved for the wholesaler's own crop of 4½-inch-pot geraniums. When his batch is ready for 4's, he dumps the stock-plants to make room for the larger pots. After his crop of 4's has been sold, his greenhouses are cleaned and the stock-plant benches are again replanted with small plants obtained from specialists in propagating stock or with plants reserved for this purpose before the last batch of stock-plants was dumped. A few concerns maintain separate greenhouses of "cultured" and highly selected mother-block plants that are propagated and added to the production-stock-plants as they are available.

The idea that buying cuttings, rooted or otherwise, is cheaper than buying 2½-inch-pot geraniums is false—except for the initial cost. It depends on your time and your greenhouse space as to whether cuttings or plants are the more economical. You have to take into consideration that with plants, the supplier absorbs the inevitable percentage loss of cuttings. You can't look at price of cutting versus price of plant as an exact comparison. If *you* grow from cuttings, you are likely to lose a greater percentage of them than the wholesaler. And again, put a price tag on your time.

The thing to do is what the big wholesalers do who establish personal relationships with their suppliers by making several trips to the suppliers' fields in the off-seasons of selling. They go to California or elsewhere, look at the propagating stock and indicate their choice. As is natural, when shipping time comes, the propagator sends his friends the best of the lot. Your local supplier will do the same for you as the two of you get to know each other, and you become to him more than a name on an order sheet when your cuttings, or more likely your 2¼'s, are sent off or packed for your pick-up.

As for your scheduling: Geraniums from 2¼-inch pots will finish out as 4- or 5-inch-pot geraniums in approximately 40 to 60 days; rooted or callused cuttings require 70 to 90 days; unrooted cuttings require another 30 days to allow for first potting—usually into 3's (4's or 5's for regals) before transfer into the larger sizes preferred for selling.

Supply and Demand

You will soon get to know sales ratios for certain varieties. Unfortunately, many a business starts with poorly selected stocks and unbalanced ratios. If you are specializing in geraniums alone, count on the zonals for 50 to 60 per cent of your sales. Whatever size pot you choose as your leading size, try to grow just about everything in that size, with the exception of the dwarfs, which are usually sold in 2¼'s, and specimen plants that may be in 5's or 6's. Uniform pot sizes go a long way toward making your nursery attractive, and they are easier for your less experienced help to care for with no special directions on watering for instance.

Even as a specialist you will find that 80 per cent of the zonals you sell will be the trade-leaders. For their complete satisfaction, encourage customers to plant beds and exposed window-boxes with these dependables. Not more than 20 per cent of zonal sales will be of the less familiar varieties, although some of these are among the most beautiful geraniums in the loveliest colors and blends.

Three to 5 per cent of the total inventory can well be of dwarfs. But, most of these should be of the larger more dependable doubles. Leave the very small ones and the variegateds to mail-order specialists unless you know you have a real demand for them.

About 5 per cent of total inventory can be of the fancy-leaved geraniums. These also should be mostly of the leading dependable five or six varieties that can be used in gardens as 'Distinction', 'Happy Thought', 'Marshall MacMahon', 'Mrs. Pollock', 'Skies of Italy', 'Wilhelm Langguth'. A collection of the rarer fancy-leaveds is excellent for creating interest and for sales to hobbyists and collectors.

As a specialist, you will be expected to have most of the novelties —Rosebuds, Cactus-flowered, Bird's Egg—but 5 per cent or slightly more of these will probably cover your requirements. These are collectors' items sold one at a time instead of by the dozen. The exception is mail order when 15 per cent of the demand might well be for these odd and unusual varieties.

The scented-leaveds are best offered in fairly small sizes. Mail-order concerns sell them in the same size they use for shipping, that is in 2½'s. In nurseries they are seldom offered in sizes above 3's unless they are sold as specimen plants. In small sizes scented-leaveds are neat and attractive. They grow into interesting shapes, often spreading widely when they adapt themselves to a location, whether they are outside or indoors. However, in a nursery, medium-sized scented-leaveds rarely develop these characteristics.

You will find that ivy-leaved geraniums continue to gain favor. There is considerable sale for 4-inch-pot plants, and you can use a great many for baskets and boxes, especially for terraces and patios.

The regals have been popular on both coasts since the 1850s and their use jumped tenfold with the introduction of the Faiss varieties in the mid 1920s. Their popularity has increased as hybridizers have brought flower and plant to present perfection with better bloom and increased re-bloom. Regal flowers and colors vary so much that you will probably find you require a larger number of varieties of these than of most other classes.

With good equipment, you can grow spectacular regals and make an excellent profit with 5- and 6-inch-pot plants sold to florists for Mother's Day and Easter. Although they sell for less than azaleas, they give an equally fine show. This means a better market than is possible for azaleas.

A few geranium species and species-crosses are popular, both for sales and show-room attraction. The Sweetheart Geranium (*Pelargonium echinatum*) is always a good seller when the little orchidlike flowers appear. The evening-scented geranium, *P. gibbosum,* is excellent for specialty work, as espaliering. *P.* × *coriandrifolium* makes a lovely bracket or basket plant, and *P. dasycaule* with its thick tortuous growth will amaze visitors to your greenhouse.

Culture for Professional Growers

Culture in the commercial establishment is the same as for the hobbyist. Quantities of plants make good sanitation all the more vital, for chance of disease increases with increase in population. If there is trouble, more often than not the remedy will be simple, although it may take time for plants to stop dying after you solve the problem. In any case, don't jump to the conclusion that some insidious disease was imported from your source of supply. This very rarely happens. If your stock looked healthy when it arrived, even though temporarily yellowed or wilted, it most likely was perfectly healthy. If you had doubts about the stock, you should have isolated it at the start and notified your supplier at once of your doubts.

Other chapters in this book deal with good culture and coping with pest and disease but here are a few suggestions on the most serious problems of commercial growing. These are (1) lack of nitrogen in the soil—a lack geraniums will not tolerate. According to Fred Bode if the pH is low, that is, much below 6 it can be remedied by applying a solution of calcium nitrate—1 tablespoonful to 1 gallon of water—or weak manure water can be substituted. If the pH is high, 6.3 to 7.5 give a solution of urea—1 teaspoon to 1 gallon of water—or a weak solution of blood meal. (2) too low pH (acidity)—if below 5.5 geraniums cannot assimilate essential food chemicals because of the form of phosphorus present at this reading; to correct this situation, apply hydrated or other lime in solution or lightly scratched into the surface of the soil. Of course, if nitrogen is lacking, you can correct that condition and raise the pH at the same time with the calcium nitrate suggested above. (3) lack of lime (calcium)—500 ppm (parts per million) are necessary for good pot culture, even though 225 ppm is sufficient in garden soils. Correct this lack the same way you raise the pH as above.

In general, light soils rapidly become deficient in nitrogen—with a maximum limit of about thirty days. Decomposed granite soils often lack zinc; sandy loams can be deficient in magnesium; soils that have been farmed often need more of the trace elements, especially copper. In general, use a *complete* fertilizer which includes trace elements. Usually humus-rich soils taken near the surface of wooded areas are well supplied with all food elements except nitrogen; yet, even the nutritive substances they have do not always suffice for good pot culture. To these add:

5 pounds bone meal or superphosphate per cubic yard (3 ounces per cubic foot)

7-10 pounds organic fertilizer as hoof and horn meal per cubic yard
   (5 to 6 ounces per cubic foot)
10 pounds dolomite or other lime per cubic yard (6 ounces per
   cubic foot)

As for disease of geraniums, you will need to keep up with litera-
ture on this subject and with the discoveries of plant pathologists.
These are important to the industry, and especially to the producer
of propagating stock. Many retail growers never see most geranium
diseases if their source of stock is good. In fact, almost all losses are
due to poor culture, but this may end in disease. *Disease seldom
strikes healthy plants.*

There are two exceptions to this statement, and the commercial
grower needs to be constantly aware of these. One is verticillium,
discovered in 1940, and fatal to geraniums but only a weakening
disease for most other crops. Verticillium takes up to eight months
to kill a plant. This means that cuttings may die during the rooting process, that saleable plants sometimes are struck down, and
that plants often are not lost until after they are planted in a customer's garden.

Before verticillium was recognized as fatal to geraniums, losses
were often blamed on bacterial stem-rot which has similar symptoms. However, verticillium is a soil-borne fungus that enters
through roots. While more than 125 kinds of plants are hosts to
verticillium, soils are more likely to be infected when composites
like dahlias have been grown in them. Soils used for the nightshade
or solanum family (tomatoes, for example) are almost as bad and
the mint family make a close third. Most commercial growers, but
not all, find that soils for potting should be sterilized (at least to
200 degrees), or used from wooded areas that are entirely weed
free.

The second important disease you need to recognize is bacterial
stem-rot, commonly known as splash-bacteria because, until recently, it was supposed to be spread almost wholly by splashing

water. Now we know that white flies spread the disease over a much wider range and much more quickly. Bacterial stem-rot is a world-wide type of bacteria, and white flies entering the greenhouse are likely to be carrying the disease. Watch for these tiny flies that look like flecks of cigarette ash. When disturbed they flit from the plant they are on to one several pots away. Plants dying from the effects of white flies never have flies on them. By the time they have killed, the flies have colonized on another plant. Losses by bacterial stem-rot go right back to cultural methods and are the end result of bad sanitation.

Selling and Advertising

Good salesmanship can be the strongest aspect of your business, beyond the primary necessity of quality plants. As a specialist, be well versed in your subject, but remember, don't let your enthusiasm run away with you so that you wear out or confuse your customers with too much talk. A novice can take in only a certain amount in a few minutes. If the discussion drifts to areas that need long explanation, suggest a book that you have available to sell. As soon as a customer reads a book on geraniums, you can be sure he is well on his way to becoming a full-fledged enthusiast—and so a more profitable customer for you.

A common weakness of plantsmen is charging too little, and so limiting their possibilities. This is the main reason that so many small nurseries are so dull and the owners so harried with no time to do interesting plant work. A realistic profit is fair, and you must be sure to get it.

Advertising is vital to your success. In periods of good seasonal sales, you can limit this to a small ad in local papers. In making up your ad, have only the word GERANIUMS set in large type. A smaller line covering the kinds you sell, as "Very Large Assortment," or, "In Bloom for Planting Now," acquaints the reader with the fact that you have what he wants. Keep name and address small; if the reader is interested, he will read carefully the who and where. Local mail-order offers can be different: the ad should contain a popular offer at a given postpaid price.

Try to write down the name and address of every customer "as a condition of his guarantee or for a drawing," or any other agreeable reason you can give. These names become your invaluable mailing list. Each spring make a mailing to this list just before sales time. A printed letter form is best; don't make this a catalog, but rather a friendly, enthusiastic invitation to come to see your interesting stock.

If you have enough stock, your letter can take the form of an invitation to an open house. Open-house programs have been successful in many areas. One concern in Michigan has open house on Mother's Day. There, planting starts just a couple of weeks after Mother's Day. In Salt Lake City a retailer holds open house before Easter. That is a locality that sells at least one-fourth of the geraniums well before planting time. In California a prominent retailer holds open house in June, and this selling in June extends the sales season. At the time of the open house retailers sometimes take orders but do not allow plants to be taken out immediately. However, most open house programs permit as many purchases as possible. Some wholesalers who supply immediate areas simply let the public come in to see the masses of color.

Growers as Lecturers

Garden clubs are a fine source of word-of-mouth publicity. Why not work up for them an interesting lecture of 35 to 45 minutes (not a minute longer), using plants or slides for demonstration. If you are a good photographer and have good slides, people will delight in them; but never show anything short of first-quality pictures. Rather, demonstrate with plants in flower or with some odd geraniums. Show a species like *Pelargonium frutetorum* to demonstrate the ancestors of our present-day geraniums. Then show 'Mrs.

Kingsley', 'Rollisson's Unique', or some of the other species-type flowering scented-leaveds that were the rage in the 1800s. Discuss the single zonals, the ivy-leaveds, and the regals that were developed through the middle 1800s, and the fancy-leaveds and double zonals developed from the middle to late 1800s. Touch on how all this resulted in the present multiplicity of flower forms—Rosebuds, Cactus-flowering, Bird's-Egg, and other unusual classes.

After bringing your story up to the present-day rugged mass-blooming zonals and the giant ruffled regals, give a brief but understandable few minutes to soils, proper watering, and aeration. Demonstrate how to make a cutting, using actual material. If there is time, suggest new ways to use geraniums in the landscape as well as in containers.

My last word on this business of "going commercial" is that few people ever get wealthy from geraniums, although many do very well—and some have had remarkable returns from growing fields turned into real estate. However, it is astonishing how many *healthy* eighty- and ninety-year old men and women are active in horticulture—aren't these the rich ones, indeed?

Chapter NINETEEN

How to Photograph Your Geraniums

Gardening and photography are companion hobbies. At one time or another most of us have the desire to preserve forever some flower, plant, or garden scene in its moment of glory. Fortunately, this is possible by means of a camera and today's high fidelity films. The geranium hobby has hardly gone full circle until you have learned to photograph your best plants. In years to come, as you turn through album pages or review color slides on a screen, you will have the satisfying experience of seeing your own geranium hall of fame.

There are practical reasons, also, for learning to use a camera. At a flower show or on a garden tour you may see a specimen plant or a display that you want to copy in your own garden. A click of the shutter and you have more information on record than you could achieve by taking notes.

Color enlargements of your best geranium pictures will make

handsome wall prints. A color portrait 11 x 14 inches, made from a 35mm film transparency, costs about eight dollars. Smaller color prints are available for less than two dollars, making possible a veritable gallery of geraniums to decorate a favorite room. Naturally, if you are going to make an investment like this, you will view the slides critically through a projector to be sure they are in razor-sharp focus. The man in your camera shop can be a big help in selecting the slides that will be most likely to enlarge into dramatic prints.

Every artist who grows geraniums, and every gardener who dreams of one day painting pictures, can make good use of color photography. Consider, for example, a regal specimen, in full bloom in spring. You cannot possibly find time to paint it then, but you can make a color transparency or print. When you are ready to work with oil paints or watercolors, the photograph serves as a true-to-life model.

A visual record of your progress with geraniums helps you share the pleasures of this hobby with friends and correspondents all over the world. Photographs may be enclosed in letters or shown to others through the pages of the International Geranium Society's magazine, *Geraniums Around the World.* That publication always welcomes black-and-white photographs in sharp focus, accompanied by a few words of description or explanation, and manuscripts explaining details of various phases of geranium culture. As you gain more experience as a grower, a series of how-to-do-it photographs might be an interesting assignment for you and your camera. For instance, you could show your favorite method of taking and rooting cuttings. Start with a picture of the needed equipment and tools arranged in a pleasing composition. Then follow with a series of photographs showing essential steps. Finish with a portrait of a mature plant you have grown from cuttings by your method.

If you wish to succeed at growing geraniums as a business, you will need photographs of your plants. Good pictures of well-grown geraniums can be invaluable sales builders.

Selecting a Camera

The kind of camera to use will depend to some extent on what sort of pictures you want to make. Pictures to place in an album, color film slides for projection at home or for illustrated lectures, color prints and enlargements for albums and display, and black-and-white enlargements suitable for magazine reproduction—each may call for somewhat different camera equipment. Simple cameras, costing under twenty dollars, take excellent flower pictures, though usually not close-up. Talk to a reputable dealer in photographic equipment. Most horticultural photographers prefer a high-quality, single-lens, reflex-type camera. You look through the lens and see the subject in full color as well as the size of the resulting photograph right up to the instant when the picture is taken. This is a great aid to composition and focusing.

Regardless of the eventual use of your pictures, you will probably want some close-ups in addition to the usual views of individual plants and home and garden scenes. For close-ups, a special lens of long focal length is a useful but expensive piece of equipment; your camera dealer can advise you about this, too. For a simple camera, you will have to experiment with an inexpensive portrait lens used as an attachment to the regular lens.

Pointers for Success

Whether you take a distance shot of geraniums growing in the outdoor garden, a portrait of one specimen plant, or a tight close-up view of a flower, quality depends on a balance of several factors. These include arrangement of the subject, choice of background, camera angle, composition, lighting, focus, and correct exposure.

Use a background that is plain, not distracting, one that will clearly delineate the leaves and flower parts. Pastel blue matteboard from an art store makes an excellent background. If you are photographing in natural color, a yellow, blue, or green background may provide effective color contrast with the plant. Usually dark-colored backgrounds are effective for plants with pale or white flowers, and the reverse when dark-colored plants are photographed.

When photographing in black and white, consider the tonal values of various colors. If you use common black-and-white film to photograph an orange- or red-flowered geranium, remember that it will reproduce red flowers and green leaves in almost indistinguishable tones of gray. Expert photographers use a green filter over the lens in such cases, so that red flowers will be reproduced by a lighter tone of gray.

Photographs of white or pale yellow flowers on plants with dark green leaves may show excessive tonal contrast. The light-colored flowers record much more readily on the film than the green leaves, so that the resulting prints show details in the light flowers with the foliage only a cloudy mass, or else details in the leaf and stems while the flowers are "washed out" and rather formless. The way to avoid this result when photographing white or pale-yellow flowers is to use "flat" or front lighting and reduce the contrast of the illumination even further by diffusing it with cheesecloth or something similar. Avoiding underexposure will also help to prevent excessive contrast.

Part of the fun of photography comes in experimenting to obtain various effects. The selection of different camera angles produces different results. Sometimes a plant looks best when photographed straight on, but if it is very tall, try getting down low and photographing up in order to dramatize the height. Often an extremely odd angle may be necessary to record certain parts of plant or flower, particularly in close-up views. As in any other hobby, practice makes perfect, and your unsuccessful pictures, if studied closely, will give you clues to making better pictures next time.

Lighting variations affect photographs as much as the angle from which you shoot. Handbooks on photographic lighting prove as helpful for flower photography as they do for portraits of people. Back-lighting or spot-lighting from the rear may be necessary to show the hair on stems or petals, or to outline the parts of flowers. Outdoor sunlight may provide the quality of illumination needed in some cases, but frequently it is necessary, even outdoors, to use a supplementary light source in the form of a reflector, flash bulb, or electronic flash lamp. When a supplementary flash is used in shooting an outdoor scene, the camera setting is not affected since the overall illumination is unchanged. For close-ups, it usually is necessary to subdue the supplementary or filler light with a diffuser, such as a handkerchief placed over the flash attachment.

Today's fast films, sensitive to relatively small amounts of light, have provided increasing opportunity to photograph with existing light. Geraniums growing by the light of a window can be photographed, for example, as they look to us every day. They need not be flood-lighted unnaturally to produce enough illumination to suit the needs of the available film and camera.

Composition is a challenging aspect of good photography. Many technically excellent photographs would be vastly improved by a slightly different arrangement of the scene elements. Brilliant color tends to dazzle the senses and often makes us overlook composition. Consequently it is a good idea for beginners to start with a simple and inexpensive camera. Then composition and lighting can be practiced, and the mechanics of lens focus and the adjustment of exposure mastered without a large initial investment.

Use of a tripod is vital to good composition and virtually a necessity in flower photography, indoors or out. Set the camera on a tripod and move it or the plant (if the plant is in a pot) about until you find the best camera angle to show what you want to show. This is determined by looking through the finder lens, or simply by closing one eye and sighting with the other from alongside the camera and as close to the lens as possible. In this way, you will continually see things about the composition that require changing—a leaf turned the wrong way, a fleck of soil on a petal or the table, or a flower that does not stand just right. If you must put down a hand-held camera to make such adjustments, arranging the picture can become so irksome that good composition may never be achieved.

Perfect focusing is no problem with either a reflex camera or a "range-finder" camera. Even with such precision equipment, expert photographers often use a tape measure to check the lens-to-subject distance.

A light meter is a necessity to determine the proper exposure, but modern cameras have built-in photoelectric exposure controls that relieve the photographer of concern about exposure. When using a simple camera, or when making flash exposures with any camera, it is good practice to take one picture using the setting indicated by the meter, then one at the setting above, and a third at the setting below. This procedure multiplies your chances of obtaining a properly exposed picture, particularly with color photography, and generally two or more of your pictures will be usable.

Chapter TWENTY

Pest and Disease to Avoid or Control

The pests and diseases of plants has never been an area of major interest for me, although for some amateurs—and I think of African violet enthusiasts—it seems to have a great fascination. But then the African violet attracts more enemies and gets more ills than the geranium. Indeed, the careful window gardener or the small greenhouse owner with a limited number of geraniums will probably never become acqainted with the various unpleasantnesses considered here. Except for verticillium and similar soil-borne fungi, good culture avoids all, and I am told that whatever the species of nematodes is that thrives in California, they do not attack geraniums.

My own experience among these horrors has been happily limited. I know about edema on the ivy-leaveds because of my previous tendency to overwater and overmist plants, especially when I am nervous—which seems to be most of the time, especially

268

if I am writing a book. And I know about spider-mites because they are a frequent end-result for plants in an advanced state of edema. For these Sel-Kaps and Scope give me new hope. I know about fasciation or "witches brooms." I have found it twice on zonals but not on dwarf zonals, which are supposed to be more prone to attack than the standards. However, the eye was hardly quicker than the hand in giving an immediate heave-ho to the fasciated plants which then had same-day removal by the garbage man. As for white flies, I am sure they would never have found my geraniums if the nearby heliotrope and lantana had not issued the invitation.

In a word, or say a nutshell, avoid trouble by obtaining plants from reputable growers and most of them are just that—and then take care to provide regularly the prime requisites of good culture: full light or sun in season; water and extra feeding *as needed;* and a fresh atmosphere. (For detailed scientific information consult the manual "Geraniums" presently available for $2.00 from the Editor, John W. Mastalerz, 207 Tyson Building, The Pennsylvania State University, University Park, Pennsylvania; make check payable to the Pennsylvania Flower Growers.)

Actually, when plants flower sparsely or not all, they probably haven't "got" anything, but are just suffering from a poor environment—maybe it's too warm, especially at night in a living-room window in cold weather, or perhaps plants in active growth are hungry and want a square meal plus more sunlight. Through dull weeks in January and February in the East, without fluorescent lights, a geranium has to be supercharged to put on much of a show in the average home.

Prof. Frank P. McWhorter, to whom I am particularly indebted for information on the virus diseases of geraniums, writes that these are principally problems for wholesalers who grow cuttings in the field and for florists who handle a great many plants in green-houses. The amateur needs to know symptoms simply to avoid buying virus-infected plants. The responsibility for controlling virus diseases really rests on the commercial man.

Prof. McWhorter is presently examining a strange bacterial malady, the "fasciation" disease, that occurs sporadically on the zonals; he finds it particularly on the dwarf zonals. In fact, there is some evidence that the fasciation bacteria is partly responsible for their being dwarfs. This may be a case where a little disease is a fine thing, as with the serrated petals of some Fiats and the brilliant zoning of some of the fancy-leaved geraniums.

DISEASES

BACTERIAL LEAF-SPOT AND STEM-ROT (*Xanthomonas pelargoni*)

Symptoms: Serious and contagious, primarily a disease of the zonals and ivy-leaveds; domesticums are resistant. There is an indefinite latent stage when a plant can be infected and infect other plants while showing no symptoms. Cuttings from such plants may rot, sometimes just before rooting.

The *active* stem-rot stage may be preceded by a leaf-spot stage with variable symptoms, but usually there is first a sudden yellowing or wilting, or both, of lower leaves, often on just one branch. The yellowing or wilting is rapid, with a noticeable change in twenty-four hours. At this time, or within the next day or two, water-soaked areas appear on the stem, usually just below points of attachment of the affected leaves. These areas enlarge, turn brown, often split and exude a very infectious bacterial ooze. Later stems blacken and shrivel, sometimes retaining a few unhealthy leaves at the top. The sudden yellowing or wilting of lower leaves, and water-soaked areas on the stem, occurring together, give reliable diagnosis.

Control: In the latent stage, the disease is spread by tools used in taking cuttings and in pruning. In the leaf-spot stage and stem-rot stage, it is spread by splashing water, by white flies, slugs and snails, by handling, and probably through the air when plants are crowded. The period of bacterial ooze is the most dangerous. Soil in which an infected plant has grown can transmit the disease to a clean plant or infect the potting soil supply.

There is no cure. Discard the soil and sterilize the used containers. Immediately destroy all infected plants and wash your hands before handling other plants. If a knife is used for taking cuttings, it can be sterilized as laboratory workers do, by dipping the blade into strong alcohol which is burned off by touching the tip to a flame. Less risky and perhaps as effective in sterilizing the knife is a rinse in laundry bleach, after which the blade is wiped dry.

Keep in mind that the responsible bacteria is everywhere and when soil is low in nutrient content and the air is warm, humid, and stale, the stage is set for bacterial leaf-spot and stem-rot. Bordeaux and other copper sprays are used in commercial greenhouses to control the bacteria.

BOTRYTIS BLIGHT

Gray mold is caused by the fungus, *Botrytis cinerea,* which lives primarily on dead and decaying leaves, flowers, and broken stems. or stubs left when cuttings are taken. Under poor culture, succulent growth of healthy plants is subject to attack.

Symptoms: Flowers fade and dry prematurely; central flowers often are the first affected. In high humidity, gray-brown masses of spores may cover blossoms and flowers mat together. Next, botrytis-blighted petals fall on leaves and leaf-spot appears, often in the outline of the flower part that fell upon it. Wet leaves and high humidity cause spots to enlarge, becoming irregular, brown, and water-soaked, and covered with gray-brown spore masses. Air currents carry these spores to many plants, as does splashing water or handling.

Spores of botrytis are so generally prevalent that even if they do not become active on mature plants, they often lodge on stems, and when cuttings are made, the spores germinate, causing a cutting rot, light to dark brown, not to be confused with the shiny black of pythium black leg.

Control: Promptly remove all affected parts. Space out plants to allow freer air circulation, provide ample sunshine, avoid excessive heat and humidity and keep water off the foliage. Remove withered flower heads and yellowing leaves.

Botrytis is not likely to trouble the hobbyist. In a large greenhouse, apply a protective fungicidal spray of zineb or captan every week.

Virus Diseases

Ring-spot types of the disease called "yellows" are prevalent in the Eastern states, and leaf-breaking types are most serious in the West. In ring-spot, leaf areas become yellow in circular or irregular areas from very small to very large, and center along main leaf veins, forming arcs, half arcs, rings, and concentric rings. The symptoms of virus infection are characteristic of the virus present. Some cause "mosaic," a mottling of the leaf with light green and dark green areas. Some cause "leaf curl" (also termed "measles" or "crinkle"), showing white spots up to ¼-inch diameter accompanied by ruffled, crinkled, malformed, or dwarfed leaves.

The yellowing of leaves, called chlorosis because chlorophyll is absent from affected areas, can be light green in young leaves, and sometimes you have to hold old leaves up to the light to see the spots. Heat above 70 degrees F generally produces clear yellow markings; at 60 to 65 degrees F the virus is masked. In a favorable environment, chlorosis often shows within seven to fourteen days on mature leaves directly below a pinch.

Etiolation, a complete or almost complete lack of chlorophyll in the upper leaves, is a form of chlorosis, and the condition is increased in constant high heat, as 85 degrees F. However attractive this "albino" effect may be, after four or five weeks the pure white areas give way to browning and desiccation.

Control: There is no cure for virus disease. Immediately discard and burn infected plants. Virus infection is spread primarily by insects, and by careless handling and the use of infected tools. Insure good culture and take cuttings only from plants that appear healthy.

FASCIATION

At this time there is no agreement on fasciation, which is a proliferation of small shoots and buds usually from the stem near the soil. Some growers claim that a number of their most popular commercial varieties almost always show some fasciation, even under controlled conditions in spotless greenhouses, and that if the growths are *completely* removed—both above and below the soil line—plants continue their healthy development. Mary Ellen Ross wonders if fasciation is not stimulated by the use of hormones on cuttings. Commercial growers are advised to destroy plants infected by *Corneybasterium fasciana,* the cause of this seldom seen disease.

CROWN GALL

Symptoms: Galls and knots on roots and crown of plant are caused by *Agrobacterium tumefaciens,* a bacterial disease. Growth is checked.

Control: Plants should be destroyed, the pots and soil sterilized or discarded.

CUTTING ROT OR BLACK LEG

Caused by several species of the *Pythium* fungus, this disease rarely attacks when sanitary propagation procedures are followed.

Symptoms: Brown water-soaked areas at base of cuttings blacken and become slimy for some 3 inches upwards. Leaves turn yellow,

·petioles rot, leaves fall, and cuttings decay. Easily confused with the cutting-rot phase of bacterial stem-rot; both diseases may be present in the same block of plants. Black leg has a coal-black, shiny, slimy, wet appearance; rot progresses rapidly, sometimes killing cuttings within a week. In contrast, bacterial stem-rot is dull to dark brown and progresses slowly not killing for several weeks.

Control: Take disease-free cuttings from the tops of healthy plants; dip them in a fungicide, as zineb (Dithane Z-78, Parzate-65 per cent wettable powder); or captan (50 per cent wettable powder), 8 teaspoons per gallon; or ferbam (Fermate 76 per cent wettable powder), 6 teaspoons per gallon. Insert cuttings in clean coarse sand. Or use coarse vermiculite, which is sterile and can be purchased in small quantities at garden-supply stores. Avoid propagating geraniums during hot, damp weather.

Edema (Oedema)

This unsightly and common condition particularly in ivy-leaved geraniums is generally considered to be entirely a cultural problem, not a disease, although it looks like a disease.

Symptoms: Water-soaked spots that get reddish brown and corky appear on leaves that turn yellow and fall. Corky ridges may develop on petioles and stems.

Control: Avoid overwatering at any time but particularly in cloudy, damp weather. Raise heat, lower humidity, space out plants, and in window gardens do not mist foliage. Be sure soil is not deficient in potassium or calcium. In cloudy weather in late winter if soil is moist and warm, and air is moist and cool, plants rapidly absorb water but loss from leaves is slow; extra moisture backs up and cells burst. Indoor plants usually recover when set outside, but heavy rains and hot muggy weather may produce edema in basket plants outdoors in summer. When you bring affected plants indoors in fall, cut out worst areas but don't entirely denude plants—they must have *some* leaves—then grow them very dry.

Give all light and air possible. Do not mist tops and carefully apply water only to the surface of the soil. Water well then let drain. And don't water again until soil is very dry. With such treatment, my plants have recovered and put up clean new growth —but not quickly.

Zonals are sometimes troubled by edema when pots are set on wet, spongy material like peatmoss; pea-gravel is less likely to promote edema. Heating coils or pipes under greenhouse benches or heat from a radiator under a window garden may encourage edema. To avoid it, place a buffer such as air-conditioning wool or building paper, even a board, between the heat source and the surface on which pots rest.

William E. Schmidt, a California hybridist, writes me that he is sure that more than careful watering is involved. "For one thing, high humidity such as we have here most of the year is one reason for edema. Then, too, a fungus may enter the open edema spots and cause a worse condition than the edema itself, although not a fatal condition. There seems to be a correlation between edema and mites—possibly the open spots attract mites, I don't know. But this certainly would be a worthy subject for university investigation." And to the last, we will agree.

Verticillium Wilt

This is not associated with poor culture, but is a fungus disease that kills even well-grown plants if infected soils are used (or if host plants are nearby). The composites—chrysanthemums and dahlias; the solanums—tomatoes and potatoes; as well as the mints, are notable carriers.

Symptoms: Pale streaks occur along principal veins of leaves, sometimes accompanied by slight wilting. Later bright yellow spots appear on the streaks near center of leaf blades or on and near edges of leaves. Vigorous plants may show symptoms suddenly with yellow spots at points where leaf blades join petioles. Leaves fall and bare stems are exposed. Decay begins at the ends of affected shoots. Partially decayed stems affected by a bacterial blight may recover and produce terminal leaves but not if verticillium is the bacteria. Verticillium may also cause stubby, dwarfed growth with numerous very short nodes and small leaves but no wilt.

Control: Burn infected plants. Buy plants from reputable growers who take every precaution to provide disease-free stock. Use soil sterilized to 200 degrees F. Try to develop a keen eye for signs of disease; be sure to take cuttings only from healthy plants.

PESTS

Although *possibilities* are numerous, few pests prove troublesome since all-purpose house-plant or greenhouse sprays—applied in time—rout the invaders. Generally speaking, malathion may be used safely and satisfactorily to control most pests. It is an organic phosphate that is inoffensive, and almost no one is allergic to it. The best method of cleanup for the hobbyist is dipping a badly infested plant in a solution of malathion, or malathion and DDT, or in Isotox, or any combination of these. A very small portion of Dreft or Vel in the solution insures complete coverage.

In the West, Fred Bode says commercial growers can now control most pests without resorting to such chlorinated insecticides as DDT, Toxaphene, or Kelthane. The only insecticide used on the vast Bode fields is a new organic phosphate (that geraniums like) in the form of a systemic poison. This develops an internal protection but is so highly toxic its use is restricted to professional growers. Where chlorines severely stunt geraniums and cause yellowing of foliage, the organic phosphates, which are more expensive, applied to roots seem to promote health. However, except for malathion, sprays of highly toxic organic phosphates are dangerous to man and death to valuable predators, just as the chlorines are.

Proper use of a systemic insecticide absorbed by plant roots makes it possible to check small infestations and yet not injure natural predators. Thus, wasps, which search plants for worms or moths, and ladybird beetles, which go after mites and the eggs of mites, are valuable beyond any comparison with chemical controls. Thrips, mites, and other minute pests have little chance against the industrious ladybird beetles.

Scope is the trade name of one systemic insecticide widely available today in granular form. For potted plants, the present label recommendation is one rounded teaspoonful per 6-inch pot, mixed well into the top soil and drenched with water. Roots drawing the chemical up into the plant make its juices toxic to sucking insects that try to feed on it, as aphids, spider mites, thrips, and white flies.

While systemics are today's brightest hope among pest controls, gardeners will be pleased to hear that Japanese beetles are poisoned by the blossoms of white geraniums. In a recent experiment, 51 to 80 per cent of red spiders and aphids on cotton plants were killed within twenty-four hours after plants were covered with a 2 per cent emulsion spray of geranium oil—or isn't using the geranium oil in a *spray* "organically" fair?

Aphids

Symptoms: Tiny black or green bugs (called "plant lice") on new growth weaken the plant, distort foliage, and may transmit virus.

Control: If you have only a few plants, plunge stems into warm soapy water. Hold a thick cover of newspaper over the soil. Usually this does the trick. Otherwise, use a house plant bug bomb, or malathion as spray or dip. A systemic like Scope, *applied according to package directions,* is also effective and not so messy but dangerous to use in the home.

Caterpillars

Symptoms: Rolled or webbed areas on the underside of leaves indicate the presence of leaf rollers and leaf tiers, generally light green. In autumn, cabbage looper may also be present.

Control: Hand pick from a few infested plants; for many plants, spray with DDT or methoxychlor.

MEALYBUGS

Symptoms: Colonies of white, cottony, sucking insects cluster in leaf axils, behind stipules, between veins on underside of leaves. In severe buildup, sticky honeydew is secreted on which sooty fungus thrives.

Control: Go after first offenders with cotton swab dipped in rubbing alcohol or strong witch hazel. Use malathion as spray or dip; for a heavy infestation, three applications at ten-day intervals may be required.

ORANGE TORTRIX

Symptoms: Tender new growth is damaged and leaves are webbed with caterpillars inside, whitish, yellowish, or greenish, with brown heads. Disturbed, they wriggle or dangle by a silken thread. They bore into buds and terminal shoots.

Control: Use malathion or DDD.

PLUME MOTH

Known from coast to coast, this is prevalent where vegetables are grown. Brown moth looks like an airplane when it rests with wings extended for an overall inch, with wings at right angles to the needlelike body. In flight wings are plumelike.

Symptoms: Half-inch worm, pointed on both ends, drills through stem crosswise at node so that hole is hidden by petioles. Seldom more than one egg is laid in each young flowerhead; worm drills through bud once, making a tiny crosswise hole. Flowers are distorted, or turn brown or pale yellow.

Control: If you see a plume moth in the greenhouse, kill it immediately, or spray with DDT to kill both moth and worm. If you suspect moths, examine outdoor plants before bringing any of them in, and treat accordingly.

RED SPIDER

Symptoms: A generally dull look and a grayish-yellow tint to the leaves are first signs. In heavy infestations, you can see webbing on underside of leaves. To see the "spiders" you need a magnifying glass.

Control: To prevent spread of mites, remove and burn affected leaves. Hot, dry conditions encourage red spider. In hot summer weather, try to keep greenhouse bench or ground outside moist, not wet. Spray with malathion or Isotox, use Spectracide which controls both mites and insects, or consider a systemic like Scope for effective mite control over a period of weeks.

ROOT KNOT

Symptoms: Plants look sickly but no disease or insect is apparent. Examination of roots reveals unnatural galls or swollen portions; nematodes may be present.

Control: Immediately burn infested plants; do not take cuttings from them. Use sterilized soil.

SLUGS AND SNAILS

Symptoms: Holes and notches in leaves, trails of gray, slimy mucous indicate these pests are present.

Control: Use commercial bait containing metaldehyde and calcium arsenate. If infestation is serious, spray or dust soil surface and injured plants with metaldehyde. Be sure you are not growing plants too warm and humid. Keep debris cleaned up.

TOBACCO BUDWORM

Symptoms: Holes in buds and terminal shoots or ragged areas in unfolding leaves and flowers are caused by ½-inch greenish or pinkish caterpillar. This has emerged from an egg laid by a fawn-colored moth. In southern California, damage appears in April or May and continues into December. Caterpillars are tiny when hatched; they bore into the side of an opening bud and feed on inner petals and stamens; they may damage several flowers before they grow long enough to live outside. Even then they are hidden in the center of the umbel and difficult to get at.

Control: Hand-gather eggs and worms from a few plants or apply a 5 per cent DDT dust weekly. Use DDD if the orange tortrix is present also, or malathion, but this is less effective than DDD or DDT.

WHITE FLY

Symptoms: When a plant is shaken, tiny white insects swarm out. Leaves are pale, stippled, and sticky (sometimes with sooty mold) on upper surfaces. It is the pale wingless nymphs on the underside of leaves that do the damage and excrete the honeydew. Worst of all, white flies spread bacterial stem-rot.

Control: Use a malathion spray or dip every five days until all traces of flies are gone. If you spray, be sure to cover underside of foliage. A systemic insecticide like Scope gives effective control of white flies for weeks.

CROOKNECK

A condition in which flower stems droop down, not caused by disease or insects. It is usually the result of dryness when buds are forming. Sometimes in bright spring weather if plants wilt a little in the sun, crookneck occurs even though the soil is not dry. Some varieties, notably 'Olympic Red', are more prone to this reaction than others.

Chapter TWENTY-ONE

$\mathcal{S}$ocieties, $\mathcal{M}$agazines, and $\mathcal{S}$hows

Your pleasure in pelargoniums may come various ways. If you must be among people more than you like, the time you spend working with your plants is an occasion of spiritual resource. Alone, you relax and renew your strength. Many gardeners turn to their flowers for this special and excellent reason.

Others want to share their delight. They incline to take their avocation more seriously, perhaps as a hobby to be pursued along rather definite lines. They want to study this plant group and compare their experiences in growing geraniums with those similarly enthralled.

With both attitudes I have sympathy but since the Alone-Group is a law unto itself, it is the Share-Group only to whom these further suggestions for enjoyment are offered. With its arrangement of classes the pelargonium is a natural for the collector. But you must specialize or else be overwhelmed by the material available.

281

It has been estimated there are, including synonyms, some eight thousand species and varieties.

An obvious way to proceed is to collect only garden or *P.* × *hortorum* varieties. Then reduce choices to either singles or doubles and perhaps in one or two colors only, as pink and lavender singles, or red and white doubles. Or what appeals more to me is a collection of unusual kinds, such as Bird's Egg, Cactus-flowered and Rosebud or these plus or minus the dwarfs.

With the scenteds you could concentrate on the rose or mint section or the oak-leaved kinds if the whole seventy-five scenteds couldn't find house and garden room with you. This class is delightful and besides you seem to meet such amusing people who are thoroughly concerned with it!

Or, how about the colored-leaved varieties? There are not too many of these around today. Yet once you are mindful of them, you will find yourself discovering an unknown every time you take a trip. This happened to me when I visited a remote garden in Santa Barbara and again when I just happened to stop in a New England village beyond Springfield.

Because they are difficult to grow well in the East, the ivy-leaveds and regals are better left to Western collectors. It would be fun among regals to round up the darker ones or the near-whites. And this would lead, as it has most of the regal enthusiasts I've known, right into hybridizing, another pleasant aspect of pelargoniums as a hobby.

But long before you reach this point you will want to compare notes with others who are growing these plants seriously. Perhaps you can interest your local garden club in taking on geraniums as a project for several years. Members then can divide into groups for investigation and comparative growing of the different classifications. This seems to me an excellent way to channel garden club effort. And it is always interesting to the gardeners concerned since practically everyone loves geraniums.

Flower show committees have discovered this. Boston had an exhibit of scenteds some years ago that drew crowds who practically defoliated the plants pinching the leaves to identify scents. And now, the geranium has been discovered by arrangers. It is a "homey" flower, they find, with special affinity for containers of wood, copper, brass, and iron, and unexpectedly good for contemporary designs, too. Arrangements featuring geraniums appear more and more frequently in show schedules.

Of course you will want to join the International Geranium Society and so share in this delightful world-wide interest in your favorite plant. There's a quarterly magazine, that is sent to members, with interesting articles from growers, far and wide—both amateur and commercial. When I read my copy, I always feel the world is a friendlier—and safer—place. People who direct their energies to *growing* are rarely the ones bent on destroying.

Besides the magazine, every year since 1953 a convention has been held, and from 1954 on, also a national geranium show. There are members in nearly every state, and many foreign countries are also represented. The Society's full range of activities includes regional directors, affiliation with other plant societies, nomenclature studies, question and answer departments—all this beside the magazine, "Geraniums Around the World."

With so many benefits, you'll probably want to send your check for $4.00 right off to the Membership Secretary, Mrs. Vernon Ireland, 1413 Bluff Drive, Santa Barbara, California. You will be in mighty nice company if you do!

How to Ship Geraniums

Increasing interest in geraniums, spurred by correspondence with other growers, leads naturally to a desire to exchange or share plants and cuttings. If your stock is pest- and disease-free, you can send it by mail within your state without a special permit. To ship out-of-state, it will be necessary for a government inspector to ex-

Figure 72. How to Wrap a Plant. Label the plant and cover the soil with a wad of moist sphagnum moss. Slip pot into a plastic bag; secure with rubber bands. Roll in two or three sheets of newspaper. Fold up paper at the bottom; leave open at top; fasten with rubber band or string. *Stand upright* in a strong carton with more newspaper wedged around plants. Seal with gummed tape and put label *on the top* of the box.

amine and approve your plants. Get in touch with the Department of Agriculture in your state to find out about this.

Fresh cuttings, rooted or unrooted, are prepared for mailing by wrapping a handful of moist sphagnum moss around the base of each and extending the moss up the stem for about 2 inches. Cover the moss with a square of aluminum foil crumpled around it, or use a piece of polyethylene held in place with a rubber band. Roll in a piece of newspaper, leaving the top open so that air can reach the leaves. Pack the wrapped cuttings in a corrugated shipping container of adequate size. Wad pieces of crumpled or shredded newspaper around the cuttings to hold them firm in the box. Check this by shaking the box vigorously several times, adding more packing until there is no shifting about inside.

Geranium plants are usually at a good size for shipping when they are growing well in 2¼-inch plastic pots. Water the night before or far enough ahead for the soil to be evenly moist, neither dry nor dripping wet. Thrust a label down into the soil of each plant. Pack a layer of barely moist sphagnum moss over the soil in each pot, tucking it in around stem and pot rim. Slip each pot inside a small plastic bag, and fasten this securely with a rubber band around the stem at top of the pot. Or you can wrap the pot in waxed paper, fastening at the top with a rubber band or in aluminum foil carefully crimped into place over the rim and close to the stem.

Next, roll each plant in two or three sheets of newspaper, until four or five inches of paper remain. Fold up the lower end neatly around the bottom of the pot, but leave the top open as you finish rolling. Fasten the paper with rubber band or string, just above the pot rim so the paper wrinkles in sufficiently to hold the plant in place. *Stand upright* in shipping container, and wad crumpled newspaper into spaces until plants are held securely in place.

Close the lid and apply gummed tape carefully so that no corners or tag ends are left to invite damage in transit. In warm

Figure 73. For the Santa Barbara, California, Flower Show, geraniums are exhibited in pockets carved out of a big piece of feather rock—'Dark Beauty' at top and lower right, 'Pink Harry Hieover' center, and 'Mrs. Pollock' below left. Photo by Hort-Pix.

weather, punch some holes in the upper part of the shipping container to admit fresh air. Put the address label on the top of the box. This way there is good chance that in the handling of the box, it will be kept right side up.

One grower who ships geraniums all over the country recommends that they be sent Insured Parcel Post, Special Handling. This way is convenient, inexpensive, and about as fast as First Class Mail. Special Delivery is advisable for long distances. The extra cost of 30 to 45 cents may save a full day in transit time. If you ship valuable varieties for a distance, Air Parcel Post is the answer; it is fast but expensive.

Usually plants show some reaction to shipping. Plants that are in transit three days or less usually show little effect of shipment except some rumpling of the leaves and an occasional broken flower stalk. Plants that are in transit four to six days may show some yellowing of the leaves. There may also be blighted flower buds. It is normal for the plants to seem to get worse for a few days after they are unpacked. Often some leaves are lost. This sort of damage is not so serious as it appears. Usually the plants leaf out quickly, and often are bushier than they would have been otherwise. Flowers that open in transit or shortly after arrival may be abnormal in color or form.

Geranium Show Business

Success with geraniums and membership in the International Geranium Society can lead to but one thing if you are the outgoing type: Show Business. The Society, under the leadership of Harry P. May, chairman of the Judging Standards Committee, has issued some suggestions for setting up and judging geranium and pelargonium shows.

General rules and the organizational structure are the same for a geranium show as for any public display of flowers where entries

Figure 74. 'Gay Baby', the miniature ivy-leaved geranium with lilac-tinted flowers, is appropriately placed in a cradle for an exhibit in a California flower show. Plant by Clara May, cradle by Harry Neal. Photo by Fred Bode.

are made on a competitive as well as an educational basis. Classifications for a geranium show will be based to some extent on the type and number of entries expected. Mr. May, writing in "Geraniums Around the World," suggests these classifications:

CLASS

1 Zonal, single flowered
2 Zonal, double flowered
3 Pelargonium (Lady Washington)
4 Ivy Leaf
5 Fancy Leaf (bicolor or gold leaf)
6 Fancy Leaf (tricolor)
7 Scented Leaf
8 Dwarf Zonal, single flowered
9 Dwarf Zonal, double flowered
10 Any Other

This system can be doubled in scope by having one set of classes for 4-inch pots or under, and another set for larger containers. You will probably want to add other classes for flower arrangements, for hanging baskets, totems, standards, espaliers, bonsai, and other specialties.

Judging for your geranium show can be based on the official score card of the Society, reproduced for your convenience in this chapter. To merit an award, the Society suggests this scale of points:

1st Place	90 to 100
2nd Place	85 or over
3rd Place	75 or over

Honorable Mention: An excellent plant that for some reason did not quite capture 3rd Place

INTERNATIONAL GERANIUM SOCIETY
Official Score Card—November 1, 1962

CLASSES	ZONALS		DWARFS							Geraniaceae Various genera and species and cultivars
	Hortorum	Fancy Leaf	Semi-dwarf	Dwarf (Emphasis on Dwarfness)	Min.	Rosebud, Cactus, etc.	Regal	Ivy Leaf Peltatum	Scented Leaf	
PLANT Condition, form, size, floriferousness	30%	30%	35%	40%	40%	25%	20%	30%	30%	30%
UMBEL Size, form (and number of flowers)	20%	5%	10%	10%	10%	15%	20%	20%	5%	10%
FLOWER Form, substance and size	20%	10%	15%	15%	15%	30%	20%	15%	5%	15%
FLOWER COLOR	20%	5%	20%	15%	15%	20%	25%	15%	10%	15%
FOLIAGE Typical form and size	10%	50%	20%	20%	20%	10%	15%	20%	50%	30%
TOTAL PER CENT	100%	100%	100%	100%	100%	100%	100%	100%	100%	100%

A seedling must be tested for a minimum of two years and will be judged against a typical plant of its class.

A seedling should be scored against a typical plant of its class.

Join the International Set

There is a world-wide interest in geraniums, and as your desire for sharing the hobby increases, you may want to join other groups. There's the Geranium Society of England, and they, too, publish a most interesting *Bulletin.* To subscribe, send a Post Office Money Order for 10 shillings to the Editor, Mr. R. P. Burrows, 4 Old Hale Way, Hitchen, Herts, England. It was Mr. Burrows who wrote me that he kept two copies of my geranium book on hand, one he read on Sunday, and one on weekdays, so, of course, you know how I feel about him.

The Australian Geranium Society has grown steadily since its formation in 1956. Early *Newsletters* have given way to a quarterly *Journal,* issued March, June, September, and December. For information about membership, write to Mr. W. H. Heytman, International Correspondent, the Australian Geranium Society, P.O. Box 57, Armadale SE 3, Victoria, Australia.

The Australian Geranium Society N.S.W. Division is another society with many American members. It publishes a quarterly *Journal* and lends color transparencies of plants to members. For membership information, write to Mrs. G. Thomas, President, The Australian Geranium Society N.S.W. Division, 11 Watson Street, Neutral Bay, New South Wales, Australia.

To all of you garden enthusiasts who travel, or plan to, let me say you have friends everywhere, though you may not know it. Just let the secretaries of plant societies know you are coming and what you want to see, and you will discover that the way will be open.

Plants are indeed harbingers of friendship.

Finder's List of Species and Selected Varieties

From each classification of geraniums, I have selected and described those that are both desirable and available. From these lists, you can select with confidence plants of the types you like and in the colors you prefer. Some varieties have remained on the lists now for twenty years; many are newcomers, particularly among the ivy-leaved and the regals, for there has been considerable hybridizing in these classifications since the 1957 edition of this book was published. The zonals have also been supplemented and, in the intervening eight years, the dwarfs have become one of the most important of all groups. These small plants are indeed attractive with their abundance of bloom while the plants themselves require so little space. There are fewer new ones among the fancy-leaved and the scented-leaved varieties.

More species and Latin-named hybrids are included than before, and, to make the groups more useful, I have made separate lists of the species that are scentless and those that have fragrant foliage. I hope you will try some of the species in your window gardens. They are such thoroughly interesting plants, and each unfamiliar one that I have tried has given me pleasure. But then all geraniums do.

PLANTS THAT ARE ILLUSTRATED

Plant	*Figure No.*
abrotanifolium	40
acerifolium	28, 35
'Always'	1
angulosum	43
'Apple Blossom Rosebud'	20
australe	43
'Beauty'	47
bicolor	42
'Black Vesuvius'	27
× *Blandfordianum*	40
'Cesar Franck'	49
'Charles Turner'	26
'Comtesse de Grey'	49
cordifolium	12
cotyledonis	6
crassicaule	5
crispum	34, 43
crispum Gooseberry Leaved	28
crispum 'Minor'	34
crispum 'Prince Rupert'	20, 34, 46
cucullatum	43, 44
'Dark Beauty'	73
'Dark Red Irene'	18, 46

Plant	Figure No.
denticulatum	40
denticulatum 'Filicifolium'	28
'Double Poinsettia'	24
echinatum	10
Endlicherianum	12
'Fiat'	26
'Fiat Enchantress'	14
'Fiat Supreme' ('Dawn')	14
'Flame'	3, 19
× *fragrans*	40
frutetorum	11
fulgidum	42
'Gay Baby'	74
gibbosum	1, 7
× *glaucifolium*	42
glutinosum	28, 43
graveolens	46, 47
graveolens 'Camphorum'	29
graveolens 'Minor'	29
graveolens 'Red-Flowered Rose'	30
graveolens 'Rober's Lemon Rose'	29, 46
grossularioides	38
'Intensity'	49
'Jeanne'	24
'Jeanne d'Arc'	49
'Joseph Warren'	49
'L'Elegante'	51
× *limoneum* 'Lady Mary'	28
'Little Darling'	27
'Madame Fournier'	27
'Madame Jaulin'	20
'Madame Layal'	53
'Magnificent'	1
'Mexican Beauty'	1, 46
'Mrs. Banks'	49
'Mrs. Henry Cox'	46
'Mrs. Kingsley'	28
'Mrs. Pollock'	73

Plant	Figure No.
'Mrs. Taylor'	28, 47
× *nervosum*	36
odoratissimum	28, 43
'Old Scarlet Unique'	45
papilionaceum	44
'Party Dress'	1
'Pigmy'	27
'Pink Harry Hieover'	73
'Pretty Polly'	28
'Prince Bismarck'	46
quercifolium	47
quercifolium 'Giganteum'	41
quercifolium 'Prostratum'	39
quercifolium 'Village Hill Hybrid'	39
radens	28, 32
radens 'Skeleton Rose'	20, 29
reniforme	46
'Rollisson's Unique'	37, 62
'Rosebud'	20
× *rutaceum*	20, 42
'Santa Paula'	1
scabrum	31
scandens	9
'Silver Lining'	46
'Snowflake'	20
× *Stapletonii*	20
tetragonum	8
tomentosum	25, 33
vitifolium	43
xerophyton	5

UNSCENTED PELARGONIUM SPECIES AND LATIN-NAMED HYBRIDS

These species are important as collectors' items or as the parents of popular hybrids. The dates of introduction to horticulture in England are cited when known.

acetosum. Sorrel Cranesbill.

Smooth shiny scalloped gray-green leaf with an acid flavor, used in salads; narrow-petaled, spidery rose-pink flowers; spreading growth somewhat like *peltatum* indoors but a compact bush in the wild. Introduced England before 1724.

alternans. Parsley-leaved Geranium. (Sweet III, 286)

One of the succulent-stem Geranium group that also includes *carno sum, crithmifolium,* and *dasycaule;* usually grown with cacti and other desert plants. It has tiny wedge-shaped pinnate leaves and white flowers streaked with red on the upper petals.

✕ *ardens.* Glowing Storksbill. (Sweet I, 45)

Fleshy with variable oblong heart-shaped, unequally-lobed leaves. Peduncles few to 8-flowered, about 4 inches long, from a thick base; flowers nearly sessile, bright scarlet, tinged darker. (*P. lobatum* ✕ *P. fulgidum.*) I find it a pretty house plant. Introduced England 1817.

carnosum. Fleshy-stalked Cranesbill. (Sweet I, 98)

A thick trunk from which grow pinnate leaves that are soft and downy; tiny, creamy-pink flowers. Introduced England before 1724.

✕ *coriandrifolium.* Coriander-leaved Cranesbill.

A name once used for a hybrid called *Jenkinsonia pendula* by Sweet. The plant I have under this name is a lovely basket trailer at my window with branching dark green pinnate leaves giving a fernlike effect. Introduced England before 1724.

crassicaule. Thick-stalked Cranesbill. (Figure 5; also Sweet II, 192)

Thick, fleshy leaves rising directly from the crown. Umbels of white flowers, sometimes spotted on all five petals, sometimes only on the upper two. Introduced England 1786.

crithmifolium. Samphire-leaved Geranium. (Sweet II, 179)

Succulent green stems 1 inch in diameter both base and tips; leaves finely divided, resembling the common glasswort; huge clusters of pink-striped white flowers; climber.

cucullatum. Hooded Cranesbill. (Figures 43, 44)

Famous ancestor of the regals. Very tall and shrubby, sometimes to above 5 feet; heart-shaped cupped denticulate leaves; many-flowered panicles on long stems; big crimson-purple flowers, upper ones larger than purple-feathered lower ones. Introduced England 1690.

dasycaule.

Thick succulent stems, noticeably swollen at joints; fleshy compound leaves; small red-spotted creamy flowers, extremely odd. Mine likes to remain leafless too long in summer.

× *divaricatum.* Absinthe Geranium.

Small erect but spreading plant; shiny fleshy finely divided gray-green leaves; pale pink flowers, larger upper petals spotted purple. Introduced England 1820.

echinatum. Sweetheart Geranium, Prickly-stalked Geranium. (Figure 10; also Sweet I, 54)

Silky, roundish leaves, 3- to 5-lobed and toothed in tufts at end of branches; gray, stubby, permanent succulent stems with spiny stipules and slender, branching flowering ones; notched, inch-wide flowers, white or purple (sometimes both on the same plant) with maroon markings. Fascinating plant but unlovely during its moulting season.

frutetorum. (Figure 11)

Wide, dark center area of almost circular, soft hairy leaves on tall plants; single, salmon-pink flowers. Much used by hybridizers today for its shade tolerance, colorful foliage and masses of bloom. Introduced England 1932.

fulgidum. Celandine-leaved Storksbill. (Figure 42; also Sweet I, 69)

Oblong, wooly, gray-green 3-lobed toothed leaf; elongated and di-

vided terminal lobe; thick stemmed with large pointed stipules; tuberous roots; small crimson flowers have contributed their color to
many bright scarlet hybrids. Introduced England before 1732.

gibbosum. Knotted or Gouty Storksbill. (Figures 1, 7; also Sweet I, 61)
Gray-green brittle foliage, not so fine as × *rutaceum;* lower two sections of leaf separated by about an inch of midrib from 3-lobed upper
section; tan, corky, jointed stems with prominent swellings at the
joints; tuberous roots; evening-scented greenish-yellow flowers; stark
framework during dormancy; climber. Most interesting but not for
a small window. Introduced England before 1712.

× *glaucifolium* (Figure 42; also Sweet I, 354)
(*P. gibbosum* × *P. lobatum.*) Large, ruffled leaf somewhat like *gibbosum,* 3-lobed to pinnately lobed but not pinnate; tuberous roots;
small maroon, yellow and green flowers in spring are not spotted at
the base; climber. Sad sight in summer dormancy.

× *hortorum.* Zonal or Fish Geranium.
L. H. Bailey gave this useful collective name to the zonal pelargoniums, also called garden or bedding geraniums, derived mainly from
inquinans, zonale, frutetorum and others.

inquinans. Scarlet-flowered Cranesbill.
One of the ancestors of modern garden types. Large, slightly crenate
light green leaf; narrow-petaled vermilion flowers on long stems; tall
vigorous plant. Bailey states flowers sometimes white or pink. Introduced England before 1714.

lateripes. Ivy-leaved Cranesbill.
An old species that has figured in ivy-leaved hybrid geranium heritage. Similar to *peltatum* but petiole is not inserted into the blade
and margins of leaves are slightly dentate; pink flower. Introduced
England before 1787.

peltatum. Ivy-leaved Geranium, Peltated Cranesbill.
Variable in the wild, this is the ancestor of the ivy-leaved group,
producing the shield leaf and trailing form or climbing to 3 feet.
Thin stems, branching, scrambling growth; smooth, fleshy bright
green leaves, 5-lobed stars suggesting Hedera or ivy; big lavender to
white umbels, broad upper petals marked carmine. Introduced England before 1701.

rapaceum. Caraway-leaved Cranesbill. (Sweet I, 18 and II, 135)
An oddity from the stemless *Hoarea* section of Pelargonium with
annual leaves rising from the tuberous-rooted crown. Two entirely

different plants have been offered under this name. Flowers are like miniature sweet peas, the lower petals lying close together, the upper ones bent backwards; the leaves are pinnately divided into slender segments. Introduced England 1788.

reniforme. (Figure 46)

Stems are wiry, branching and without the spines that characterize other *Cortusina* pelargoniums, the section having white hairy undersurfaces of the leaves. Leaves are small, gray, kidney-shaped and velvety with slight lobing and long petioles; small purple-rose flowers on stems more than a foot long. Nice to edge a plant tub in summer, or for my window basket.

$\times$ *saepeflorens.* Frequent-flowered Storksbill. (Sweet I, 58)

Bluntly notched flat cordate leaves, tomentose below, pubescent above; shrubby, spiny succulent brown stem; rosy red-spotted flower. Rare and perhaps no longer available. (*P. echinatum* $\times$ *P. reniforme.*)

salmoneum.

Very tall plant with fleshy blue-green truncate leaves; single salmon-pink flowers.

scandens. Climbing Geranium. (Figure 9)

The true species does not appear to be available in the United States. Round, crenate, slightly-zoned shiny dark leaf; spidery magenta single flowers in clusters with linear petals.

$\times$ *Stapletonii.* Miss C. Stapleton's Storksbill. (Figure 20; also Sweet III, 212)

Double hybrid of *P. echinatum* and *P.* $\times$ *saepeflorens.* Leaves 5-lobed, crenate, cordate; stems glossy with spiny stipules bent downwards; shrubby growth; petals cerise or rose, the two upper ones white at the base, all five spotted with red.

tetragonum. Square-stalked Jenkinsonia or Cranesbill. (Figure 8; also Sweet I, 99)

Few, very small round crenate "rubbery" leaves; unequal quadrangular stalk, sometimes triangular; disproportionately large 4-petaled rose and white flowers; climber. Introduced England 1774.

triste. Mourning Geranium, Night Geranium, Night-smelling Cranesbill.

Only occasionally offered by dealers, this unusual species was unavailable when Prof. H. E. Moore's review of the Pelargoniums cultivated in the United States was published in 1955. Subsequently, Logees listed it in 1960. The dull brown-yellow flowers with dark spots are fragrant at night. Probably the first to be cultivated in Europe, this Pelargonium was brought to England by Tradescant before 1632. It is a medium-sized plant with tuberous roots; the rough thick leaves are finely divided.

zonale. Horseshoe Geranium, Common Horseshoe Cranesbill.
Widespread in South Africa and probably the first to reach Europe via Holland. An important ancestor of the extensive *P.* × *hortorum* group of garden geraniums, providing the zone in the leaf when there is one. Some zonal hybrids have plain green leaves. Woody below and succulent above, this plant may go beyond 5 feet. Cordate leaves, according to Mr. Clifford, are "not distinctly zoned." Single flowers are 5-petaled, generally considered to go from white through rose-red. On my plant purchased under this name they are bright red. Introduced England 1700.

THE ZONAL GERANIUMS

Name of introducer and date of introduction are stated when known. Not *all* of the good varieties could be included.

'Afterglow'
Single large clusters of salmon darkening to old rose in the maturing flowers. Miller 1939.
'Alice of Vincennes' (Painted Lady Group)
Single large bright red flowers shading to a white center; medium to large grower and an excellent pot plant. Hill 1901.
'Always' (Figures 1, 59)
Double flowers, cream-white to deeper pink in center; large flowers in large clusters; year-round bloom on a very handsome pot plant; needs some shade in garden or may burn out. A favorite of mine, and I am not alone. Miller 1948.
'A. M. Mayne (synonym 'Springfield Violet')
Double large rich crimson-purple flowers on a fine strong plant; requires extra feeding and some pinching to keep shapely; resents overwatering; very handsome when well grown. Most popular of the purple-flowered zonals. Bruant 1913.
'Ann Sothern' (Painted Lady Group)
Single dark fuchsia-pink shading to a veined white center, unusual coloring and very beautiful. Rober 1940.

'Apache' (Irene Group)
Semidouble flowers, darkest of the trade-type reds; much larger flowers than the previously popular 'Dark Red Irene'. Bode 1964.

'Apple Blossom' (Painted Lady Group)
Single flowers, scarlet to a veined white center, very lovely. (Not the same as 'Madame Jaulin'.)

'Apple Blossom Rosebud' (Rosebud Group; Figure 20)
Double flowers.

'Aztec'
Semidouble large vermilion flowers of an unique shade, freely produced on a bushy, medium-sized plant with some useful trailing stems. Miller 1947.

'Berkeley Belle' (Painted Lady Group)
Single, very large rounded light-red flowers with white center. Jory before 1946.

'Better Times' (Better Times Group)
Double rich-crimson flowers with a center splash of lighter color. Mrs. J. D. West calls this "one of the 'Fords' for her Midwest area," a nice color and excellent for the long autumn there. A sport of 'Edmond Blanc'; introduced about 1935.

'Blaze' (Irene Group)
Semidouble but more double than most; one of the fastest-growing Irenes; seems to shatter less and is a clearer red than 'Irene' itself. Wilson 1960.

'Bode's Coral-Pink Bird's Egg' (Bird's Egg Group)
Single flowers. Bode 1955.

'Bode's Light Pink Bird's Egg' (Bird's Egg Group)
Single flowers. Bode 1952.

'Bougainvillea' (Painted Lady Group)
Single lovely purple-crimson flower with white center; considered one of this hybridizer's best. Miller 1938.

'Canadian Pink and White'
Double white rose-edged flowers on a tall strong plant; an old favorite. Rober before 1945.

'Carmel'
Single white flowers with rosy picot edge; charming medium-sized free-flowering plant.

'Cerise Carnation' (Carnation-Flowered Group)
Double, cerise-to-light-crimson clusters of medium-sized flowers; the

most carnationlike of the class, the petals being sharply toothed; not very free-blooming.

'Challenge' (Figure 59)

Double large dark-scarlet-and-crimson, white-centered flowers on a medium-sized plant; free-blooming but needs some shade. Miller 1957.

'Cheerio' (Painted Lady Group)

Single coral-salmon flowers shading to white; cheerful, showy, and very free-flowering. Miller 1949.

'Dawn' (probably 'Fiat Supreme')

'Debonair'

Double soft lavender-pink flowers with white center; large flowers and a large plant of the French type. Miller 1952.

'Double Dryden'

Double lovely bright-red flowers with white centers; large flowers and a strong pot plant. An old variety by the 1900's. Listed by Paul Howard 1911.

'Double New Life' (New Life Group; synonym 'Stars and Stripes')

Double scarlet-and-white flowers, fun to have. Knight 1878.

'Double Poinsettia' (Cactus-Flowered Group; Figure 24)

Red flowers.

'Dreams' (Figure 59)

Double salmon-coral, fine large waxen flowers; free-blooming fast-growing plant; one of Miller's best hybrids. Miller 1942.

'Ecstasy' (Phlox Group)

Single white flowers lightly flushed salmon with coral eye; large flowers on a medium-sized plant that requires good culture and some shade; very lovely. Schmidt 1947.

'E. H. Trego'

Double large bright orange-red flowers; big glossy leaves, a cross between a zonal and an ivy-leaved geranium but plant is medium-sized and does not trail. Introduced by 1911, origin unknown.

'Elenore S. Rober'

Single lovely soft salmon flowers shading to lighter edge; sturdy plant. Rober by 1942.

'Emile Zola'

Single soft apricot-salmon, large round flowers in big umbels; grow in part shade for good color. A lovely variety but it requires care; flowers freely but does not produce many branches. Probably French; U. S. by 1913.

'Fantasy' (Painted Lady Group)
Single large purple-rose to white flowers in big clusters on a tall plant. Miller 1949.

'Festival' (Figure 59)
Double very large salmon-apricot flowers on long, strong stems; free-blooming, sturdy and handsome; needs good culture; open, not free-branching, growth. Miller 1951.

'Fiat' or 'Pink Fiat' (Fiat Group; Figure 26)
Semidouble to double lovely large salmon-coral flowers on a small to medium plant; the progenitor, strongest of them all. Bruant 1908.

'Fiat Enchantress' (Fiat Group; Figure 14)
Semidouble to double soft-salmon flowers, perhaps the most beautiful in the Fiat group, free-blooming, somewhat delicate.

'Fiat King' (Carnation-Flowered Fiat Group)
Semidouble to double medium-pink serrated flowers on a tall plant; lighter shade than 'Pink Fiat'; a sport of 'Fiat Queen'. Eisenbart 1959.

'Fiat Queen' (Carnation-Flowered Fiat Group)
Semidouble to double bright salmon-coral flowers, first to show serrated petals; floriferous plant, sport of 'Pink Fiat'. Hinsdale about 1942.

'Fiat Supreme' ('Dawn'; Carnation-Flowered Fiat Group; Figure 14)
Semidouble to double lovely serrated soft salmon-coral flowers, somewhat slow and compact, exacting but free-flowering when successful. Summers 1942.

'Firebrand' (Irene Group)
Semidouble large clear red flowers, heavy winter bloom. Bode 1964.

'Fireglow'
Double large orange-scarlet flowers in profusion; medium to large plant. Miller 1947.

'Flame' (Figures 3, 19)
Single very large scarlet flowers on a fine tall free-blooming plant. Wilson 1960.

'Flare'
Single large dark-salmon to salmon-red flowers on a large strong plant. Miller 1947.

'Forest Maid'
Double shapely brilliant rose-pink flowers of large size on a low compact unusual plant, a zonal ivy-leaved hybrid. As growth matures it tends to cascade over pot or basket; excellent in garden or for baskets

or pots in summer, as on my terrace or in my Plant Room. Germany
and Australia; Bode 1963.

'Frances Perkins'
Double rose-colored flowers with white center; large sturdy grower.
Before 1900.

'Fred Bean'
Single very large light salmon-coral flowers with a waxen sheen. By
1913.

'Gallant'
Semidouble large free-flowering red; strong medium-sized plant of
the French type; richer coloring than old 'Alphonse Ricard' and a
slightly smaller plant. Miller 1948.

'Garnet'
Double dark red flowers, almost black in bud, free-flowering on a
medium-sized compact plant. Miller 1959.

'Genie' (Irene Group)
Semidouble large rose flowers with a white eye; strong well-formed
plant; profuse bloomer; excellent for Midwest gardens.

'Gertrude Pearson'
Single rose-pink with white eye; excellent in Midwest. Pearson before 1897.

'Gypsy'
Double dark crimson with small white center; tall and free-flowering. Miller 1949.

'Halloween' (Figure 59)
Double apricot-orange with a white center, one of the best in this
color pattern for indoors or out; large flowers and clusters but medium-sized plant with free-blooming habit; so delightfully named.
Miller 1951.

'Harvest Moon'
Single large white-centered soft orange flowers, a popular color; medium to large plant. Miller 1958.

'Helen Van Pelt Wilson'
Single light lavender-pink with white center; medium-large flowers
in good clusters on a plant of moderate size; blooms year-round for
me and is very pretty; I do like my namesake. Rober 1945.

'Holiday' (Painted Lady Group)
Single large soft red flowers with white centers, on a free-blooming
plant. Miller 1954.

'Honeymoon'
   Single big round flowers of fine form with apricot centers and a
   near-white eye, shading through pink to blush petal edges; small to
   medium plant. A real beauty. Schmidt 1941.

'Inspiration'
   Semidouble cream flowers with a salmon-pink suffusion; large very
   beautiful flower in medium clusters on a fast-growing plant, small
   for the French type; profusion of blooms is fine for arrangements and
   corsages; outstanding among light-colored varieties. Miller 1949.

'Irene' (Irene Group)
   Semidouble clear-red-to-crimson flowers; the progenitor of this great
   commercial family; a trusted winter bloomer. Behringer about 1942.

'Jeanne' ('Skelly's Pride'; Carnation-Flowered Group; Figure 24)
   Single vibrant salmon-pink flowers in steady profusion on a medium-
   sized plant; good for pots. I am very fond of this one. Excellent for
   winter bloom.

'Joy' (Figure 59)
   Double, one of the lovely tinted geraniums, margined and flecked
   salmon; free-flowering and a small bushy plant. Miller 1952.

'Lady of Spain' (Painted Lady Group)
   Single large soft coral-pink flowers beautifully shaded to white centers; one of the prettiest of the off shades, and with a lovely name;
   a tall plant. Schmidt 1947.

'Lady Ruth' ('Rudyard Kipling')
   Single magenta flower, scarlet splashed; free flowering; valuable in
   dry areas; good performer in Midwest. Incorrectly called 'Wicked
   Lady'. England 1899.

'La Fiesta'
   Single large vivid orange-scarlet blooms on a low free-flowering
   plant; noteworthy for the Northwest. Rober 1937.

'Lavender-Pink Bird's Egg' (Bird's Egg Group)
   Double flowers.

'Lavender Ricard' (Ricard Group)
   Double very large lavender-rose white-centered flowers on a strong
   tall plant; lovely with other light shades.

'Lullaby'
   Double medium-sized pale-salmon flowers often with lighter margins;
   color varies considerably with culture; blooms freely; for pots or gar-

den if well fed and watered and grown in partial shade. Schmidt 1947.

'Luster'
Single carmine, sometimes violet-shaded rounded flowers on a small to medium-sized plant. Miller 1952.

'Madame Jaulin' (sometimes called 'Apple Blossom'; Figure 20)
Semidouble cupped white flowers shaded salmon to darker centers (opposite of real apple-blossom coloring); strong bushy plant; fine old favorite, color best in partial shade. Bruant 1894.

'Madame Thibaut' (Carnation-Flowered Group)
Single, white in the bud, pink in the older flower, edges sharply cut. Very old, origin unknown.

'Magenta Ruby' (Better Times Group)
Double purple-crimson flowers with the same splash of scarlet as 'Better Times'; one of the best, most rugged zonal purples. This may be an old variety renamed.

'Magnificent' (Fiat Group; Figure 1)
Semidouble, enormous light rosy-salmon flowers on a large strong plant requiring more food and water than most. Blooms year-round as a pot plant for me. I love it but it is too rangy for a small window garden. Bode 1955.

'Marguerite de Layre'
Single white flower with slightly ruffled petals and pale pink buds; sturdy medium-tall plant; flowers freely with good clusters; an old and treasured variety, one of the most beautiful of all geraniums, I think. Several different varieties are offered under this name; impossible to say which, if any, is the original. 'L'Aube', 'Snowdrop', and 'Snowflake' are similar; see also 'Starlight'. Bruant 1889.

'Maria Wilkes'
Double large light rose-pink flowers with some white in center. Very pretty and free-blooming on a bushy medium-sized plant; slightly lighter pink than the old 'Berthe de Pressily'. Rober 1941.

'Marquis de Montmort'
Double fairly large purple-crimson flowers with well-zoned foliage; a handsome plant, but not a good choice for outdoors where summers are very hot or wet. Bruant before 1901.

'Masure's Beauty' (sometimes called 'American Beauty')
Double rosy-red, glorious clear color like the rose of the same name;

big in flower, truss, leaf, and plant, readily trained to climb or as a standard. About 1930.

'Maxime Kovalevski'
Single glowing vibrant orange, striking and free-flowering; low spreading plant; excellent in New England but select something else for warm dry areas. Lemoine 1906.

'Merry Gardens White'
Double white seldom with a pink tint; selected strain from various whites; unzoned light green leaves on a bushy plant; free-flowering even in winter. (It has been difficult to develop satisfactory semidouble and double pure whites.) Merry Gardens first listed 1955.

'Morning Star' (Cactus-Flowered Group)
Double soft-salmon flowers. Smith 1953.

'Mr. Wren'
Single light red with brushed-on white edge, a charming novelty that O. N. Conn of Carlsbad, California, obtained from the garden of a Mr. Wren; may be a very old variety renamed; often reverts to an all-red single, and once, for Holmes Miller, to an all-red double. Conn 1952.

'Mrs. E. G. Hill'
Single clear salmon flowers with divided petal groupings of the "primitive" type; an outstanding single; blooms year-round for me; also good outdoors in the Midwest. Apparently there are three geraniums under this name; mine appears to be this old one. Bruant 1889.

'Mrs. J. J. Knight' (Bird's Egg Group)
Single white-to-pale-pink flowers, all petals spotted, probably freest blooming of the Bird's Egg group. Knight before 1948.

'My Beauty'
Double crimson of French type; free-flowering, medium-sized plant. Brown 1941.

'New Life' ('Peppermint Stick'; New Life Group)
Single scarlet-and-white flowers. Cannell 1876.

'New Phlox' (Phlox Group)
Single white flower, flushed salmon in maturity, with vermilion eye; popular for its very free flowering indoors and out; medium-tall plant. Miller 1942.

'Nimbus'
Semidouble wide-petaled flowers, white flushed salmon, darker toward center, medium to large plant. Miller 1961.

'Noel' (Cactus-Flowered Group)
Double white flowers. Smith 1948.

'Nouvelle Aurore' (Painted Lady Group; Figure 59)
Single orange-to-white; a glorious flower but an exacting plant, requiring some shade and extra feeding; I dote on this one; it's hard to find and hard to grow. Lemoine about 1920.

'Orange Ricard' (Ricard Group)
Double large orange-to-scarlet flowers on a big free-flowering plant; most dependable.

'Painted Lady' (Painted Lady Group)
Single cerise flower shading to a veined white center; a beauty and a favorite, strong and sturdy.

'Party Dress' (Irene Group; Figure 1)
Semidouble striking rose-pink, mass bloom and strong plant. Flowers well in winter for me. Bode 1962.

'Patience'
Double white-centered purple-rose flowers in profusion on a bushy plant of medium size. Miller 1955.

'Paul Crampel'
Single brilliant scarlet on a fine compact free-blooming plant that responds to fluorescent light. (Not always possible to get true variety.) Lemoine 1892.

'Penny' or 'Penny Irene' (Irene Group)
Semidouble flower similar to 'Irene' but the color has more pink toward spring; very popular.

'Persian Rose'
Single dark purple-rose with a little white in center; free-flowering on a bushy plant. Rober before 1946.

'Phlox New Life' (New Life Group, Phlox Group)
Single white sometimes slight pink flush, with coral eye; medium-sized flowers; mass bloomer and excellent for pots. Frequent sport of 'New Life' and probably occurred about the same time but if a name was given then, it is not known today. Probably England about 1877; named by Miller 1948.

'Pink Cloud'
Double large salmon-pink flowers on a rugged free-blooming plant bred to endure Midwest heat; fast grower suited to short seasons. ('Red Cardinal', 1961, is of the same type.) Dr. E. C. Voltz, Iowa State College 1955.

'Pink Giant'
Semidouble enormous rose-pink white-eyed flowers on a strong low-growing plant; a very fine pink and preferable to the old 'Jean Viaud'.

'Pink Poinsettia' (Cactus-Flowered Group)
Double flowers.

'Pink Rosebud' (Rosebud Group)
Double flowers, blooms freely.

'Pride of Camden' ('Camden Nutt')
Double dark velvety red flowers freely produced on a fast tall rampant grower under culture it likes; avoid overwatering; one of the best dark reds.

'Princess Fiat' (Carnation-Flowered Fiat Group)
Semidouble to double, large lovely pastel of white lightly touched salmon, serrated petals; free-blooming, small compact plant; sport of 'Fiat Queen'. Eisenbart 1947.

'Radiance' (Figure 59)
Double large red-to-salmon white-centered flowers on a tall free-blooming plant; best of the red-and-whites. Miller 1948.

'Radiant' (Irene Group)
Semidouble light brick-red, large round and somewhat cupped flowers; heavy-wooded, fast growing, and as good a bloomer as the famous 'Irene'. Bode 1964.

'Red Rosebud' or 'Scarlet Rosebud' (Rosebud Group)
Double flowers.

'Rose-Pink Bird's Egg' (Bird's Egg Group)
Single flowers.

'Royal Fiat' (Carnation-Flowered Group, Fiat Group)
Semidouble to double, serrated petals, soft salmon-coral blending to lighter margins; considered finest of carnation type; sport of 'Princess Fiat'. Eisenbart 1951.

'Royal Times' (Better Times Group)
Double, softer lighter crimson than 'Better Times' from which it sported. Bode 1954.

'Shimmer'
Double large soft apricot-salmon flowers with white centers; free-blooming medium-size plant; better with some shade. Miller 1958.

'Shocking'
Double large ball-shaped shocking pink flowers on a big plant; good

in Midwest and desert; excellent in Connecticut in hot weather, and blooms well in winter. Hartsook 1961.

'Silver Star' (Cactus-Flowered Group)
Single white flowers. Miller 1948.

'Souvenir de Mirande' (Painted Lady Group)
Single red to white; famous as a free-blooming winter pot plant. Herlaut 1886.

'Springtime' or 'Springtime Irene' (Irene Group)
Semidouble, the choice among salmon-pinks and remarkable for heavy blooming; excellent in Midwest.

'Starlet' (Cactus-Flowered Group)
Double coral flowers. Smith 1956.

'Starlight'
Single white, free-flowering; smaller more compact plant than 'Marguerite de Layre', which compare; of rather slow growth. I love this one; nice for a window garden; these single luminous whites are worth close observation.

'Star of Persia' (Cactus-Flowered Group)
Double purple-crimson flowers. Smith 1956.

'Summer Cloud'
Semidouble large free-flowering pure white from faintly pink buds; strong, low compact pot or garden plant. Miller 1956.

'Tangerine' (Cactus-Flowered Group)
Double vermilion flowers.

'Thomas E. Stimson' ('Olympiad')
Single soft cerise, free-blooming on a rather small plant. California about 1955.

'Toyon' (Irene Group)
Semidouble very large clear red, for me more scarlet than crimson; flowers last for weeks on the plant. Bode 1963.

'Tresor '
Double large unique variegated salmon-and-white flowers on medium-sized plants; appreciated by collectors. Gerbeaux before 1901.

'Velma'
Single very large umbels to 6 inches, and velvety dark red flowers on outdoor plants; good for arid regions; too large a plant for some uses. By 1945; perhaps an old variety renamed. Not Bruant's white 'Velma'.

'Verité' ('Springfield White')
Double large white flowers with orange pollen. An old variety,

stronger perhaps than 'Madame Buchner' which is so commonly planted. To U.S. by Good and Reese 1941. (It has been difficult to develop good double whites. 'Madonna' or 'White Madonna' may be preferred in North; 'Snowball' with larger plant and flower than 'Madame Buchner' is favored in the South. If a faint blush tone is acceptable, 'Gardenia' with a satin sheen is fast-growing, free-blooming, and excellent for pots.)

'Vesuvius' (New Life Group)
Single scarlet, the progenitor of the New Life Group. (Not 'Black Vesuvius'.) Smith 1868.

'Welcome'
Double large somewhat cupped salmon-apricot flowers freely borne; excellent foliage on strong compact plant for pot or garden. One of the best. Miller 1950.

'White Magic' (Figure 59)
Semidouble large glistening pure white flowers; bushy medium-sized plant; one of the most beautiful of double whites but requires special attention to culture and feeding, also needs some shade. Miller 1950.

'Will Rogers'
Single vivid purple-crimson with intense scarlet splash on each petal; one of the darkest shades among geraniums; very large clusters on a thick-stemmed very tall plant; stunning variety. Rober before 1946.

THE FANCY-LEAVED ZONAL GERANIUMS

'Alpha' ('Golden Harry Hieover').
Prominent, narrow, red-brown zoning on small yellow-green shiny leaf; compact, low-growing plant but taller than most dwarfs; narrow-petaled, single vermilion flowers. England by 1873.

'Attraction' (possibly 'Gaines Attraction').
Silvery-green leaves with narrow creamy borders; small single red flowers; large bushy plant. England from 1863.

'Blazonry'.
Brightest of silver tricolors with silvery-green leaves bordered with ivory and broadly zoned rose-red and purple-brown; small single vermilion flowers on a slow-growing tall sturdy plant. Miller 1961.

'Bronze Beauty No. 1'.
Large round scalloped yellow-green leaves with a rather narrow red-brown zone; slow-growing bushy plant; small single salmon flowers. Possibly an old variety renamed.

'Bronze Beauty No. 2'.

Brighter greenish-yellow foliage with a wide red-bronze zone, more attractively lobed; smaller plant; single scarlet flowers.

'Cloth of Gold' ('Golden Bedder' listed by Grieve).

Fine, unzoned yellow-green foliage; single bright pink flowers. Mentioned by Grieve but not described. See also 'Yellow Gem'.

'Contrast'.

Golden tricolor; bright, yellow-edged green leaves with a wide zone splashed with scarlet, crimson, and brown; small, single scarlet flowers. Compare with 'Mrs. Pollock'.

'Crystal Palace Gem'.

Yellow-green leaf with a bold irregular splash of dark green in center; bushy spreading grower; single red bloom. Grieve describes it as "rosy scarlet and an improvement upon 'Cloth of Gold'." By 1868.

'Damon's Gold Leaf'.

Large golden leaves have a crenate edge and a light brown ring; blooms are orange-red.

'Dark Beauty'. (Figure 73)

Mutant form of *P. frutetorum,* dark scalloped leaves with black central area; single salmon flowers on a free-blooming plant.

'Display'.

A beautiful tricolor but not easy. Wide yellow border with bright zones of scarlet, crimson, and brown on large flat leaves; small, single scarlet flowers; slow-growing plant. Worth an effort. Miller 1948.

'Distinction' ('One-in-a-Ring')

Small dentate round bright-green leaf with distinct black circle near outer edge; red flower. Probably England by 1880.

'Dwarf Gold Leaf'.

Large yellow-gold leaf without zoning; rather tall plant, not dwarf but slow-growing; small single scarlet flowers. Intolerant of full sun. Possibly English variety 'Gold Leaf'; before 1860.

'Filigree'.

Silver tricolor nicely lobed; silvery green leaves with a wide creamy border lightly zoned pink and brown; spreading, moundlike plant. Small single dark-salmon flowers. Intolerant of hot dry weather. Hybrid of *P. frutetorum.* Miller 1953.

'Flower of Spring'.

Scalloped silvery-green leaf with very wide cream border; tall and shapely plant; vermilion flowers. Perhaps finest of all the silver-leaved. Before 1860.

'Freak of Nature'.
Ivory leaves with ruffled edging of bright green; stems, leaf, and flower stalks white. Rarely do the single small red flowers appear; slow-growing and bushy. England about 1880.

'Golden MacMahon'.
Yellow to yellow-green leaves with pale brownish zones and sometimes pink markings; compact, slow-growing, and a little difficult; will not tolerate full sun.

'Golden Oriole'.
Shiny scalloped yellow-green leaves with bronze zones; single salmon flowers freely produced on a small bushy plant. Arndt about 1954.

'Greetings'.
Silvery-green leaves with wide creamy borders and narrow bright rose-red and purple-brown zoning (except in hot weather); small single dark-salmon flowers on a medium-sized bushy plant. Hybrid of *P. frutetorum*. Miller 1964.

'Happy Thought'.
Irregular ruffled bright green leaf with yellow center and "butterfly" zoning of brown and orange; single rosy-red flowers; medium-sized plant. England about 1876. (Not same as Grieve's 'Happy Thought'.)

'Hills of Snow'.
Silvery-green flat leaf with very narrow edge of white; flowers double, light pink with white center suffusion. Sport of 'Mrs. Parker'.

'Jubilee'.
Golden-green leaves with broad red-brown zones; small single salmon flowers; tall plant. England 1887 or 1897 presumably to honor Queen Victoria's Jubilee.

'Lady Cullum'.
Described by Grieve as "uniquely beautiful by the remarkably broad and rich leaf-zones." Today's plant is certainly not the original; a tricolor but hardly one of the best; single red blooms. Grieve 1858.

'Lass O'Gowrie'.
A silver tricolor with narrow cream edging and wide purple-brown zone splashed rose-red; small single scarlet flowers on a medium-sized bushy plant. Not so bright as other silver tricolors but stronger and more heat-tolerant. England by 1868.

'Madame Salleron'.
Toothed, gray-green leaf, regularly cream-edged; never known to flower; small plant. Probably a sport of 'Mangle's Variegated' found by Pierre Mathieu in France, 1840-1850.

'Magic Lantern'.

Strong red, yellow, and light-green zoning; single salmon flowers; excellent for baskets. Hybrid of *P. frutetorum*. Both, Australia.

'Marechal MacMahon'.

Large yellow-green leaves with broad bronzy zones; small single scarlet flowers; bushy medium-sized plant. England about 1871 if this is the true variety.

'Medallion'.

Yellow to yellow-green leaves with large red-brown center markings; bushy spreading habit; fine for baskets; small single dark-salmon flowers. Hybrid of *P. frutetorum*. Miller 1956.

'Miss Burdett Coutts'.

Tricolor with green center, purple-zoned and pink-splashed leaf, cream-colored variable margins, much broader than a rim; small, slow-growing plant; single vermilion flowers, although leaf pink. England about 1860, described by Grieve. Compare 'Mrs. Henry Cox' with red in leaf and salmon in flower.

'Mosaic'.

Dark well-zoned foliage sometimes splashed light green; single salmon flowers; good for baskets. Both, Australia.

'Mountain of Snow'.

Whitest of the green-and-whites; light-green leaf, irregular wide cream border; small single scarlet flowers. Tall somewhat difficult plant. By 1860.

'Mrs. Henry Cox'. (Figure 46)

Truly brilliant tricolor, medium-green leaf center with vermilion and purple zone, light yellow edge; tall and fast-growing plant, needs pinching. Single salmon flowers. Handsomest of all the colored-leaveds and my favorite. England about 1879.

'Mrs. J. C. Mappin'.

Silvery-green leaves with wide creamy borders; unusual single red-veined white flowers; bushy plant; quite rare. Townsend 1880.

'Mrs. Parker' ('Chelsea Gem').

Silvery-green leaves deeply and irregularly margined cream; low, well-branched plant; double soft-pink flowers in abundance. By 1893.

'Mrs. Pollock'. (Figure 73)

Medium-green leaf center, dark red- and orange-splashed, irregular zoning with brilliant yellow scalloping; *single* vermilion flowers, sturdy medium-sized plant. Grieve origination, England 1858. Grieve

states, "from this and 'Sunset' doubtless descended the entire race of Golden Variegated Zonal or Golden Tricolor Pelargoniums."
'Mrs. Strange' ('Double Mrs. Pollock').
Almost identical to 'Mrs. Pollock' but with double flowers. England about 1883.
'Pastel'.
Silvery-green leaves with a deep ivory border, widely zoned with coral-pink splashed purple; single salmon-coral flowers match the zone; small, slow-growing bushy plant. A little difficult but very lovely. Miller 1954.
'Pink Happy Thought'.
Apparently a sport of 'Happy Thought' with similar leaves but light-pink flowers in profusion. A weaker less bushy grower than 'Happy Thought'.
'Prince Bismarck'. (Figure 46.)
Large-lobed yellow-green leaf with broad brilliant rust-red zone. Compare the smaller more scalloped leaf of 'Bronze Beauty No. 2'. Medium-sized handsome plant; single salmon flowers.
'Silver Lining'. (Figure 46)
Gray-green leaves *deeply* splashed with white, the young ones having a pink flush. Sport of 'Wilhelm Langguth'. Merry Gardens 1964.
'Silver Ruby'.
Silvery-green leaves with narrow white margin; double clear-vermilion flower; sturdy plant with good heat resistance; similar to 'Wilhelm Langguth'.
'Skies of Italy'.
Most brilliant after 'Mrs. Henry Cox' and 'Miss Burdett Coutts'. Sharply-lobed dark-green leaf, dark-zoned with crimson-and-orange splashes, narrow yellow edging, small single vermilion flowers; suggests a maple leaf.
'Sophia Dumaresque'.
Large green yellow-bordered leaves with wide scarlet-and-brown zoning; small single scarlet flowers on a medium-to-large plant much like 'Mrs. Henry Cox' but not so bright and considered a stronger grower. England before 1869.
'Verona' ('Pink Cloth of Gold').
Gold leaf with bronze zoning in good light; pink flowers on a tall compact plant. In Canada by 1900.

'Wilhelm Langguth'.

Silvery-green cream-edged dark-zoned leaf; attractive medium-sized plant; double clear-vermilion flowers. By 1898.

'Yellow Gem' (incorrectly 'Cloth of Gold').

Yellow to yellow-green leaves without zoning; small single red flowers; a sport of 'Crystal Palace Gem'. Bushy plant of medium size, easiest and best general-purpose variety of the gold-leaveds.

THE DWARF ZONAL GERANIUMS

'Black Vesuvius'. (Figure 27)

An appealing single orange-scarlet with very dark foliage. It grows slowly with a profusion of small to medium-sized flowers on a quite small plant; particularly good in winter. Darkest of all and now three-quarters of a century old, it continues to hold its own. Gnarled in age, it has pronounced leaf zoning. Early listings placed it among the fancy-leaved geraniums. It counts as a tiny one. England about 1890.

'Brooks Barnes'.

Single pink flowers; dark, strongly-zoned leaves that suggest a tiny *P. frutetorum;* a good grower but difficult to keep very small. Arndt about 1950.

'Bumblebee'.

Single light red, relatively large flowers on a larger plant; good as pot plant or, like most of the Rober varieties, excellent for outdoor bedding. Rober about 1949.

'Dancer'.

Very large single salmon flowers often lighter shaded at the petal edge; effective large clusters which tend to come and go in heavy spurts of bloom; dark leaves beautifully zoned on a fast-growing strong-stemmed bushy plant. Don't crowd this one but allow a 4-inch pot. (Probably largest flowers of all the dwarfs; only 'Prince Valiant' and 'Meditation' are comparable.) Miller 1957.

'Dopey'.

Large single white-centered rose-red flowers, the apple-blossom type; half-inch leaves on a fairly fast-growing plant that is good-sized like most of the fine Rober varieties. Rober about 1949.

'Emma Hossler'.

Large, double, white-centered rose-pink flowers in big clusters; green leaves on a robust fast-growing free-blooming plant of proven excel-

lence. Larger than most true dwarfs and best in 4- to 6-inch pots. 'Tu-Tone' from Wilson is similar but the flowers are in varying shades from light to dark pink. Dutch origin from Wilson about 1946.
'Epsilon'.
Evenly spaced petals form a large rounded white-centered soft-pink flower like an apple blossom, very lovely; pale green leaves on a moderate grower. I do like this one. Arndt about 1950.
'Fairyland'.
Single, small scarlet flowers but not freely borne, with small silver tricolor leaves, gray-green bordered ivory and splashed rose-red. Best of Miller's fancy-leaved dwarfs, a bushy plant, very slow growing with a light root system. Difficult to propagate but once started rather easy to maintain as a tiny plant for several years; grown mainly for its interesting foliage, a challenge to collectors. Miller 1951.
'Fleurette'.
Semidouble to double, deep coral-pink flowers on a fairly large plant that is almost always in bloom; deservedly a favorite. Case 1955.
'Flirt'.
Double, cream-white with reddish-salmon shadings, medium-sized flowers of variable coloring. Fast-growing bushy plant with dark leaves. Most reliable among larger dwarfs. Miller 1961.
'Goblin'.
Large double scarlet flowers in good-sized clusters above dark leaves. Strong fast-growing plant but one that can be kept attractively small for at least two years in a 3-inch pot. Kerrigan about 1955.
'Gypsy Gem'.
Double ruffled cerise flowers, a lovely color; scalloped medium-green leaves on a fast-growing larger plant. Wilson 1961.
'Imp'.
Single, salmon-pink flowers; very dark leaves. A good bloomer that stays tiny for years and years. Pleasing at the window with its frequent clusters of surprisingly good-sized blooms on so diminutive a plant. Miller 1951.
'Jaunty'.
Large double white-centered red flowers with olive-green leaves; a free-flowering, showy larger dwarf, faster growing than 'Perky'. Miller 1961.
'Kleiner Liebling' ('Little Darling'; Figure 27)
Tiny single rose-pink flowers with a little white in the center; clear

green zoneless leaves; bushy compact fast-growing plant. One of the older dwarfs. German origin about 1925.

'Lyric'.

Very lovely large white-centered double orchid-pink flowers in large clusters freely produced; most attractive among the paler colors; dark green leaves; fast-growing bushy plant. Miller 1961.

'Madame Fournier'. (Figure 27)

Bright single scarlet flowers and very dark leaves. Fast growing habit, not easily kept small. An important ancestor. Lemoine 1895.

'Minx'.

Distinctive large, double crimson-purple flowers in many big clusters; color is variable, reminds me of the one I know as 'Battle of Gettysburg'; lobed black-green leaves; bushy moderate grower. Miller 1955.

'Mr. Everaarts'.

Large, double white-colored cyclamen-pink flowers in large clusters; medium-green leaves; fast growing and almost everblooming, larger than most true dwarfs, an excellent big one. Dutch origin from Wilson about 1946.

'North Star'.

Lovely single white sport of 'Polaris' with radiating pink veinery and rose-colored pollen; flowers in groupings of twos and threes. Moderate grower. Merry Gardens 1962. (The faster-growing 'Rober's Snow White' is another lovely single.)

'Orange Imp'.

Double bright orange-like flowers of 'Maxime Kovalevski' but with darker green leaves; strong bushy fast-growing plant and free-blooming. Schmidt 1964.

'Perky'.

Single white-centered bright-red flowers, the two color areas well defined; plain olive-green leaves; a slow grower but so free-flowering it needs extra feeding to keep going; one of the best of the Miller small ones. Miller 1952.

'Pigmy'. (Figure 27)

Distinctive and one of the prettiest, small double vivid-red flowers steadily produced in full sun; small light-green scalloped leaves; bushy plant that appears very dwarf when young. A moderately fast grower soon attaining medium size. Requires more water and food than other dwarfs—nearly twice as much. Past losses of 'Pigmy' may have been due to accidental dryness since the dense growth makes it difficult to check the soil. The tiny cuttings are easy to propagate and sometimes take root in a week. Unknown origin.

'Pride'.
Large single salmon blooms on a lusty plant; one of the larger dwarfs. Eisley by 1950.

'Prince Valiant'.
Large single bright crimson flowers with dark leaves; fast-growing, bushy and free-flowering; very showy. Excellent larger dwarf. Schmidt 1959.

'Rober's Lavender'.
Large single pale-orchid flowers held well above medium-green leaves, most attractive; medium-sized to large plant. Rober about 1949.

'Ruffles'.
Semidouble medium-sized salmon flowers, somewhat ruffled, a real beauty; dark leaves on a slow-growing small spreading plant, pretty for a basket. Can be kept tiny for a long time if started from hardwood cuttings. Miller 1952.

'Salmon Comet'.
Unusually narrow-petaled single clear shrimp-pink flowers in contrast to black-zoned leaves; interesting for variety of flower form; medium-sized plant. Arndt early 1950s.

'Small Fortune'.
Large double white flowers with slight pink markings in good-sized clusters; small dark olive-green leaves; the profusion of two-toned blooms offers nice contrast among self-colored dwarfs. Stays small and compact if grown slowly until rootbound. Miller 1958.

'Snow Baby'.
Many delightful double white flowers borne above plain dark-green leaves; one of the best of the scarcer whites; almost constant bloom on a sturdy medium-sized plant. Case 1960.

'Sorcery'.
Small single orange-scarlet flowers freely produced; dark centered olive-green leaves; a big low-spreading grower among dwarfs and a good basket plant. Miller 1960.

'Sparkle'.
Large semidouble brilliant vermilion flowers borne freely in fine clusters above very dark-green serrated leaves. A taller open fast-growing plant. A lively note in any collection. Miller 1955.

'Sprite'.

A silver-leaved miniature probably the easiest and best of the small variegateds—and still fairly rare—with charming, pink-tinged green-and-white foliage on a rather slow-growing but bushy plant. The abundant coral-pink single flowers are in pretty association with the colorful leaves, not always true of the double colors of fancy-leaved plants. Miller 1950.

'Twinkle'.

Double good-sized coral-rose flowers in profuse clusters close to foliage; dark leaves on a bushy spreading fast-growing plant, nice for a basket. Miller 1954.

'Variegated Kleiner Liebling' ('Variegated Little Darling')

Lives up to its name. A sport of 'Kleiner Liebling', it has smaller white-bordered, gray-green leaves and it grows a little more slowly, but is so robust that it soon needs a 4-inch pot. Single rose-pink flowers, white-centered, suggest a small star phlox and come in short-stemmed clusters. In any greenhouse bench, this stands out. For contrast among your other dwarfs, keep young plants coming along from cuttings. Miller 1956.

'Venus'.

Double light-pink flowers of bright hue, one of the rare pale pinks; blooms well on a rather fast-growing plant with strongly-zoned foliage. Arndt early 1950s.

'Whitecap'.

Charming single white medium-sized flowers borne in profusion in large clusters; olive-green leaves; slow-growing bushy plant. Miller 1952.

SCENTED-LEAVED PELARGONIUM SPECIES, LATIN-NAMED HYBRIDS, AND VARIETIES

abrotanifolium. Southernwood-leaved Geranium. (Figure 40; also Sweet IV, 351)

Strongly pungent; silvery finely-feathered growth of small leaves. Tiny white flowers, upper petals each with a double carmine dot. (Synonym *P. artemisiaefolium* is used, but incorrectly.) Introduced England 1797.

acerifolium. Maple-leaved Geranium. (Figures 28, 35.)

Pungently spicy; light green rough deeply 5-lobed leaf resembling maple; handsome tall grower; lavender flowers, carmine markings on upper petals. (Synonym *P. aceroides* is sometimes used, but illegitimately.) Introduced England before 1784.

australe. (Figure 43)

From Australia, Tasmania, New Zealand, etc., similar to Cape species. Spicy scent; soft dark-green heart-shaped leaves with slight lobes; many long-peduncled flowers with narrow blush red-spotted and feathered upper petals, broader lower red-lined white petals; low branching growth from base. Introduced England 1792. (This is not the 'Australis' that has been offered in the United States.)

× *Blandfordianum* (*P. graveolens* × *P. echinatum;* Figure 40)

Strongly pungent; 7-lobed deeply cut gray leaf; rangy plant; white flowers, upper petals maroon-marked. Good contrast specimen in a mixed scented planting. Produced in England in 1805.

'Brilliant'.

Slightly pungent; cordate crenate dark-green leaf; spreading plant; fine medium-sized cerise flowers, upper petals broad, deeply-veined and gleaming, center of blossom light. Seedling brought from California by Dorcas Brigham.

capitatum. Rose-scented Geranium.

The name of this species is very generally misapplied to hybrids of *P. graveolens* ancestry that are grown in Algeria and elsewhere for the extraction of "rose" oil for perfume. The true species with slight rose scent is a sprawling plant; leaf 1½ inches, lobed and ruffled, serrated, hairy; flowers lavender. Introduced England 1690.

'Capri'.

Slightly pungent; triangular dentate leaf with brush of hairs on serrations; hoary stems; beautiful plant suggesting *domesticum* varieties; richly-colored, medium size cherry flowers, upper petals orange-red with dark spots and veins, darker petals.

× *citrosum.*

A name assigned to replace the name *P. citriodorum* that was incorrectly used by Henry Andrews at the start of the 19th century for hybrids derived from *P. crispum.* The true *citriodorum* is the same as *P. acerifolium.*

'Clorinda'. (Figure 1)

Pleasantly pungent, perhaps eucalyptus-scented; rather large 3-lobed crenate leaves; largest flowers among scented-leaved geraniums; resembles *domesticum* varieties; brilliant cerise, orange-flushed flowers.

cordifolium. Heart-leaved Storksbill. (Figure 12; also Sweet I, 67)

Sometimes inaccurately called *P. cordatum.* Upright, narrow plants with leaves deep green above, silvery beneath; large umbels of pale lavender flowers of good size marked with darker color; blooms over a long period; stems shrubby, erect with few branches. An attractive house plant in my collection. Introduced England 1774.

crispum. Lemon-scented Geranium, Curled-leaved Cranesbill. (Figures 34, 43)

Marvelous lemon scent; small curled and fluted leaves, crisp green with long petiole; tall, narrow plant resembling a miniature evergreen; pale lavender flowers, upper petals brushed purple. Prof. Moore found plants sold under this name to be definitely of hybrid origin. Introduced England 1774.

crispum, Gooseberry leaved. (Figure 28)

Slightly pungent; *crispum*-like leaves, some yellow-marked; compact plant; free-flowering pale lavender, cerise feathering on upper petals.

crispum 'Minor'. Finger-bowl Geranium. (Figure 34)

Strong citronella scent; tiniest leaves of all *crispum* hybrids; leaves stemless; plant growth like *crispum* but flowers paler and smaller.

crispum 'Prince Rupert'. (Figures 20, 34, 46; also Sweet IV, 383)

Lemon scent, strong and pleasant; small, smooth crenate leaves; largest of *crispum* group; lavender flowers, upper petals carmine-veined.

crispum 'Prince Rupert Variegated'.

Lemon scent less pronounced than 'Prince Rupert'; white to yellow-edged leaf; finer growth; same flower. (Also called 'French Lace'.)

× *decipiens.*

A name sometimes used in error for hybrid forms of *P. denticulatum.*

denticulatum. (Figure 40; also Sweet II, 109)

Fine rose- or pine-scented; 5-lobed much cut dentate light green leaves; plant a filmy mass (next finest to *P. denticulatum* 'Filicifolium'); small lavender flowers, upper petals with 2 vivid carmine-brushed marks; distinguished from *P. radens* by smooth leaves, notched upper petals.

denticulatum 'Filicifolium. Fern-leaf Geranium. (Figure 28)

Pungent; sticky 5-lobed finely-cut ferny leaves; tall spreading plant; most finely cut foliage of all the scented-leaved geraniums; tiny blush-pink flowers, upper petals each two carmine streaks.

× *domesticum*.

Useful collective name given by L. H. Bailey in 1907 for the regal, fancy, and show pelargoniums. Mostly derived from *P. cucullatum* and other scented-leaf geraniums. (Synonym Florists or Martha Washington Pelargonium.)

× *fragrans*. Nutmeg-scented Geranium. (Figure 40; also Sweet II, 172)

Spicy; small, slightly lobed round crinkled gray leaves; rangy grower; clusters of very tiny white flowers, upper petals brushed red.

× *fragrans* 'Old Spice'.

More compact and larger leaves than *P.* × *fragrans*; predominately apple-scented; cordate, velvet texture leaf; tiny, red-brushed flowers. (*P. ordoratissimum* × *P.* × *fragrans*.)

× *fragrans* 'Snowy Nutmeg'.

Variegated green and white.

glutinosum. Pheasant's Foot Geranium, Clammy Cranesbill. (Figures 28, 43)

Pungent; narrow, deeply-toothed leaf with 3 lobes, like *P. quercifolium* but tips are pointed instead of rounded. Weak, open grower; rose flowers with carmine dots; named for resemblance to a pheasant's footprint in snow. (*P. viscosum* is an invalid synonym.) Introduced England about 1777.

'Godfrey's Pride'.

Mint, strong and delightful; large, bold 5-lobed, not deeply indented, yellow-marked leaf; prostrate grower; light pink flowers.

graveolens. Old Fashioned Rose Geranium, Attar of Roses Geranium. (Figure 47)

This is the old-fashioned rose geranium with the fine true rose scent; it was used as a perfume substitute for attar of roses. Deeply cut, pubescent, heart-shaped leaf, finer than *capitatum*; small orchid flowers, purple-veined. Introduced England 1774.

graveolens 'Camphorum'. Camphor Rose Geranium. (Figure 29)

Camphor scent; 5-lobed leaf, otherwise similar to *graveolens*.

graveolens 'Elkhorn'.

Strong rose scent; 3-lobed leaf with large divisions further separated; tall strong plant; small orchid-pink flowers.

graveolens 'Giganteum'. Giant Rose Geranium.

Less fragrant than the species *graveolens*; larger leaf, less divided and not particularly gigantic, despite the illegitimate name.

graveolens 'Gray Lady Plymouth'.

Good rose scent; regularly cut like *graveolens* but gray cast with fine white line edging the leaves; vigorous plant, handsomer than 'Lady Plymouth'; typical flower.

graveolens 'Lady Plymouth'.

Rose scent; very irregular gray leaves, splotched white; less vigorous than but same flower as 'Gray Lady Plymouth'.

graveolens 'Large Leaf Rose'.

Strong rose scent; large, 7-lobed crenate light green leaves; tall grower; large heads of rosy purple flowers.

graveolens 'Little Gem'.

Pungent; tri-lobing of leaf, very marked with finer divisions, light green, pubescent; compact, low-growing plant; attractive clone and very like 'Schottesham Pet'; free-flowering, lavender-rose, upper petals spotted deeper and veined purple. (Sometimes called *P. terebinthinaceum.*)

graveolens 'Minor'. Little-leaf Rose Geranium. (Figure 29)

Strong rose scent; smaller leaf than typical *graveolens;* low, compact plants; tiny rose flowers with deeper upper petals, flowers darker than type.

graveolens 'Red Flowered Rose'. (Figure 30)

Slight rose scent; 3-lobed, small crenate leaf, very crinkly when young; compact plant; bright cerise flowers, upper petals deep and black-spotted. (Formerly 'Vandesiae', but not Sweet's 'Vandesiae' I, 7.)

graveolens 'Rober's Lemon Rose'. (Figures 29, 46)

Lemon-rose scent; very irregularly lobed leaf; lavender flowers with double brush marks on upper petals.

graveolens 'Variegatum'. Mint-scented Rose Geranium.

Rose-mint scent; deeply lobed, gray-green leaf, cream edged; compact; flowers typical.

grossularioides. Coconut-scented Geranium. (Figure 38)

Sometimes offered as *P. parviflorum,* which is a discarded name for a different species. Also a shrubby, lemon-scented plant called *P. crispum* 'Variegatum' is sometimes sold as *P. grossularioides.* The true species has coconut-scented, slightly crenate smooth small dark leaves; small, compact plant with rangy branches; easily grown from seed; clusters of infinitesimal magenta flowers. Introduced England before 1731.

X *jatrophaefolium.* (Sweet II, 118)
(*P. denticulatum* X *P. quercifolium.*) Oily, pungent scent; sticky, toothed 5-lobed leaf; tall, shrubby and vigorous plant; rose flowers, carmine dots and streaks.

'Joy Lucille'.
(*P. tomentosum* X *P. graveolens.*) Strong mint scent; bold, triangularly lobed, light green "felt" leaf; rangy, rampant grower; pink flowers, not showy.

X *limoneum.* Lemon-scented Geranium.
Strong lemon scent; fan-shaped, toothed leaf; small lavender flowers, upper petals garnet-brushed.

X *limoneum* 'Lady Mary'. (Figure 28)
Slight lemon scent; rather small hairy leaf, less sharply toothed than *limoneum;* compact growth; handsome for specimen use; free-flowering magenta blossoms, upper petals with large carmine spots and streaks.

X *melissinum.* Lemon Balm Geranium. (Not Sweet VI, 5)
Lemon-balm scent; tri-lobed, light green crenate leaf; handsome sturdy plant, good for background foliage mass in a narrow border; too large for a window garden; small lavender flowers, double purple brush marks on upper petals.

'Mrs. Kingsley'. (Figure 28)
Slightly pungent, perhaps mint; small leaf almost round, much ruffled and silvered, suggests curly parsley; compact growth; flowers deep rich cerise, rather like 'Brilliant'. Sometimes misspelled 'Mrs. Kingsbury'.

'Mrs. Taylor'. (Figures 28, 47)
Pungent; much crinkled, deeply lobed leaf; free-flowering with fine, small, bright red blossoms, upper petals black-brushed, unusual color in this group.

X *nervosum.* Lime-scented Geranium. (Figure 36)
Excellent lime scent; small, smooth, deep green sharp-toothed leaf, similar to 'Toronto' but smaller and more sharply dentate; compact growth; lavender flowers, darkly marked.

odoratissimum. Apple-scented Geranium, Sweet-scented Cranesbill. (Figures 28, 43; also Sweet III, 299—modern material has tiny red spots.)
Apple-scented; crisp, light green oval crenate velvety leaf; compact

plant with vinelike flower branches; tiny white flowers, upper petals with red pin points. Introduced England before 1724.

'Old Scarlet Unique'. (Figure 45; also Sweet I, 69)

Pungent; wooly, pointed-lobed, grayish leaf; rangy plant providing few cuttings; rare, handsome; large scarlet flowers with striking black markings, free-blooming. Probably a variety of *fulgidum*.

papilionaceum. Butterfly Cranesbill. (Figure 44)

Striking flowers, butterfly form, upper white petals very large, purple-marked, lower petals short and unmarked; large rounded leaf, deep green; stiff grower. Introduced England before 1724.

'Pretty Polly'. Almond-scented Geranium. (Figure 28)

Pungent, questionably almond; 5-lobed cordate leaf, resembling *domesticum;* crisp, fresh look to compact mounds of the plant; flowers rare but lovely, pink upper petals maroon-spotted and brushed.

'Prince of Orange'.

Orange-scented; quite small, crenate leaves; compact showy plant, large among scented varieties; free-blooming, pale orchid flowers, upper petals lavender with a large maroon "feather" on each; 1½-inch florets.

quercifolium. Oak-leaved Geranium, Great Oak-leaved Cranesbill. (Figure 47)

The true species may not be obtainable today but many hybrids are offered. It differs from *P. glutinosum* in the rounded rather than pointed tips of the leaf lobes. Introduced England 1774.

quercifolium 'Beauty'. (Figure 47)

Pungent with hint of mint; rough 5-lobed rather light green brown-marked leaf; low spreading plant, can be trained as climber; tiny rosy flowers, upper petals spotted deeper and brushed purple.

quercifolium 'Fair Ellen'.

Pungent scent; bold, round-lobed purple-marked rough-textured leaf; leaf and stem sticky; medium size lavender flowers, spotted darkly on upper petals.

quercifolium 'Fringed Oak'.

A difficult, poor grower, not worth having.

quercifolium 'Fringed Oak' × 'Fair Ellen'.

Pungent; smaller leaf than 'Fair Ellen', some leaves more definitely 3- than 5-lobed, sometimes slightly contrasting midrib colorings; more ranging plant, less sturdy and upright than 'Fair Ellen'; tiny lavender flowers, purple-brushed; hairy petioles and stems.

quercifolium 'Giganteum'. Giant Oak Geranium. (Figure 41)
 Pungent; 3- to 5-lobed variable leaf form, older leaves with deep purple veins; coarse, tall grower, excellent for standards; stems somewhat sticky; rather small rose flowers.
quercifolium 'Prostratum'. Prostrate Oak Geranium. (Figure 39)
 Excellent pungent scent; small, distinct 5-lobed leaf, blotched purple; low, spreading growth; small lavender flowers, upper petals distinctly veined purple.
quercifolium 'Skelton's Unique'.
 Pungent; small, rather round leaf, slightly scalloped and hairy; rangy,
 prostrate growth; typical *quercifolium* flower.
quercifolium 'Staghorn Oak Leaf'.
 (Formerly called 'True Oak'.) Pungent; 5-lobed, very distinctly divided leaf, narrow purple veining; more prostrate than 'Fair Ellen',
 fine hanging sort of plant; this and 'Village Hill Hybrid' finest cut
 of *quercifolium* varieties; 'Fair Ellen' best marked; flowers typical.
quercifolium 'Village Hill Hybrid'. (Figure 39)
 Pleasantly pungent; 5-lobed narrow crenate leaf, new ones like moss-
 curled parsley; small, showy lavender flowers, veined purple; rare.
quercifolium 'Variegatum'.
 (Also called 'Harlequin'.) Similar to *P. quercifolium* 'Giganteum'
 only variegated with streaks of white; difficult to grow, and rare.
radens. Crowfoot Geranium. (Figures 28, 32)
 (Formerly *P. Radula* and *P. revolutum*.) Pungent rather than mint
 scent; fine-toothed like 'Skeleton Rose' but grayer, lobed leaf with
 triangular divisions; compact growth; freest-flowering of all scented-
 leaveds; small rosy flowers, upper petals spotted magenta and distinctly brushed purple; flowers best removed from small plants or
 tendency to bloom to death before any size attained. Distinguished
 from *P. denticulatum* by "harsh hairy leaves" with inrolled margins
 and entire upper petals.
radens 'Skeleton Rose'. (Figures 20, 29)
 (Also 'Dr. Livingston'.) Lemon-rose scent; fairly large, 7-lobed, finely
 cut leaf; vigorous plant; lavender flowers with 2 purple spots on upper petals.
'Rollisson's Unique'. (Figures 37, 62)
 Mint- rather than pepper-scented; leaf pubescent, somewhat like *P.
 rapaceum* but larger and less crinkled; rangy grower, readily climbing

if supported and tied, specimens reach 5 feet; brilliant flowers of
pleasing magenta, size medium-to-large, zonal in flower and truss,
abundantly borne in spring and sporadically at other times. Sweet
IV, 371 mentions William Rollisson's nursery at Tooting near London but misspells the name by omitting one "s."

'Round Leaf Rose'.

(Possibly a variety of *P. graveolens*.) Rose-scented; round, light
green leaf with shallow lobes; small lavender flowers.

'Round Leaf Rose Variegated'.

(Also called 'Snowflake'.) Strong rose scent; crenate hairy leaf
streaked and splashed white; one branch of a plant sometimes much
more white variation than any other branches, many of which are
almost entirely green; large, prostrate grower; tiny lavender flowers,
deep markings. Compare with 'Godfrey's Pride'.

× *rutaceum*. Rue-scented Storksbill. (Figures 20, 42; also Sweet III,
279)

Rue scent; gray-green ferny leaf; knotty, fruticose stem and 10- to
12-inch petiole; tuberous root; 3-inch umbel of fragrant, evening-
scented maroon-petaled flowers with yellow rim and base; climber.

scabrum. Rough-leaved Cranesbill.

Plants sold under this name have been identified by Prof. H. E.
Moore of the Bailey Hortorium as hybrids, possibly of *P. graveolens*.
The true species may not be available. It has small leaves with 2 or
3 lobes, deeply cut, nearly to the base. Introduced England 1775.

scabrum 'Apricot'. (Figure 31)

(Also called 'M. Ninon'.) Pungent, doubtfully apricot; dark, glossy,
rather pointed leaf, deeply toothed and irregular; large, lovely brilliant deep rose flowers with darker pencilings.

× *Scarboroviae* 'Countess of Scarborough'. Lady Scarborough's Geranium.

Pleasant fruity, strawberry scent; small, crinkled tri-lobed leaves suggesting *crispum* but larger; plant difficult to grow and propagate; red
calyx and tube with bright rose flowers, upper petals garnet-veined.
(Resembles Sweet II, 117 but leaves of modern plant more dentate,
flowers same.)

'Schottesham Pet'. Filbert-scented Geranium.

Filbert scent; 5-lobed, further divided, rather pointed pubescent leaf,
light green; frosty, hairy stems; rosy flowers.

'Shrubland Rose'.

   Pungent; large heavy glossy leaf, less finely cut to 5 crenate lobes than 'Fringed Oak' × 'Fair Ellen'; tall vigorous and spreading plant; handsome when showy rose flowers open, free-flowering.

tomentosum. Peppermint-scented Geranium. (Figures 25, 33; also Sweet II, 168)

   True refreshing mint scent; large, velvety "grape leaf"; widely procumbent grower; tiny white flowers with purple veinings.

'Toronto'. Ginger-scented Geranium.

   Pungent, slightly ginger; round leaf with toothed edge, gray, frosted stems; similar to lime but leaf larger, lighter green and less sharply-toothed; flowers showy, rose lavender.

tricuspidatum. Three-pointed Cranesbill.

   Records at the Bailey Hortorium indicate the species introduced England in 1780 is not available in the United States. My plant bearing this label may be a form of *P. scabrum* except for its narrower, more pointed leaves, dark green, stiff and upright. The flowers are white, carmine-brushed on the upper petals. I do like this plant.

vitifolium. Balm-scented Cranesbill. (Figure 43)

   A very old species with scented leaves, still commonly grown. Erect stems bear large leaves that are harshly hairy. Introduced England before 1724.

THE IVY-LEAVED GERANIUMS—PELARGONIUM PELTATUM

'Apricot Queen'.

   Double soft salmon-pink to white with shaded umbels; fair-sized flowers open bright pink and fade to shell-pink to give a multicolor effect; small-wooded while young but with a larger future. Fine for pots or baskets. Use alone for small garden areas and trim a little to control it. Bode about 1955; probably already in Australia.

'Barbara Wirth'.

   Double cerise sport of 'Galilee'; strongest plant in this color; medium-sized plant of various uses. Wirth 1961.

'Barbary Coast'.

   Double delicate orchid flowers with light crimson markings on upper petals; excellent color; a 'Galilee' sport; medium trailer of many uses. Breitner 1957.

'Beauty of Eastbourne'.

Double cerise-red and very fine; medium trailer for pots and baskets; you will love it. From England by Schmidt 1960.

'Carlos Uhden'.

Double bright-red flowers opening to a white center; good medium trailing plant; a very popular red, few ivy-leaveds in this color. By 1914.

'Charles Turner'. (Figure 26)

Double large rose-pink flowers; long strong grower, familiar and reliable; excellent for pots or for extensive lawn plantings; all-purpose basic pink. About 1880.

'Comtesse de Grey'. (Figure 49)

(Apparently the English 'Madame Crousse'.) Semidouble soft pink violet-marked flowers with petal reverses deeper; fine as pot or basket plant, excellent also for slopes and lawns; a favorite; rugged long trailer. 'White Mesh' is a version of this; 'Mrs. Banks' is the albino form; 'Mexican Beauty' the dark or melano form. Characteristics are rugged mite-resistant plants rather open, even straggly, before they produce their fine long-trailing small-wooded growth; very free-blooming with good-sized rather papery-textured flowers.

'Corona del Mar'.

Semidouble to double brilliant scarlet flowers; long trailing for slopes and lawns but also a fine basket plant. Bode 1960.

'Double Lilac-White' ('Madonna').

Double white flowers, in hottest weather flushed palest lavender around center of rosebud-type blooms; free-flowering best "white," general use and dependability; medium growth. By 1939.

'Galilee'.

Double clear pink; free-blooming sturdy medium-sized plant; one of the very best; progenitor of such excellent varieties as 'Barbary Coast', 'Barbara Wirth', and 'Cliff House'. Florists like it and so do I for pots, baskets, small outdoor areas. Characteristic of the 'Galilee' group are plants of solid growth, medium-spreading habit while young; moderately thick wood and sturdy foliage; flowers of good size and quality with free and early bloom. France before 1882.

'Gay Baby'. (Figure 74)

Miniature; double ragged lilac-tinted, violet-striped flowers; thick dark-zoned close-set leaves; small in every way; slow growing, compact, thin-stemmed plant. This is a novelty, to grow for fun; doubtless more miniature ivy-leaveds will appear. I know of only one other, so far unnamed. From Australia by Bode 1961.

'Giant Salmon'.

Double very large clear-salmon flowers; sturdy compact plant, blooming late in North; very handsome for baskets. ('Double Salmon' similar but larger.)

'Hummel's Monselet'.

Double large cerise flowers in big clusters on a moderate-sized plant, fine for pots and baskets. This discovery by Mr. Hummel seems to fit the old descriptions of 'Charles Monselet' better than the red-cerise plant generally known by that name since 1900. Either 'Monselet' is excellent. Hummel about 1955.

'Intensity'. (Figure 49)

Semidouble bright red flowers, excellent plant with long growth; mite-resistant; fine for lawns and terraces. France by 1913.

'Jean Roseleur'.

Double cerise flowers; very lovely, a larger plant than most rosebuds; one of the finest of this type; lovely for baskets. Probably Jones 1895.

'Jeanne d'Arc'. (Figure 49)

Single pale-lavender, red-striped flowers; does not bloom long into summer; bushy, dark foliage; good for espaliers, tree climbing, or great lawns; mite-resistant and strong. By 1930; not the older *double* white.

'Jester'.

Double large orchid-rose flowers; free-blooming, best of penciled-petal types; compact growth, excellent for pots or small garden areas. Schmidt 1947.

'Joseph Warren'. (Figure 49)

Double large purple flower with real brilliance; have noted pot plants blooming year-round; fast but compact and the best in this color; good also for lawns if kept free of mites. By 1938.

'La France'.

Double large lovely purple-marked lavender flowers on a strong healthy plant; one of the very best, not to be missed; a universal variety; for pots, baskets, or small ground areas. From England by Schmidt 1960.

'Lucky Strike'.

Double large rosy-pink flowers; profuse-blooming, compact version of 'Charles Turner'; most satisfactory; young foliage has a yellow cast. Schmidt 1940.

'Mexican Beauty'. (Figures 1, 46)
Semidouble intense dark red flowers; a dark sport of 'Comtesse de Grey'; long-trailing handsome variety but because so dark does not show up well in garden; spectacular for baskets. From Mexico by Arndt in 1950s.

'Mrs. Banks'. (Figure 49)
Semidouble white flowers with lilac undertone, violet or crimson-veined; albino form of 'Comtesse de Grey'; best of long-trailing whites. Before 1910.

'Nutmeg Lavender'.
Double lavender flowers with a reddish center; peach-scented foliage, or is it *nutmeg*?; blooms profusely, charming pot plant, trailing, short-jointed grower with dense foliage, darkly zoned.

'Pink Rampant'.
Double medium-pink flowers on a notably strong plant; select this for heat endurance; late in North but dependable in South; a cross of 'Galilee' and 'Charles Turner'. Bode 1958.

'Ryecroft Surprise'.
Semidouble but rosebud type, soft-pink flowers; favorite specialist's variety for baskets. Probably England 1895.

'Santa Paula'. (Figure 1)
Semidouble bright lavender-blue flowers in a riot of color; low-growing, well-branched, fairly solid foliage; trailing but compact; enduring favorite for pots, baskets, small groundcover; good show plant. Before 1950.

'Scarlet Beauty' ('Corden's Glory').
Semidouble clear red flowers on a hybrid ivy-leaved plant; somewhat upright but with recurving stems; profuse blooming; one of the very best of the basket ivy-leaved geraniums. Since 1898.

'Sybil Holmes'.
Double rose-pink, rosebud-type flowers slow to open, often taking a month from first color to final unfurling; not for foggy areas; avoid overwatering or the very double flowers will mold; otherwise rugged; fairly fast grower but also branching; compact, near-dwarf. Rober by 1941.

'The Blush'.
Semidouble large white, rose-penciled rosebud-type flowers, some-

what weak-petaled in very hot spells but otherwise a mass bloomer; small-wooded compact plant for baskets and wall pockets.
'The Duchess'.
Semidouble large lilac-white, pink-lined and red-marked flowers, color deeper in sun; free-flowering; compact growth; weak-petaled in hot weather. Schmidt 1941.
'Valencia'.
Semidouble pink flowers, exceptionally free-blooming medium-sized small-wooded plant of many uses. Schmidt 1940.
Variegated Ivy-leaved—Lilac-White Flower. (Figure 51)
Single large silvery white-to-lilac blooms on a small-wooded low trailer; green and white, also rosy, leaves if allowed a little too much sun and some dryness; good for pots, baskets, small areas; consistent show-winner and an old favorite. This has long been called 'L'Elegantc'. England by 1868.
Variegated Ivy-leaved—Pink Flower.
Double tiny rose-pink flowers in profusion on a green-and-cream, sometimes pink-foliaged plant; likes full sun; a dependable house plant. Often called 'Duke of Edinburgh'.

THE REGAL GERANIUMS—PELARGONIUM DOMESTICUM

Also called Show, Florist's, Martha Washington, and Lady Washington Pelargoniums. Number of petals is given; and time of bloom as early, very early, or relatively continuous. The low growers make fine pot plants.
'Amour'.
5-6 petals; very early; fine pale, white-throated orchid with purple markings; compact free-blooming pot or garden plant. Schmidt 1959.
'Applause'.
6 petals; relatively continuous; very ruffled white-centered and white-edged pink; medium high and long blooming; patented variety. Schmidt 1963.
'Apple Blossom'.
5-7 petals; very early; blush pink flushed darker, like the flower that inspired its name; profuse bloomer. Cassidy 1939.
'April'.
6-7 petals; early; fine "clean" white, upper petals with tiny crimson spots; excellent plant. Brown.

'Autumn Haze'.

5 petals; early; flat flowers, salmon pink with orange glow and white center; medium tall, long blooming. Schmidt 1963.

'Azalea'.

6 petals; early; glowing rosy-red flowers on a low bushy plant, with heavy periods of bloom spring and fall. Popular in South and warm areas of California; good pot plant in East. I love it. Faiss before 1925.

'Aztec'.

5 petals; relatively continuous; rose-flushed-to-white border with velvety brown markings in center of petals; profuse flowering on a low compact plant. Schmidt 1962.

'Black Magic'.

6 petals; very early; ruffled and completely black, a *tour de force* in regal coloring; fine for pots and beautifully compact in garden. Schmidt 1961.

'Break O'Day'.

6 petals; early; fine white with large light-pink markings on upper petals, the kind of pale romantic coloring I like. An excellent plant. Schmidt 1961.

'Carisbrooke'.

5-7 petals; very early; ruffled medium-pink with carmine markings on up to 9 flowers in an umbel; long straight stems, excellent for cutting; "England's best." Large plant, good for pots or garden. England 1928.

'Carmen'.

5 petals; very early; ruffled wild-rose flowers with black markings on upper petals; a medium-tall plant. Schmidt 1963.

'Chorus Girl'.

6 petals; relatively continuous; lavender with salmon markings but the effect is brilliant salmon. Mass bloomer, favorite in Midwest where it is almost continuously colorful, as in Iowa. May 1957.

'Confetti'.

6 petals; relatively continuous; ruffled lavender-to-rose, darkly veined; low and compact; up to 6 periods of bloom. May 1962.

'Conspicuous'.

5 petals; relatively continuous; wavy dark-but-brilliant red with darker petal markings. Large, showy, well-formed plant; fine for pot or garden. Brown 1947.

'Corsage'.

5-6 petals; very early; fine medium-sized orchid flowers in profusion on a compact plant. Of course, good for cutting. May 1958.

'Country Girl'.

5 petals; early; soft candy-pink, feathered red; low shapely plant. Schmidt 1963.

'Delores'.

6-8 petals; early; peach-pink without markings; an excellent medium-high plant that blooms late into the season. Schmidt 1960.

'Destiny'.

5 petals; very early; pure white, considered the best white, an excellent plant. (Other good whites but with markings and not included here: 'Mrs. Mary Bard', 1938; the English 'Victoria Regina', 1959; and the nearly white 'Moon Rapture', 1964.) Schmidt 1963.

'Dubonnet'.

6 petals; very early; ruffled red the color of the wine, but with brilliance; a reliable repeat bloomer; popular pot plant in all parts of the country. May 1957.

'Easter Greetings'.

5-6 petals; relatively continuous; cerise with black markings, superb and constant bloomer, probably heaviest of all, large flowers to 4 inches; valued by florists both North and South and the best winter bloomer in Florida. Faiss before 1925.

'Edith North'.

5-6 petals; very early; bright medium-sized salmon flower, orange-suffused and crimson-marked. Tall and good for special garden uses; as a pot plant needs early pinching; will be in second bloom in North before other varieties are in first. Source unknown.

'Fifth Avenue'.

7-8 petals; relatively continuous; very dark red with a near-black overlay in the center, a velvety flower; long-blooming, bushy grower, one of the best of the very dark ones. Horner 1951.

'Firedancer'.

6-8 petals; early; brilliant ruffled crimson flowers covering the well-formed upright plant on all sides; profuse bloomer, for bedding. Bode 1953.

'Gardener's Joy'.

7-8 petals; early; blush-white with some rose markings and stripes;

upright, compact and showy plant. An old but exceptionally good variety. Germany 1913.

'Gay Nineties'.
6-7 petals; early; ruffled white with dark-rose markings; excellent for pots or garden; in continuing favor. Schmidt 1947.

'Geronimo'.
6-7 petals; early; vermilion Christmas-red flowers that make it invaluable although the small stiff plant is hardly among the best. Kerrigan 1954.

'Grand Slam'.
5-6 petals; early; rose-red flowers in profusion on a compact plant; consistent winner of awards and the leading favorite for more than ten years. Schmidt 1950.

'Grossmama Fischer'.
6 petals; early; ruffled clear-salmon, longtime favorite of florists; a good repeater for pots or garden. Faiss before 1925.

'Halo'.
6 petals; very early; frilly clear-salmon with small dark markings and a narrow lavender edging; profuse bloomer. May 1963.

'Heartbeat'.
6-7 petals; early; white-edged rosy-pink, a lovely flower on a tall spreading grower. This sport of 'Springtime' sometimes reverts to it, either part or all the plant. Kerrigan 1947.

'Holiday'.
7-8 petals; early; ruffled gleaming white with rose markings; fine plant, good performer in East. Generally considered one of the finest and now preferred to the older 'Mrs. Mary Bard'. Jack Evans.

'Josephine'.
5-6 petals; relatively continuous; medium-sized rose-and-white flowers, sparse plant but in bloom at my window from April on, and intermittently in summer garden. Popular from coast to coast. Cassidy 1945.

'Joy'.
5 petals; relatively continuous; small, frilly-edged, dark-salmon flowers, white throats. Long sprays have good keeping qualities in bouquets or in the garden. Schmidt 1955.

'King Midas'.
5-6 petals; very early; ruffled-edged salmon with a golden glow. Excellent for pot or garden. May 1956.

'La Paloma'.
 6-8 petals; early; white, light flush in hot weather; pale mauve markings on top petals; compact grower; free-blooming and popular in
 East. Schmidt 1957.
'Lavender Grand Slam'.
 5-7 petals; early; lovely deep-lavender flowers on a fine compact plant.
 Like 'Grand Slam' a winner of many awards. Extremely popular
 with florists and for gardens. Schmidt 1953.
'Mackensen'.
 6-8 petals; early; rose-pink, crimson-veined and marked, profuse. in
 bloom that covers a good plant over a long season, for pot or garden.
 Tried and true. Faiss before 1925.
'Madame Layal'. (Figure 53)
 5 petals; very early; the old favorite Pansy Geranium with small
 pansy-faced blooms, upper petals purple, lower ones mainly white,
 and they literally cover a compact well-grown plant. A pleasant contrast among regals and a darling window plant for spring. Other
 Pansy Geraniums include: 'Baby Snooks', 'Earliana', and 'Little
 Rascal'; 'Seeley's Pansy' makes largest plant with predominately
 white flower; 'Salina' has largest flowers, pink to crimson; but they
 are all quite similar. France 1870s.
'Marie Rober'.
 6-7 petals; very early; though an old one, still perhaps the finest of
 the dark purples with very large flowers; almost constant bloom on
 a rather tall plant but still good for pots as well as gardens. Rober
 1937.
'Mary Elizabeth'.
 5-8 petals; relatively continuous; cerise flowers in long sprays of
 heavy spring-and-fall bloom and with intermittent color between seasons. Fine tall garden plant that may start blooming indoors at a
 window in February. Cassidy 1942.
'Melissa'.
 6-8 petals; very early; soft deep-pink in a continuous bloom; excellent pot, garden, or basket plant. Bode 1956.
'Mood Indigo'.
 6 petals; very early; dark lavender but with brilliance and deeper
 velvety petal markings; strong free-blooming plant even in windy
 places. (Pink or lavender regals near it will "soften the mood.")
 May 1958.

'Neuheit Carl Faiss'.

5 petals; early; an old "novelty" of a great German hybridizer, this silvery lavender with dark markings is lovely. I think 'Lavender Grand Slam' and 'Mood Indigo' are generally considered superior, and are more deservedly popular with florists, but I am fond of 'Neuheit'. Faiss before 1925.

'Parisienne'.

5 petals; relatively continuous; white-centered mauve, the general impression is blue; repeated flowering on an open plant. Schmidt 1963.

'Pink Gardener's Joy'.

5-6 petals; early; rich pink with deeper veinings and markings. An old German variety of proven excellence popular with florists. Faiss before 1925.

'Rapture'.

5-7 petals; relatively continuous; apricot (an "improved" and larger 'Dawn', although it hardly seemed possible that lovely thing could be improved). Masses of flowers that hide the plant. A gorgeous regal, one of Mr. Schmidt's greatest triumphs. Schmidt 1963.

'Rogue'.

6 petals; very early; crimson-to-black flowers on a compact, free-blooming pot plant. Schmidt 1953.

'Roulette'.

5 petals; very early; glistening white with dark, clear markings. Good plant and perhaps superior to the older 'Gardener's Joy' and 'Victoria Regina'. May 1960.

'Vin Rouge'.

6 petals; very early; frilly, clear dark-red flowers, deeper at the center and with a sparkling quality; mass bloomer on compact plant. May 1963.

'Waltztime'.

6-7 petals; relatively continuous; lavender, ruffled double-appearing flowers of crisp texture in large clusters. Strong upright plant, popular with florists and gardeners. Schmidt 1947.

Glossary

Anther. The small sac carried on a thick thread emerging from the center of each flower is an anther. It splits to release the pollen grains containing the male elements of the plant.

Axil. The angle between a branch or leaf and the stem from which it springs. It is this part of a pelargonium plant which is highly attractive to mealy bugs.

Bipinnate. A pinna is a feathery leaf part. *P. rutaceum* has a bipinnatifid leaf. When the sections of a leaf are not only arranged on each side of a midrib but themselves similarly divided the leaf is *twice pinnate* or bipinnate.

Cordate. A leaf form roughly heart-shaped and notched at the base is termed cordate. The Old Fashioned Rose Geranium, *P. graveolens*, leaf is cordate.

Crenate. When the margin of a leaf is cut into rounded scallops, it is described as crenate. The Apple Geranium, *P. odoratissimum*, has crenate leaves.

Crock. A fragment of a broken earthen flower pot is called a crock (sometimes a potshard). If you fit a few overlapping pieces together in the bottom of a container to form a drainage area through which water but not soil will pass, you call it "crocking."

339

Cultivar. The term is applied to plants that have originated or are maintained only in cultivation. Cultivar names should not be in Latin nor printed in *italic* type. They are invariably capitalized words, usually enclosed in 'single quotes' unless preceded by the abbreviation cv. The use of the term cultivar, its abbreviation cv., or the single quotes is recommended by the International Code of Nomenclature for Cultivated Plants to distinguish cultivated plants from those originating in nature.

Cutting. This is a piece cut or broken from a parent plant for the purpose of obtaining additional plants of the identical type of the parent.

Dentate. A leaf with a toothed margin is dentate. The Pheasant's Foot Geranium, *P. glutinosum,* has deeply dentate leaves while *P. denticulatum* is so finely cut as to be filmy.

Dormant. When a plant is inactive either because of some unfavorable condition like cold or lack of sun, or it reaches the end of a growth cycle and a natural season of inactivity occurs, it is said to be resting or dormant.

Flat. This is a shallow box in which seeds or cuttings are started. Light plastic containers are often used in the home.

Florescence. This is the state of being in bloom or blossoming; also refers to the *period* of blooming.

Floret. Liberty Hyde Bailey gives this definition: "very small flowers that make up a very dense form of inflorescence." Following him, I formerly called the individual parts of a geranium cluster "florets." The International Geranium Society, following other authority, uses the term "flower," which I now accept.

Fruticose. This means shrub-like or bushy.

Genus. (The plural is *genera*). A Plant classification between family and species; a group of structurally related species. Thus *Pelargonium* is a genus within the family of *Geraniaceae.* This is an internationally accepted arrangement to simplify identification and to indicate relationship. The structural characteristics common to pelargoniums are "irregular" flowers, five petals and a nectar tube adnate to the flower stalk for almost the whole length.

Germination. When seeds start to grow into little plants, we say germination has taken place. The rate of "bursting into life" depends not only on cultural factors but also on the innate disposition of the seeds. Pelargonium seeds usually germinate about fourteen days after planting.

Hybrid. This is an individual resulting from the crossing of two species or two parents that differ basically in some strongly marked characteristic. 'Scarlet Beauty', 'Alliance', and 'Milky Way' are hybrid pelargoniums resulting from the crossing of varieties of *P. hortorum* and *P. peltatum,* natural hybrids.

Inflorescence. The general arrangement of flowers on an axis; the manner of development of the flowers, the *type* of bloom; the wisteria, a panicle.

Internode. The spaces between the tiny swellings along the stems of plants where leaves emerge. (See *nodes* also.)

Lath Shade. This is a screen to protect soil and plants from direct sunlight. It is frequently made by nailing lattice strips to a light board frame.

Linear. A long leaf or petal, uniform in width, is called linear. The 'Poinsettia' geranium has such petals which are of uneven lengths.

Lobe. A division of a rounded leaf form. The Camphor Rose Geranium has a 5-lobed leaf; 'Skeleton Rose' a 7-lobed.

Midrib. The central vein of a leaf which appears as a ridgelike extension of the petiole or leaf stem is the midrib.

Node. If you run your finger along the stem of a plant you will feel at regular intervals little swellings or joints. These are called nodes. They are the points of growth for leaves and buds. In taking a geranium cutting, for example, you are urged to select pieces of growth with two or three nodes and to make the cut just at the base of one of them.

Ovate. Egg-shaped leaves attached to stems at the broad end are called ovate. (cf. cordate leaves which are similar but notched at the base.)

Palmate. When the sections of a leaf radiate from a common point, the leaf is called palmate or handlike.

Pan. This is a broad, shallow flower pot, good for seed growing indoors but especially used for growing bulbs.

Peduncle. The flower stem or stalk that supports the inflorescence.

Peltate. Shield-shaped leaves with leaf stalks attached at a point within the circumference of the lower leaf surface. *P. peltatum,* the ivy-leaved geranium, has such leaves.

Petiole. The leaf stalk by which a leaf is attached to a main stem is called the petiole. .

Pinch. If with thumb and finger you nip out the end growth of a branch or remove tight little buds to make development fuller or to delay flowering, you are "pinching" it.

Pinnate. When leaflets are arranged on each side of the midrib, as in *P. denticulatum* 'Filicifolium', the Fern-leaf Geranium, the leaf is described as pinnate. The word means featherlike.

Pistil. The ovule bearing organ which receives pollen and develops seeds is the pistil.

Plunge. When you sink the flower pots in which plants are growing up to their rims in soil, you are plunging them. Such is a safer summer practice than removing pots and letting roots range.

Pollen. The fertile, usually yellow dust, released from the anthers is pollen.

Potbound. When a plant actually fills with roots the container in which it is growing, we say it is potbound and needs more root room. If the pot is lifted from such a plant, a potbound condition is indicated by a mass of roots covering the outside of the soil in a frantic search for food.

Prune. When you cut off part of a plant to keep it shapely or almost all of it to induce fresh new growth from the roots, you are pruning it.

Pubescent. A covering of down, not matted, is termed pubescent in contrast to the thicker covering called tomentose. P. 'Torento', the Ginger-scented Geranium, has pubescent stems.

Reniforme. This means kidney-shaped.

Sessile. Lacking a stalk or support.

Shifting. Installing a plant in a next larger size container with a little more soil but the least possible disturbance is termed shifting. This is in contrast to repotting which may involve replacement of worn-out soil with a fresh mixture, the improvement of drainage conditions and even some cutting back of roots. Shifting is for healthy young plants on their way to maturity. Repotting is for established plants in need of reconditioning. In repotting a larger pot may be provided, the same one used again, or even a smaller one selected, if the pot in which the plant grew was so overlarge that it suffered indigestion from too much soil and water for its size.

Species. This is something nature produces. It is a group of plants sharing certain distinct characteristics that indicate a common parent or genus. In a plant name the first word indicates the genus, the second the species to which it belongs, the third the variety, as *Pelargonium domesticum* 'Mary Elizabeth'.

Spine. Less woody than thorns, sharp-pointed and rigid outgrowths on stems are called spines. *P. saepeflorens* has a "spiny" stem.

Stamen. This consists of the anther and the filament and bears the male fertilizing cells.

Stigma. The sticky part of the pistil of a flower which receives the pollen grains in the first step of fertilization.

Stipule. The pair of little wings attached to the base of the leaves of many plants. In cactus-stemmed varieties of pelargonium these are hard and thorny.

Style. The stalk or tube that connects the stigma with the ovary.

Terminal. The end of a stem or foliage branch or shoot bearing a flower cluster.

Tomentose. A dense, matted covering of short, soft, wooly hairs makes a leaf, and sometimes a stem, tomentose. *P. tomentosum,* the Peppermint Geranium, is tomentose.

Trifoliate. Leaves divided into three main sections.

Truss. A compact flower cluster at the top of a stem.

Umbel. A flat or round flower cluster.

Variety. Most gardeners and nurserymen use the term to designate hybrids and other individual or groups of plants distinguishable from others maintained in cultivation. The botanical term variety, usually abbreviated *var.*, is an English translation of the Latin term *varietas,* denoting a self-perpetuating variant of a species that occurs usually in the wild.

Sources of Plants

Buy and ship pelargoniums preferably in cool weather. They are poor travelers in times of excessive heat. Do not be alarmed if plants arrive with yellow leaves or if leaves turn yellow in a few days. This is not the grower's fault. With proper care plants will soon recover.

RETAIL FIRMS IN THE UNITED STATES

Bitzig, Gustave F., 317 S. Finley Avenue, Basking Ridge, New Jersey 07920
   Scented-leaved, fancy-leaved, specialist in dwarfs. List.
Crane, Mrs. Bruce, Sugar Hill Nursery, 45 Main Street, Dalton, Massachusetts
   Extensive list of dwarfs including Rober's; also ivy-leaveds. No catalog, no shipping.
Hall's Geraniums, 3202 Memorial Highway, Tampa 9, Florida
   Zonal, ivy-leaved, unusual. No catalog, no shipping.
Logee's Greenhouses, 55 North Street, Danielson, Connecticut
   Zonal, dwarf, scented-leaved, ivy-leaved, unusual. Catalog.

Manhattan Garden Supply, 305 North Sepulveda Boulevard, Manhattan Beach, California
    Zonal, fancy-leaved, dwarf, scented-leaved, ivy-leaved, regal. Catalog.
. Merry Gardens, 1 Simonton Road, Camden, Maine
    Zonal, fancy-leaved, dwarf, ivy-leaved, regal, unusual, species, seed.
    Excellent catalog for hobbyist 25¢.
Miller, Holmes C., 280 West Portola Avenue, Los Altos, California
    Zonal, fancy-leaved, dwarf, unusual. Catalog.
Park, Geo. W. Seed Co., Greenwood, South Carolina
    Seed, 'Nittany Lion Red' strain, Read's Little Strain. Catalog.
Road Runner Ranch, 2458 Catalina Avenue, Vista, California
    Zonal, fancy-leaved, dwarf, ivy-leaved, regal, unusual, species, seed.
    Catalog.
Schmidt Nursery, 355 Lambert Avenue, Palo Alto, California
    Fancy-leaved, dwarf, scented-leaved, ivy-leaved, regal. No catalog,
    no shipping.
Wilson Bros., Roachdale, Indiana (Greenhouses at Raccoon, Indiana)
    Zonal, fancy-leaved, dwarf, scented-leaved, ivy-leaved, regal, unusual.
    Catalog with color.

WHOLESALE FIRMS IN THE UNITED STATES

Bode's Geraniums, Southern California Geranium Gardens, Route 4,
    Box 403, Escondido, California 92025
Wilson Brothers, Roachdale, Indiana 46172

FIRMS IN ENGLAND

Anthony C. Ayton Ltd. "Constables", Southborough, Kent
    Zonal, fancy-leaved, scented-leaved, ivy-leaved, regal, unusual. Catalog.
Caledonian Nurseries, 20 Maidstone Road, Rainham, Gillingham, Kent
    Zonal, fancy-leaved, dwarf, scented-leaved, ivy-leaved, unusual. Catalog.
Clifton, W. 'A. R.—The Geranium Nurseries, Cherry Orchard Road,
    Chichester, Sussex
    Zonal, fancy-leaved, scented-leaved, ivy-leaved, regal. Catalog.
D. & M. Jackson, Woodville Nursery, Cragg Vale, Nr. Halifax, Yorkshire

Greybridge Geraniums, Common Road, Evesham, Worcestershire
  (Distributor for F. G. Read releases) Zonal, dwarf, ivy-leaved, regal.
  Catalog.
Jiffy Grown Plants, Trulls Hatch, Rotherfield, Sussex
Telston Nurseries, Telston Lane, Otford, Sevenoaks, Kent
  Zonal, fancy-leaved, dwarf, scented-leaved, ivy-leaved, regal, unusual.
  Catalog.

FIRMS IN AUSTRALIA

Danson's Home Service, Main Eltham Road, Research, Victoria
  Fancy-leaved, dwarf, scented-leaved, ivy-leaved, regal, unusual. Cata-
  log.
F. R. E. Coates Nurseries, Cavanagh Street, Cheltenham, S 22, Victoria
Green Fingers, 1723 Pittwater Road, Mona Vale, Sydney, N.S.W.
  Zonal, fancy-leaved, ivy-leaved, regal. Catalog with color illustra-
  tion 7/6.
Morf's Margot Nurseries, P. O. Box 89, Belmont, N.S.W.
  Zonal, fancy-leaved (a few), ivy-leaved, regal. Catalog.
Tunia Service, Box 1091 J, G P O Adelaide, South Australia
  Zonal, fancy-leaved, dwarf, scented-leaved, ivy-leaved, regal, Hybrid
  Staphs, 'Fingered Flower'. Catalog.
W. H. Wood Rosebank Nursery, Beaumaris Parade, Highett, Victoria
  Limited list of fancy-leaved, dwarf, regal.

INDEX

Bold type indicates main discussion of subject.

'A. M. Mayne' 63, 68, **300**
'ABC Red' 41
'Abel Le Franc' 71
abrotanifolium 130, 143, 145, 229, 293, **320**
absinthe geranium 297
acerifolium 124, 136, 293, **320**
aceroides 321
acetosum 30, 175, 230, **296**
'Achievement' 49
'Afterglow' 67, **300**
Aiton, William 7, 183
'Alice of Vincennes' 47, 67, 77, 79, **300**
'Aline Sisley' 11
'Alliance' 38, 49, 50, 172, 175, 181, 224
almond-scented geranium *see* 'Pretty Polly'
'Alpha' 49, 63, 105, **311**
'Alphonse Ricard' 37, 44, 304
Alphonse Ricard Group 43, **44**
alternans **296**
'Always' 1, 2, 49, 66, 83, 293, **300**
'American Beauty' *see* 'Masure's Beauty'
'Amour' 184, 190, **333**
Andrews, Henry 4, 7
angulosum 150, 293
'Ann Sothern' 47, 77, 79, **300**
'Apache' 39, 40, 68, **301**
aphids 153, **277**
'Applause' 184, 191, **333**
'Apple Blossom' regal **333**
'Apple Blossom' zonal 46, 47, 77, 79, 240, **301**
Apple Blossom Group 77
'Apple Blossom Rosebud' frontispiece, 58, 74, 80, 83, 111, 219, 293, **301**

apple-scented geranium see *odoratissimum*
'Apricot' 328
'Apricot Queen' 164, 172, 178, 181, **329**
'April' 184, **333**
× *ardens*, 32, **296**
Arndt, Milton 114
Arnold, Paul xvii
artemisiaefolium 320
'Attar of Roses' 133
attar-of-roses geranium see *graveolens*
'Attraction' **311**
australe 33, 150 *illus.*, 293, **321**
Australian Geranium Society xv, 291
Australian Geranium Society N.S.W. Division 291
'Australis' 33, 321
'Autumn' 215
autumn care 94–97
'Autumn Haze' 183, **334**
'Avalon Beauty' 43
'Avalon Red' 41
'Azalea' 190, **334**
'Aztec' regal 184, 190, 191, **334**
'Aztec' zonal 67, **301**

'Baby Snooks' 337
bacterial leaf-spot 270–271
bacterial stem-rot 270–271
Bailey Hortorium xvi, 17, 145
balm-scented cranesbill 329
'Bandalaire' 71
'Barbara Wirth' 179, 181, **329,** 330
'Barbary Coast' 179, **329,** 330
'Bariolage' 71
'Bashful' 113
baskets 224–226
'Battle of Gettysburg' 318

'Beaute de Poitevine' 11, 37, 214
'Beautiful Forever' 99
'Beauty' see *quercifolium* 'Beauty'
'Beauty of Eastbourne' 166, 176, 293, 330
'Beckwith Pride' 106, 293
bedding geraniums 102–103, 155
Behringer, Charles 39
'Berkeley Belle' 47, 61, 77, 79, **301**
'Berkeley Raspberry' 59
'Berthe de Pressily' 37, 306
'Better Times' 40, 41, 59, 61, **301**, 306, 309
Better Times Group 38, **40–41**, 81
bicolor 149 *illus.*, 293
bicolored geraniums 98–107
'Bijou' 17, 115
Bird's Egg Group 34, 38, 69, **70–73**, 75, plate IV facing 76, 78, 83, 255, 261
'Black Lace' 186, 191, 224
black leg 273–274
'Black Magic' 334
'Black Vesuvius' 3, 108, 109, 110 *illus.*, 114, 117, 122, 228, 293, **316**
× *Blandfordianum* 43 *illus.*, 145, 293, **321**
'Blaze' 40, 61, 63, 240, **301**
'Blazonry' 311
'Blossomtime' 49
'Bobolink' 71
Bode, Fred, jr. xiv, 13, 32, 38, 39, 40, 43, 47, 70, 173, 180, 183, 208, 209, 257, 276
'Bode's Coral-Pink Bird's Egg' 70, 78, **301**
'Bode's Light Pink Bird's Egg' frontispiece, 70, 78, 293, **301**
Bohannon, Mrs. William H. 13
'Bonbon' 115
bonsai forms 227–229
Bonsai Society of Greater N.Y. 229
Both, Ted xv, 15, 32, 115, 173
botrytis blight 271–272

'Bougainvillea' 47, 68, 77, 79, **301**
'Bravo' 215
'Break O'Day' 334
'Bridesmaid' 176
Brigham, Dorcas xiii, 13, 30, 53, 157
'Bright Pixie' 32
'Brilliant' 148, **321**, 325
'Bronze Beauty No. 1' 105, **311**
'Bronze Beauty No. 2' 105, 106, plate VI facing 108, 293, **312**
Brookhaven National Lab. xvi, 216
'Brooks Barnes' 114, 122, **316**
'Bruant' 37
Bruant, Paul 37, 43, 44, 46, 77
Bruant Race 37
'Buccaneer' 40
'Bumblebee' 113, 117, 123, **316**
Burgers, Max 10, 183
Burton, Lady Irene 184, 186
business, geranium 247–261
Butterfield, H. M. 13
butterfly cranesbill 326
butterfly geraniums 105

Cactus-flowered Group 34, **75**, 79, 111, 255, 261
cactus type 25–30
'Cal' 40
California 10, 54–59, 102, 116, 168–172, 188–190, **192–201**, 219, 243–244
'Caligula' 114
'Camden Nutt' 309
'Camellia Fiat' 44
'Cameo Fiat' 44
camphor rose geranium see *graveolens* 'Camphorum'
'Camphorum' see *graveolens* 'Camphorum'
'Canadian Pink and White' 61, **301**
'Capella' 114
capitatum 128, **321**
'Capri' 321
'Caprice' 189, 191
caraway-leaved cranesbill 298
'Carisbrooke' 183, 189, 191, **334**

'Carleton's Velma' 61
'Carlos Uhden' 171, 178, 181, **330**
'Carmel' 66, **301**
'Carmen' 189, 190, **334**
Carnation-flowered Group 73–74, 79
'Carnival' 178
carnosum 18, **296**
Case, David 113, 183
Cassidy, Mr. and Mrs. A. H. 13, 183
caterpillars 277–278
celandine-leaved storksbill 297
'Celebrity' 216
'Cerise' 113
'Cerise Carnation' 74, 79, **301**
'Cesar Franck' 167, 180, 181, 293
'Challenge' 67, **302**
Chandler, Philip A. xvi
'Charles Monselet' 166, 331
'Charles Turner' 11, 92 *illus.*, 166, 168, 178, 179, 181, 293, **330**
'Cheerio' 47, 66, 77, 79, **302**
'Chelsea Gem' 314
Cherry, Elaine xvii, 85
'Chiquita' 183
chlorosis 272
'Chorus Girl' 184, 187, 190, 191, **334**
chromosome counts 36, 37, 38
'Circus Day' 183, 189
citriodorum 321
× *citrosum* 321
Citrus-scented Group 137
clammy cranesbill 323
'Cliff House' 63, 179, 181, **330**
Clifford, Derek xvi, 75, 116, 128, 175
climbing geranium see *scandens*
climbing type 19–25
'Clorinda' 2 *illus.*, 25, 131, 145, 147, 148, 293, **321**
'Cloth of Gold' **312,** 316
'Clown' 184
coconut-scented geranium see *grossularioides*
'Cody' 130

coldframe, 195–196
collector's geraniums 69–80, 104
colored-leaved geraniums *see* fancy-leaved geraniums
commercial geraniums 240
common geranium see × *hortorum*
common horseshoe cranesbill 300
'Comtesse de Grey' 63, 167, 169, 173, 179, 180, 181, 293, **330**
'Confetti' 183, 184, 191, plate XI facing 205, 293, **334**
'Conquistador' 41
'Conspicuous' 190, **334**
containers 101–102, 155, 164, **232–246**
'Contrast' 312
'Coral Glow' 49
'Coral-Pink Bird's Egg' 70, 78, **301**
cordatum 322
'Corden's Glory' 63, 332
cordifolium 31 *illus.*, 32, 293, **322**
coriander-leaved cranesbill 296
× *coriandrifolium* 33, 256, **296**
Cornell University xvi, 17, 145
'Corona del Mar' 181, **330**
'Corsage' 186, 190, 191, **335**
'Corsair' 40
cotyledonis 10, 16 *illus.*, 293
'Countess of Scarborough' 328
'Country Girl' 184, 190, **335**
Crane, Mrs. Bruce xiv, 15, 109, 113, 114, 115, 116, 119, 173, 178, 224
cranesbill 3
crassicaule 9, 14 *illus.*, 293, **297**
'Crimson Rosebud' 74, 80
'Crimson Rosette' 80
crinkle disease 272
crispum 7, 128, 135 *illus.*, 146, 150 *illus.*, 157, 159, 229, 293, **322**
  Gooseberry-leaved 124 *illus.*, 146, 293, **322**
  'Minor' 135 *illus.*, 137, 147, 204, 229, 293, **322**
  'Prince Rupert' 58 *illus.*, 101, 135 *illus.*, 137,

147, 154 *illus.*, 293, **322**
'Prince Rupert Variegated' 137, 146, 147, **322**
'Variegatum' 324
criterifolium 21
crithmifolia 21
crithmifolium 296, **297**
'Crocodile' 173, 178, 293
crookneck 280
crowfoot geranium see *radens*
crown gall 273
'Crystal Palace Gem' 100, 105, 106, 293, **312**
cucullatum 6, 150 *illus.*, 151 *illus.*, 183, 293, **297**, 323
culture
  for professional growers 256–259
  in California 192–201
  in East 53, 54, 77, 104, 116, 164, 186–188
  in Midwest 63, 64, 166, 186–188
  in pots 81–97
  in South 39, 61–63
  of dwarfs 118–120
  of fancy-leaveds 103–104
  of ivy-leaveds 162–173
  of regals 186–190
  of scenteds 148–160
'Curiosa' 73
curled-leaved cranesbill 322
Curtis's Botanical Magazine 23
cutting rot 273–274
cuttings 91, 95, 153, 196, **202–209**
'Cyclops' 46
Cyclops pelargoniums 46, 77
Czechoslovakian-type 38

'Damon's Gold Leaf' 312
'Dancer' 117, 123, **316**
'Dark Beauty' 30, 98, 226, 286, 293, **312**
'Dark Red Irene' 40, 41, 55 *illus.*, 61, 63, 101, 154 *illus.*, 173, 293, 301
dasycaule 18, 256, 296, **297**

'Daumier' 71
'David d'Angers' 71
Davis, Natalie Harlan xvii
'Dawn' regal 338
'Dawn Star' 32
'Dawn' zonal see 'Fiat Supreme'
'Debonair' 49, 67, **302**
× *decipiens* 322
'Delores' 335
'Delphin' 115
denticulatum 130, 132 *illus.*, 143 *illus.*, 293, **322, 325**
denticulatum 'Filicifolium' 124 *illus.*, 130, 293, **322**
'Destiny' 184, 190, 191, **335**
Diener, Richard 13, 183
Dilennius, J. J. 6
diploids 36
disease 153, 201, **268–276**
'Display' 103, **312**
'Distinction' 63, 105, 106, 255, 293, **312**
× *divaricatum* 297
'Doc' 113
'Dr. Livingston' see *radens* 'Skeleton Rose'
× *domesticum* 182, 193, **323**
'Dopey' 113, 117, 123, **316**
dormancy 81
'Double Dryden' 67, **302**
Double Dryden Group 38
double geraniums see zonal geraniums
'Double Lilac-White' 181, **330**
'Double Mrs. Pollock' see 'Mrs. Strange'
'Double New Life' 76, 79, **302**
'Double Pink Bird's Egg' 70
'Double Poinsettia' 72, 75, 79, 293, **302**
'Double Red' 113
'Double Salmon' 331
'Dreams' 59, 66, **302**
Dreer, Henry A. 11
Dress, William J. xvi
'Dubonnet' 184, 187, 190, 191, **335**

'Duke of Edinburgh' 175, 333
'Dwarf Gold Leaf' 103, 106, **312**
dwarf types 11, **108–123**

'E. H. Trego' 50, 176, **302**
'Earliana' 337
East, the 53, 54, 77, 104, 116, 164,
    186–188
'Easter Greetings' 184, 190, **335**
echinatum **25–27,** 26 *illus.,* 256,
    293, **297,** 299, 321
'Ecstasy' 66, 75, 76, 80, **302**
edema 165, 166, **274–275**
'Edith North' 189,
    294, **335**
'Edmond Blanc' 40, 301
'Edna' 41
Eisenbart, F. J. xv
Eisley, E. H. 73, 113
'El Gaucho' 172, 176, 181
'Elenore S. Rober' 66, **302**
'Elf' 111, 112, 122
'Elkhorn' 323
'Emile Zola' 56, 66, **302**
'Emma Hossler' 114, 117, 120, 123,
    316
'Empress of Russia' 54
'Enchantress' 176
Endlicherianum 31 *illus.,* 294
England 9, 10, 53, 99, 114, 125
English-type 36
'Epsilon' 114, 122, **317**
Erodium 3
espaliers 229–231
'Estelle Doheny' 178
etiolation 272
'Etna' 114

'Fair Ellen' 226, 326
'Fairy Queen' 32
'Fairyland' 111, 112, 117, 122, **317**
Faiss, Carl 10, 183
fancy geranium see × *domesticum*
fancy-leaved 34, **98–107,** 111
'Fanfare' 49, 59

'Fantasy' 47, 67, 77,
    294, **303**
fasciation 269, 270, **273**
fern-leaf geranium see *denticulatum*
    'Filicifolium'
fertilizing 89–90, 119, 153, 162,
    200–201
'Festival' 66, **303**
'Fiat' 37, 43, 44, 61, 66, 92 *illus.,*
    303
'Fiat Enchantress' 42 *illus.,* 43, 44,
    61, 294, **303**
Fiat Group **43–44,** 74, 81, 252
'Fiat King' 44, 73, 79, **303**
'Fiat Queen' frontispiece, 44, 73, 79,
    294, **303,** 309
'Fiat Supreme' 42 *illus.,* 44, 66, 294,
    303
'Fiery Chief' 32
'Fifth Avenue' 335
filbert-scented geranium see 'Schotte-
    sham Pet'
'Filicifolium' 124, 130, 293, **322**
'Filigree' 30, **312**
finger-bowl geranium see *crispum*
    'Minor'
'Fingered Flowers' frontispiece, 15,
    78, 80, 294
'Firebrand' 40, **303**
'Firedancer' 190, **335**
'Firefly' 113, 117
'Fireglow' 67, **303**
fish geranium see × *hortorum*
'Flag of Denmark' 76
'Flame' 8 *illus.,* 55 *illus.,* 59, 63, 67,
    221, 294, **303**
'Flare' 66, **303**
fleshy-stalked cranesbill 296
'Fleurette' 113, 117, **317**
'Flirt' 117, **317**
'Floire de Nancy' 11
Flora Capensis 4
florists pelargonium see × *domes-
    ticum*
'Flower Basket' 186, 191, 224
'Flower of Spring' 101, 106, **312**

flower shows 178–179, 184, 283, 287–290
fluorescent light **85–86,** 108
'Forest Maid' 38, 176, 224, **303**
'Formosa' 78, 80
'Fortune' 49
Fox, R. D. 11
× *fragrans* 130, 141, 143 *illus.,* 146, 157, 212, 294, **323**
  'Old Spice' 130, 141, 212, 226, **323**
  'Snowy Nutmeg' 141, **323**
'Frances Perkins' 67, **304**
'Freak of Nature' 313
'Fred Bean' 66, **304**
'French Lace' 61, 137, 322
French-type **36–37,** 39, 43, 44, 49
frequent-flowered storksbill 299
'Friesdorf' 123
'Fringed Oak' 326
'Fringed Oak' × 'Fair Ellen' 326
'Frolic' 117
Fruit-scented Group 131, **141**
frutetorum 29 *illus.,* **30–32,** 98, 175, 226, 260, 294, **297,** 298, 312, 313, 314
fulgidium 27
fulgidum 18, **27–28,** 130, 149 *illus.,* 152, 294, 296, **297,** 326

'Gaines Attraction' 311
'Galilee' 63, 168, 171, 179, 181, 294, 329, **330,** 332
'Gallant' 49, 61, 67, **304**
'Galli Curci' 41
garden geraniums see × *hortorum*
'Gardener's Joy' 184, **335,** 338
'Gardenia' 311
'Garnet' 67, **304**
'Gay Baby' 111, 179, 288 *illus.,* 294, **330**
'Gay Nineties' 184, **336**
'General Grant' 11
'General Leonard Wood' 47
'Genie' 40, 67, **304**

Geraniaceae Sweet 9
Geraniologia 7
Geranium 3
  citriodorum 136
  revolutum 132
geranium, business 247–261
  classifications 17, 131
  gardens 51–63, 155
  groups 38–50
  hedges 56
  history 4–17
  lawns 179–180
  oils 128
Geranium Records 13, 73
Geranium Society of England, 291
Geraniums Andrews 4, 7
Geraniums manual xvi, 269
Geraniums Around the World, 11, 59, 158, 263, 283
German-type 38
'Geronimo' 336
'Gertrude Pearson' 64, 67, **304**
giant oak geranium 144, 327
giant rose geranium 323
'Giant Salmon' 181, **331**
gibbosum 1, 2 *illus.,* 6, 18, 19, 20 *illus.,* **21,** 212, 229, 230, 256, 294, **298**
Gigantea Section 37
'Giganteum' (*graveolens*) 323
'Giganteum' (*quercifolium*) 144, 295, 327
ginger-scented geranium 329
'Glamour' 41
× *glaucifolium* 6, **21,** 149 *illus.,* 294, **298**
'Glory' 49
glowing storksbill 296
glutinosum 7, 124 *illus.,* 145, 150 *illus.,* 294, **323,** 326
'Goblin' 108, 114, 122, **317**
'Godfrey's Pride' 146, **323,** 328
'Gold Leaf' 312
'Golden Bedder' 312
'Golden Chain' 99
'Golden Harry Hieover' 311

'Golden MacMahon' 103, 106, **313**
'Golden Oriole' 313
gooseberry-leaved geranium 124, 146, 293, 322
'Gorgeous' 43, 44
gouty storksbill 298
'Grand Slam' 183, 186, 190, 191, **336**
'Grannie Hewitt' 111
graveolens 7, 19, 101, 126 *illus.*, 128, 129 *illus.*, 130, 133, 146, 154 *illus.*, 156, 157, 158, 212, 221, 294, 321, **323**, 325, 328
  'Camphorum' 126 *illus.*, 133, 146, 294, **323**
  'Elkhorn' 323
  'Giganteum' 323
  'Gray Lady Plymouth' 133, **324**
  'Lady Plymouth' 146, 147, **324**
  'Large Leaf Rose' 324
  'Little Gem' 133, 147, **324**
  'Minor' 126 *illus.*, 133, 294, **324**
  'Red-flowered Rose' 127 *illus.*, 133, 147, 294, **324**
  'Rober's Lemon Rose' 126 *illus.*, 154 *illus.*, 158, 221, 294, **324**
  'Variegatum' 324
'Gray Lady Plymouth' 133, 324
gray mold 271–272
great oak-leaved cranesbill see *quercifolium*
'Greengold Kleiner Liebling' 111, 122
'Greetings' 30, **313**
'Gregerson's White' 61
Grenville, Lady 10
Grieve, Peter 99, 100
Gros Bois geraniums 37
'Grossmama Fischer' 56, 183, 190, **336**
grossularioides 140 *illus.*, 146, 193, 294, **324**
'Grumpy' 113
'Gypsy' 68, **304**
'Gypsy Gem' 117, 123, **317**
'Gypsy Queen' 117

Hall, Mrs. J. B. xv, 61, 63
'Hall Caine' 11
'Halloween' 49, 67, **304**
'Halo' 184, **336**
Hamlin, Elenore Rober xiv, 113
'Happy' 113
'Happy Thought' 11, 61, 63, 103, 105, 106, 207, 230, 244, 255, 294, **313**
'Harlequin' 327
Harman, Elaine Ruth xvi
Hartsook, Frances 30, 172
'Harvest Moon' 67, **304**
'Hasse's Scarlet' 41
'Hasse's Scarlet Princess' 41
'Heartbeat' 56, **336**
heart-leaved storksbill 31, 32, 322
'Heide's White' 248
'Helen Michel' 44
'Helen Van Pelt Wilson' 64, 67, plate V facing 77, 81, 294, **304**
Henderson, Peter 11, 71
Henley, R. M. 13
Herlaut 47, 77
heronsbill 3
'Hills of Snow' 102, 105, 294, **313**
'Holiday' regal 186, 190, 191, **336**
'Holiday' zonal 47, 67, 77, 79, **304**
Holmes Miller Group 49
'Honeymoon' 36, 59, 66, 244, **305**
hooded cranesbill see *cucullatum*
horseshoe geranium see *zonale*
× *hortorum* 32, 36, 193, **298**
Hortus Elthamensis 6
Hortus Kewensis 7
Howard, Paul 13, 183
humidity 83, 148
'Hummel's Monselet' 181, **331**
Hutchinson, James 11
Hutt, David M. xvi
Hybrid Staphs 32, 115
hybridizing 212–216

'Illuminator' 100
'Imp' 108, 112, 117, 122, 228, **317**

'Improved Red Fiat' 44
'Improved Ricard' 37, 44, 61, 63
'Indian Summer' 49
inquinans 6, 36, 294, **298**
'Inspiration' 49, 66, **305**
'Intensity' 167, 168, 180, 181, 294, **331**
International Code of Nomenclature xvii, 7
International Geranium Society xv, 11, 263, 283, 287
Iowa State University 15
'Irene' 40, 63, 240, 301, **305**, 308
'Irene Burton' 184
Irene Group 38, **39**, 81
'Irma' 224
ivy-leaved cranesbill 7, 298
ivy-leaved geraniums 161–181

Jarrett, Clara Sue 13, 183
× *jatrophaefolium* 212, **325**
'Jaunty' 112, 117, 120, **317**
'Jean Roseleur' 176, 181, **331**
'Jean Viaud' 61, 214, 309
'Jeanne' 69, 72 *illus.*, 73, 79, 207, 294, **305**
'Jeanne d'Arc' 164, 167, 169, 180, 181, 294, **331**
Jekyll, Gertrude and Sir Herbert 53
Jenkinsonia pendula 296
'Jennifer Jones' 43
'Jester' 172, 176, 178, 181, **331**
'Jewel' 75
'Jeweltone' 40
'Jolly Roger' 40
Jory, Stafford 13
'Joseph Warren' 165, 167, 168, 180, 181, 294, **331**
'Josephine' 184, 187, 190, **336**
'Joy' regal 183, 189, 191, **336**
'Joy' zonal 49, 66, **305**
'Joy Lucille' 137, 146, 158, 221, 226, **325**
'Jubilee' 105, 106, 294, **313**

'Keepsake' 112, 120
Kerrigan, Howard 114, 183
'Kewense' 115
'King Midas' 190, **336**
'Kleiner Liebling' 109, 110 *illus.*, 121, **317**
knotted storksbill 298
Knuth, R. 4
Krieg, Helen B. xvii

'La Fiesta' 54, 61, 67, **305**
'La France' 166, 176, 181, 294, **331**
'La Jolla' 40
'La Paloma' 183, 184, **337**
'Lady Cullum' 100, **313**
'Lady Dryden' 47
'Lady Gertrude' 50
'Lady Lavender' xv, 165
'Lady Mary' see × *limoneum* 'Lady Mary'
'Lady of Spain' 47, 59, 66, 77, 79, **305**
'Lady Plymouth' 146, 147, 324
'Lady Ruth' 64, 68, **305**
Lady Scarborough's geranium 328
Lady Washington pelargonium see × *domesticum*
'Large Leaf Rose' 324
'Lass O'Gowrie' 100, **313**
lateripes 7, **298**
'L'Aube' 11, 306
'Lavender Gibson Girl' 184
'Lavender Grand Slam' 183, 190, 191, **337**, 338
'Lavender Pink Bird's Egg' 78, **305**
'Lavender Ricard' 25, 44, 61, 67, 221, **305**
Lawrance, Charles F. xv
'Le Negre' 75
leaf-spot 270–271
'L'Elegante' 61, 173, 175, 294, 333
Lemoine, Victor 11, 71
lemon-balm geranium see × *melissinum*
lemon-scented geranium see *crispum*

and × *limoneum*
Lemon-scented Group 131, **137**
'Leopard' 178
Les Geraniums 37
L'Heritier, Charles Louis 7
light 83, 85–86
'Light Pink Bird's Egg' frontispiece,
    70, 78, 293, 301
'Lilliput Lemon' 111
lime-scented geranium see × *ner-
    vosum*
× *limoneum* 137, 146, 159, **325**
    124 *illus.*, 141, 147,
    157, 294,
    325
'Linda Arce' 47
'Little Darling' 109, 110 *illus.*, 294,
    317
'Little Gem' 133, 147, 324
little-leaf rose geranium, 126, 133,
    324
'Little Rascal' 337
Little Read's Strain 121
lobatum 296, 298
Logee, Joy S. 13
'Lollipop' 39, 40
'Louise' 50
'Lucky Strike' 331
'Lucy Ann Leslie' 191
'Lullaby' 66, **305**
'Luster' 67, 294,
    306
'Lyric' 112, 117, 120, 122, **318**

'M. Ninon' 328
'Mackensen' 183, 190, **337**
'Madame Buchner' 56, 311
'Madame Crousse' 330
'Madame Fournier' 109, 110 *illus.*,
    294, **318**
'Madame Jaulin' 11, 58 *illus.*, 63,
    66, 295, **306**
'Madame Landry' 37, 61
'Madame Langguth' 63, 235
'Madame Laporte Bicuit' 43
'Madame Layal' 185 *illus.*,

186, 191, 224, 295,
    337
'Madame Lemoine' 11
'Madame Margot' 175
'Madame Salleron' 100, 102, 105,
    313
'Madame Thibaut' 11, 74, 79, **306**
'Madonna' ivy-leaved 330
'Madonna' zonal 102, 219, 311
'Magenta Rosebud' 74, 75, 80
'Magenta Rosette' 80
'Magenta Ruby' 41, 68, **306**
'Magic Lantern' 32, 175, 226, **314**
'Magnificent' 2 *illus.*, 66, 83, 295,
    306
'Mangle's Variegated' 313
maple-leaved geranium see *acerifol-
    ium*
'Marchioness de Bute' 184
'Marechal MacMahon' 105, 255,
    314
'Marguerite de Layre' 37,
    59, 66, 219, 295, 306,
    310
'Marie Rober' 189, **337**
'Marie Vogel' 183
'Marie Wilkes' 306
'Market Leader' 38
'Marktbeherrscher' 38
'Marquis de Montmort' 68, **306**
marshmallow-leaved cranesbill 293
Martha Washington pelargonium
    see × *domesticum*
'Marthe Dupuy' 73
'Mary Ann' 17
'Mary Elizabeth' 189, **337**
'Masure's Beauty' 53, 68,
    219, 221, 295, 306
'Maxime Kovalevski' 54, 295,
    307, 318
May, Harry 13, 179, 183, 186
'May Magic' 183, 184
'Maytime' 49
McWhorter, Frank P. xv, 269–70
mealybugs 278
measles disease 272

'Medallion' 30, **314**
'Meditation' 117, 316
'Medley' 120
'Melissa' 184, 186, 190, 191, 224, **337**
× *melissinum* 141, 146, 157, **325**
'Memories' 215
'Merry Gardens White' 66, **307**
'Mertes White' 215, 216
'Mexican Beauty' 2 *illus.*, 63, 101, 154 *illus.*, 173, 179, 181, 295, 330, **332**
Mexico 172–173
Midwest 63, 64, 166, 186–188
'Milford Gem' 50
Miller, Holmes C. xiv, 13, 30, 37, 47, 64, 76, 90, 98, 112, 118
Miller, Max 214
Miller dwarfs 109, **112**
miniature geraniums 108–123
'Minor' see *crispum* 'Minor' and *graveolens* 'Minor'
Mint-scented Group 131, **137**
mint-scented rose geranium 324
'Minx' 108, 112, 120, 122, **318**
'Mischief' 118, 123, 229
'Miss Burdett Coutts' 61, 100, 103, 105, 107, 208, 295, **314**, 315
Miss C. Stapleton's storksbill 299
'Missouri' 221
'Mrs. Banks' 63, 167, 168, 169, 179, 180, 181, 224, 295, 330, **332**
'Mrs. E. G. Hill' 36, 37, 59, 64, 66, plate V facing 77, 81, 295, **307**
'Mrs. Henry Cox' 86, 101, 103, 105, 107, 154 *illus.*, 248, 295, **314**, 315
'Mrs. J. C. Mappin' 314
'Mrs. J. J. Knight' 70, 78, 83, **307**
'Mrs. Kingsbury' 325
'Mrs. Kingsley' 124 *illus.*, 261, 295, **325**
'Mrs. Lawrance' xv
'Mrs. Mary Bard' 56, 184, 190, 191, 224, 335, 336
'Mrs. Parker' 61, 63, 105, 313, **314**
'Mrs. Pollock' 99, 100, 101, 105, 107, 230, 244, 255, 286, 295, **314**
'Mrs. Sarah Pell' 173
'Mrs. Strange' 63, 105, **315**
'Mrs. Taylor' 124 *illus.*, 145, 156, 157, 295, **325**
'Mr. Everaarts' 114, 117, 120, 123, **318**
'Mr. Wren' 78, 80, **307**
Mitchell, Mrs. Early xv, 61
mites 165, 279
'Monselet' 331
'Monterey' 216
'Mood Indigo' 184, 186, 295, **373**, 338
'Moon Rapture' 184, 335
Moore, Harold E., jr. xvi, 17, 145
'More Mischief' 118
'Morning Star' 75, 79, **307**
'Mosaic' 32, 175, 226, **314**
mosaic disease 272
'Mount Macedon' 184
'Mountain of Snow' 101, 105, **314**
mourning geranium 299
multiradiatum 21
Munnecke, Donald E. xvi
mutations 38, **216–217**
'My Beauty' 68, **307**

nematodes 279
'Neon' 176
× *nervosum* 138 *illus.*, 141, 146, 295, **325**
'Neuheit Carl Faiss' 338
'New Dawn' 166
'New Life' 11, 75, 76, 79, **307**, 308
New Life Group 75, **76**, 79, 83
'New Phlox' frontispiece, 66, 75, 76, 80, 83, 295, **307**
'New Ruby' 61
night geranium 299
'Nightingale' 71

night-smelling geranium 299
'Nimbus' 49, 66, **307**
'Nittany Lion Red' 211
'Noel' 75, 79, **308**
'North Star' 318
'Nouvelle Aurore' 47, 67, 69, 78, 79, 216, **308**
'Nova' 115
'Nugget' 111, 112, 122
'Nuit Poitevine' 295
Nut-scented Group 131, **141**
'Nutmeg Lavender' 332
nutmeg-scented geranium see × *fragrans*

oak-leaved geranium see *quercifolium*
odoratissimum 7, 124 *illus.*, 130, 141, 146, 147, 150 *illus.*, 157, 210, 212, 295, 323, **325**
oedema *see* edema
old-fashioned rose geranium see *graveolens*
'Old Mexico' 176, 178
'Old Scarlet Unique' 28, 130, 145, 152 *illus.*, 295, **326**
'Old Spice' 130, 141, 212, 226, 323
'Old Unique' 130
'Olympiad' 310
'Olympic Red' 56, 63, 212, 219, 240, 280
'One-in-a-Ring' 312
'Orange Imp' 318
'Orange Ricard' 37, 44, 56, 67, 219, 221, 240, **308**
orange tortrix 278
Oregon State University 15
Oriental-type 38
orithnifolium 21
'Our Frances' 191

'Painted Lady' 47, 77, 80, **308**
Painted Lady Group **46–47**, 69, 76–78, 79, 81

pansy geraniums 186, 337
papilionaceum 151 *illus.*, 295, **326**
'Parisienne' 191, 295, **338**
parsley-leaved geranium 296
'Party Dress' 2 *illus.*, 39, 40, 67, 295, **308**
parviflorum 324
'Pastel' 103, **315**
'Patience' 67, **308**
'Paul Crampel' 67, 295, **308**
Paulus, Albert O. xvi
'Peaches and Cream' 61
Pelargonium 3
Pelargonium Bulletin 27
Pelargoniums Clifford xvi, 33
Pelargoniums in Cultivation Moore, xvi, 145
peltated cranesbill see *peltatum*
Peltato-zonal Group 38. *See also* Zonal-ivy Group
peltatum 6, 25, 50, 161, 193, 296, **298**
Pennsylvania State Univ. xvi, 15
'Penny' 40, 63, 240, **308**
'Penny Irene' *see* 'Penny'
peppermint-scented geranium see *tomentosum*
'Peppermint Stick' ivy-leaved 176
'Peppermint Stick' zonal 76
'Perky' 108, 112, 114, 122, 317, **318**
'Persian Rose' 67, **308**
pests 276–280
pheasant's foot geranium see *glutinosum*
Phlox Group **75–76**, 80, 111
'Phlox New Life' 75, 76, 79, 80, **308**
photography 262–267
'Picardy' 208, 214, 219
'Pigmy' 109, 110 *illus.*, **111**, 117, 121, 122, 208, 295, **318**
pinching 103, 120, 153, 162

'Pink Alliance' 50, 176, 224
'Pink Cloth of Gold' 315
'Pink Cloud' 63, 240, **308**
'Pink Fiat' *see* 'Fiat'
'Pink Gardener's Joy, 191, **338**
'Pink Giant' 67, **309**
'Pink Happy Thought' 105, **315**
'Pink Harry Hieover' 286, 295
'Pink Poinsettia' 75, 79, **309**
'Pink Rampant' 164, 181, **332**
'Pink Rosebud' 74, 75, 80, **309**
planters *see* containers
plume moth 278
'Poinsettia' *see* 'Double Poinsettia'
    and 'Pink Poinsettia'
'Polaris' 318
pot culture 81–97, 118
potpourri 158
'Pretty Polly' 124 *illus.*, 157, 295,
    326
prickly-stalked geranium 297
'Pride' 113, 123, **319**
'Pride of Camden' 67, **309**
'Prime Minister Menzies' 191, 224
'Prince Bismarck' 101, 105, 154 *illus.*, 295, **315**
'Prince of Orange' 141, 146, 147,
    326
'Prince Rupert' see *crispum* 'Prince
    Rupert'
'Prince Rupert Variegated' 137, 146,
    147, 322
'Prince Valiant' 117, 122, 316,
    319
'Princess Fiat' 44, 73, 79, **309**
'Princess of Wales' 99, 184
'Princess Victoria' 176, 178
'Prize' 221
propagation 120–121, **202–217**
prostrate oak geranium see *querci-
folium* 'Prostratum'
'Prostratum' see *quercifolium* 'Pros-
tratum'
pruning 91, 93, 94, 120, 153, 198–
    200
Pungent Group 131, **145**

'Pungent Peppermint' 137

quercifolium 7, 130, 145, 146, 156,
    158, 221, 295, 325, **326**
    'Beauty' 146, 156, 157, 226, 293,
        326
    'Fair Ellen' 226, **326**
    'Fringed Oak' 326
    'Fringed Oak' × 'Fair Ellen' **326**
    'Giganteum' 144 *illus.*, 295, **327**
    'Prostratum' 142 *illus.*,
        157, 295, **327**
    'Skelton's Unique' 146, 230, **327**
    'Staghorn Oak Leaf' 327
    'Variegatum' 327
    'Village Hill Hybrid' 101, 142
        illus., 145, 212, 295, **327**

radens 124 *illus.*, 130, 132 *illus.*,
    133, 295, 322, **327**
    'Skeleton Rose' 58 *illus.*, 126
        illus., 146, 295, **327**
'Radiance' 67, **309**
'Radiant' 39, 40, **309**
Radio Group 41
'Radio Red' 41, 61, 102
Radula 7, 327
'Ramona' 216
rapaceum **298,** 327
'Rapture' 191, **338**
'Red Cardinal' 308
'Red Fiat' 43, 44
'Red Flowered Rose' 127, 133, 147,
    294, 324
'Red Meteor' 40
'Red Rosebud' 74, 75, 80, **309**
red spider 279
'Red Spider' 118
refulgent-flowered cranesbill 297
regal types 13, 111, **182–191**
reniforme 32, 154 *illus.*, 229, 295,
    299
'Reverie' 59
revolutum 327
Ricard Group 43, **44**

ring-spot 272
Rober, Ernest xv, 11, 112, 183
'Rober's Cerise' 113
'Rober's Double Red' 113
'Rober's Lavender' 113, **319**
'Rober's Lemon Rose' 101, 133
'Rober's Snow White' 113, 318
'Robin Hood' 114, 117, 123
'Rogue' 338
'Rollisson's Unique' 3, 25, 130, 131, 139 *illus.,* 141, 146, 226, 227 *illus.,* 230, 231, 244, 261, 295, **327**
'Romany' 59
'Ronsard' 43
root gall 273
root knot 279
rooting aids 208–209
'Rosamond' 71
'Rose Enchantress' 178
'Rose Irene' 40
'Rose Pink Bird's Egg' 78, **309**
rose-scented geranium 128, 321
Rose-scented Group 131, **133**
Rosebud Group 34, 69, **74–75,** 80, 83, 255, 261
Ross, Mary Ellen xiv, 113, 115, 133, 166, 273
rough-leaved cranesbill 328
'Roulette' 183, **338**
'Round Leaf Rose' 328
'Round Leaf Rose Variegated' 328
'Royal' 30, 226
'Royal Fiat' 44, 73, 79, **309**
'Royal Times' 41, **309**
'Rudyard Kipling' 305
rue-scented storksbill see × *rutaceum*
'Ruffles' 112, 114, 117, 122, **319**
× *rutaceum* 18, 19, **21,** 58 *illus.,* 146, 149 *illus.,* 212, 295, 298, **328**
'Ruth Eleanore' 189
'Ryecroft Surprise' 332

'S. A. Nutt' 11, 106

× *saepeflorens* **28, 299**
'Salina' 186, 337
'Salmon' 240
'Salmon Comet' 114, **319**
'Salmon Enchantress' 178
'Salmon Ideal' 214
'Salmon Irene' 40, 63
'Salmon Queen' 47
'Salmon Supreme' 59, 221
salmoneum 299
samphire-leaved geranium 297
'Santa Cruz' 186, 191
'Santa Monica' 296
'Santa Paula' 2 *illus.,* 63, 164, 172, 178, 181, 224, 296, **332**
scabrum 7, 32, 129 *illus.,* 296, **328**
   'Apricot' 328
scandens **23,** 24 *illus.,* 230, 296, 299
× *Scarboroviae* 'Countess of Scarborough' 147, 204, **328**
'Scarlet Beauty' 171, 176, 181, 224, **332**
scarlet-flowered cranesbill 298
'Scarlet Princess' 41
'Scarlet Rosebud' 74, 80
scented-leaved types 125–160
Schmidt, William E. xiv, 13, 175, 176, 183, 275
'Schöne Schwarzwälderin' 38
'Schottesham Pet' 147, 193, 324, **328**
'Seabright' 44, 73
seashore 57
seeds 121, **210–212**
'Seeley's Pansy' 186, 337
semidwarf geraniums 109, 116
serrated-petal geraniums *see* Carnation-flowered Group
'Seventeen' 40
Shapiro, Seymour xv, 216
'Shasta' 189
'Shimmer' 49, 66, **309**
shipping 283–287
'Shocking' 67, **309**

show geraniums see × *domesticum*
'Showpiece' 215
'Shrubland Rose' 148, **329**
side-foot geranium 7, 298
'Silver Leaf S. A. Nutt' 106
'Silver Lining' 101, 106, 154 *illus.*, 296, **315**
'Silver Ruby' 315
'Silver Star' 75, 79, **310**
single geraniums *see* zonal geraniums
'Single Pink' 70
'Single Rose-Pink' 70
Sisley, Jean 11
'Skeleton Rose' 58, 126, 146, 295, 327
'Skelly's Pride' 73, 305
'Skelton's Unique' 146, 230, 327
'Skies of Italy' 1, 63, 86, 105, 107, 230, 244, 255, **315**
'Skylark' 71
slugs 279
'Small Fortune' 108, 112, 117, 122, 228, **319**
Smith, Charles Piper 13, 73
Smith, Hubert R. xvi
snails 279
'Sneezy' 113
'Snow Baby' 113, 117, 122, **319**
'Snow White' 113, 318
Snow White and the Seven Dwarfs Series 113
'Snowball' 63, 240, 311
'Snowbank' 184, 189, 191
'Snowdrift' 176
'Snowdrop' 306
'Snowflake' scented 133, 146, 328
'Snowflake' zonal 58 *illus.*, 102, 296, 306
'Snowy Nutmeg' 141, 323
societies 281–283, 291
soil, for potting **86–89,** 119
solubile 9
'Sophia Dumaresque' 100, **315**
'Sorcery' 30, 123, **319**
sorrel cranesbill 296

southernwood-leaved geranium see *abrotanifolium*
'Souvenir de Mirande' frontispiece, 47, 61, 67, 77, 78, 80, 83, 296, **310**
'Sparkle' 123, **319**
Species Plantarum 6, 36
Spice-scented Group 131, **141**
spring care 91
'Springfield Violet' 300
'Springfield White' 310
'Springtime' regal 190, 336
'Springtime' zonal 40, 56, 63, 66, 240, **310**
'Springtime Irene' *see* 'Springtime' zonal
'Sprite' 111, 112, 117, 122, **320**
square-stalked cranesbill see *tetragonum*
square-stalked Jenkinsonia see *tetragonum*
'Staghorn Oak Leaf' 327
staining geranium 36
Standard-type **36,** 41, 47, 49
standards (tree geraniums) 53, 158, **219–224**
staphysagroides 15, 32
× *Stapletonii* 19, **28,** 58 *illus.*, 296, **299**
'Star of Persia' 75, 79, **310**
'Starlet' 75, 79, **310**
'Starlight' 66, 306, **310**
'Stars and Stripes' 76, 302
stem-rot 270–271
Stiles, Richard P. 13
storksbill 3
summer care 93, 153, 164, 234
'Summer Cloud' 49, 66, 221, **310**
'Sunset' ivy-leaved 175
'Sunset' zonal 100, 315
Sweet, Robert 7, 9, 183
sweetheart geranium see *echinatum*
sweet-scented cranesbill 325
'Sybil Holmes' 166, 168, 176, 178, 181, 224, **332**
systemics 165–166, 276–277

'Tangerine' 75, 79, **310**
'Telston's Prima' 184
temperature 83, 148, 162, 193–196
'Tempter' 117
terebinthina 324
tetragonum 7, 18, 22 *illus.*, 23, 229, 296, **299**
tetraploids 36
'The Blush' 176, **332**
'The Duchess' 172, 176, 181, **333**
'Theophile Gautier' 71
thick-stalked cranesbill 297
'Thomas E. Stimson' 68, **310**
three-pointed cranesbill 329
'Tiberius' 114
'Timothy Clifford' 114
'Tinkerbell' 115
'Tiny Tim' 186, 191
tobacco budworm 279
'Token' 67
tomentosum 3, 19, 82 *illus.*, 130, 134 *illus.*, 137, 146, 153, 157, 159, 193, 237, 296, 325, **329**
'Torento' 325, **329**
'Toyon' 39, 40, 67, **310**
'Treasure' 49
tree geraniums *see* standards
'Tresor' 66, **310**
tricolored geraniums 98–107
tricuspidatum 32, **329**
'Trinket' 113, 117
triste 4, **299**
'True Oak' 327
tubs *see* containers
'Tu-Tone' 114, 229, 317
'TV Red' 41
'Twinkle' 112, 117, 122, **320**
two-colored cranesbill 149

University of California xvi
urns *see* containers

'Valencia' 172, 176, 181, **333**
'Vandesiae' 324
Vandivert, Mrs. R. N. 13, 130, 155
'Variegated Apple' 130

Variegated Ivy-leaved—Lilac-white flower 174, 175, 178, 181, **333**
Variegated Ivy-leaved—Pink Flower 175, **333**
'Variegated Kleiner Liebling' 111, 117, 122, **320**
'Variegated Little Darling' 320
'Variegated Mint Rose' 133, 146, 229
'Variegatum' *graveolens* 324
'Variegatum' *quercifolium* 327
'Velma' 61, 68, **310**
ventilation 90–91, 120
'Venus' 114, **320**
'Verité' 66, **310**
'Verona' 106, **315**
verticillium wilt 275–276
'Vesuvius' 76, 79, **311**
'Victor Lemoine' 11
'Victoria Regina' 99, 184, 335, 338
'Victorville' 172
'Village Hill Hybrid' 101, 142, 145, 212, 295, 327
'Vin Rouge' 184, **338**
Vincent, R. Jr. & Sons 46, 71
virus diseases 74, 272–273
viscosum 323
vitifolium 150 *illus.*, 296, **329**
'Volcano' 114, 117

Walker, William C. 11
'Waltztime' 191, 338
Warner, Robert T. xv, 158, 221
'Warrior' 40
watering 84, 162, 196–198
'Welcome' 61, 66, **311**
West, Mrs. John D. xv, 64, 74, 166
'White Chiffon' 183, 184
'White Cloud' 184
white fly 153, 155, 165, 188, **280**
'White Madonna' 311
'White Magic' 49, 66, **311**
'White Mesh' 173, 330
'White Mist' 178
'White Sails' 184
'White Swan' 184

'Whitecap' 117, 122, **320**
'Wicked Lady' 305
'Wilhelm Langguth' 17, 101, 102, 105, 106, 107, 255, 315, **316**
'Will Rogers' 68, 221, **311**
Wilson Brothers xv, 13, 14, 40, 63, 114, 116, 168, 240
window boxes 237–243. *See also* containers
'Winkie' 115
winter care 81–97, 162
witches brooms *see* fasciation

'Wonderful' 76
'Wyona' 44

xerophyton 14 *illus.,* 296

'Yellow Gem' 100, 106, 107, 312, **316**
yellows disease 272

zonal geraniums 34–68
Zonal-ivy Group 49–50
zonale 6, 30, 34, 50, 298, **300**
Zonquil 15